THIN
WIRE

THIN WIRE

A MOTHER'S JOURNEY THROUGH
HER DAUGHTER'S HEROIN ADDICTION

CHRISTINE LEWRY

Matador
9 Priory Business Park,
Wistow Road, Kibworth Beauchamp,
Leicestershire. LE8 0RX
Tel: (+44) 116 279 2299
Fax: (+44) 116 279 2277
Email: books@troubador.co.uk
Web: www.troubador.co.uk/matador

ISBN 978 1780882 956

Cover image from thinkstock.co.uk.
The image is being used for illustrative purposes only;
and the person depicted in the image is a model.

British Library Cataloguing in Publication Data.
A catalogue record for this book is available from the British Library.

Printed and bound in the UK by TJ International, Padstow, Cornwall
Typeset in 11pt Adobe Garamond Pro by Troubador Publishing Ltd, Leicester, UK

Matador is an imprint of Troubador Publishing Ltd

Nobody ever becomes an addict to ruin his or her life. Addiction always begins with a desire to be *better*. Stronger. Smarter. Suaver. Richer. Braver. *More*. The promise is always of less pain and greater fulfilment, and the promise is always a lie.

– Dennis O'Neil

Introduction

Christine

It is the experiences you have in life that make you who you are, not the things that are given to you. This is true for me and for you too. Every single event in my life was something I needed to experience in order to be who I am now. But it was the difficult circumstances that changed me the most, things that are usually viewed as bad luck. During these difficult times I found the strength to carry on – to move forward and make something good come out of a bad situation. From this I have gained great satisfaction and even spiritual growth.

When my son was three and my youngest daughter four, I was diagnosed with breast cancer. The operation to remove part of my breast and twelve lymph nodes left me frail and weak. In the beginning, I struggled to find the courage to believe in a positive outcome. After surgery, chemotherapy and radiotherapy, the small things that used to irritate or worry me all seemed rather trivial. To consider your own death changes you. Every day I was free from symptoms was a joy, a blessing. I came to view my struggle as a gift that made me stronger, more conscious and ultimately more alive.

Two years later, when I found out that my eldest daughter,

Amber, then twenty-two, was a heroin addict, I had to dig deep inside for the strength to understand and cope. But the voice in my head that told me she would change was impossible to ignore. At times, when my battle to save my daughter from her addiction became desperate, I stopped and reminded myself how much worse it could be. I could be dying of cancer instead of being in remission.

The events of my past changed the way I viewed my situation, and Amber's – they affected every decision I had to make. The growth of my spiritual awareness defined me in a way that would not have been possible before I had cancer.

When Amber first decided to quit heroin, I resolved to help her, and we set off on the road together. We took things one step at a time, and we didn't step off the road until we reached our destination. Whatever that destination turned out to be, it was ours, and it was right for us – as I ultimately had to accept.

Along the road Amber lied to me – so I loved her; she stole from me – so I loved her; she tricked me – so I loved her; she let me down – so I loved her. She tried many times to stop using heroin and often she thought she had succeeded, only to be knocked back by a relapse. Other people saw this as a failure, but it wasn't. It was just a result, the outcome of events.

We made a lot of mistakes, wasted time and money, but it was all part of the process, part of life's journey. Sometimes events happen that take us on a path we never expected to travel, and we are not always equipped for the journey. I know I wasn't. But I wouldn't change a thing about my past: it brought me to this moment and led me to where I am today.

Our story is not your story. Each person struggling with drug addiction is different. Maybe there is something about our story that rings true with you, that resonates with what you are going through and that makes it a little easier. I hope this book can inspire one person on the road to recovery, or one parent struggling to understand their son or daughter's addiction. But the door to change opens only one way: from the inside. However much you want a deeply loved person to change their behaviour, only they can do it. You can't do it for them, no matter how much you want to or how hard you try.

Throughout my life, the universe has sent me lots of help in the form of people willing to assist or inspire me, or maybe more importantly to just believe in me. The universe will do the same for you in your fight to quit your addiction if you believe it, believe in yourself and forgive yourself for the mistakes you have made in the past. For the past can never be changed, but the future – your future – is there for the taking.

Part One

The Back Story

One

Christine

When did I first notice there was something different about my daughter, Amber? As a parent, you are supposed to immediately bond with your child, and the two of you are meant to have an understanding of each other, an exclusive connection. My reality fell far short of that, for no obvious reason. I found myself repeatedly asking, why does she do things I don't understand? Behave differently from the way I taught her?

Pitching up to my first parents' evening at the small Catholic school Amber attended, I pulled back the low wooden chair in front of her teacher's desk and sat down. The teacher had a kind face and a head of brown curls, a crucifix hung at the neck of her blouse. I waited for her to tell me about my daughter's progress, but my eagerness turned to disappointment when she sighed and shook her head: 'Oh, you're Amber's mother'. Her detailed account of Amber's naughty behaviour and rebellious nature made my cheeks flush. She just didn't have that inbuilt urge most children have to be good, and struggled to understand and repent when told off. It was a pattern that would be repeated over the following years. Why did I always feel it was my fault? Maybe it was.

My parents separated when I was twelve. After the divorce, my father stayed in the pub while my mother enjoyed her freedom. There was no-one to stop me from doing whatever I pleased. So I lived for the weekend, clothes and make-up, smoking and drinking, older boyfriends in fast cars. I was headstrong and independent, making my own life. Until my series of mistakes led me to get pregnant at twenty and be alone with my baby at twenty-one.

I felt trapped, like my life was over. I had lost my sparkle. Sitting on the front step watching my baby play with her toys, I tried to identify the sick feeling in the pit of my stomach. Why was I so unhappy? Why were the days so easy yet so difficult? The clouds built up and the weather changed. Spots of rain appeared on my forearm.

I yearned for a better life than this stay-at-home loneliness. I wanted things: carpet on the floor, presents for my child at Christmas. The rebel inside me – the one who had made me who I was, had made all those mistakes for me – now turned itself into drive and ambition.

So I enrolled at night school and then went on to college to study accountancy. I landed a good job, bought my own house and tried to provide Amber with the best after-school childcare. There were times when I had to leave her with people, childminders she didn't like. She would pull at my skirt, and cry and complain. I would just say 'I have to go to work'. But, while I was busy working full-time trying to make a success out of my life, Amber grew up pushing things to the edge.

Amber's father lost contact with her when she was still a baby. Birthdays and Christmases came and went with never a card from him. I didn't care that she never saw her father, didn't want him interfering in our lives. He phoned once and took her out for the afternoon. Made promises to her of a present to be sent – I guess it got lost in the post.

I had boyfriends. My loneliness made me keep them around long after I knew I didn't want them. I thought there was something wrong with me, that I couldn't sustain a relationship, until at thirty-one I accepted that I might live my life alone – after all, I already had a child. But meeting Tony changed everything. He was good-looking with a strong, square jaw and the most exquisite hazel eyes, and I felt differently about him from the start. The first night we spent together, I stayed awake until the birds sang, content to listen to the sound of his steady breathing. I wanted him like I had never wanted anything my whole life until then.

Although it didn't bother Tony that I had an eleven-year-old daughter, I packed Amber off to boarding school, 'to give her a better education,' I said. Her second-hand trunk, with the previous owner's name blazoned down the side, set her apart from her wealthy classmates. But, from Monday morning until Saturday lunchtime, I was free to enjoy my new love.

Amber's problems at school escalated. She wasn't doing any work, and when she came home at the weekends she was smoking and shoplifting. I found her so difficult that there was a part of me that didn't care. I cared what Tony thought, I cared what the people at work thought and I believed all those teachers at her school who said she was uncontrollable, devious and thick, but I never asked her why she was so naughty – I just accepted that she was. When the call came to say she had been expelled, I was embarrassed but not surprised. The bursary that I had worked hard to obtain had been lost. We talked, Amber promised to do better, and for a while she did.

Tony would tell Amber off for not helping me around the

house or for leaving her stuff lying around, but he never tried to father her. We got married and moved to a larger house, hidden from the road in a quiet cul-de-sac. I waited for the arrival of our first child with such joy – joy I hadn't felt when pregnant with Amber. I knew that this time I was ready to become a mother. Tony slept lightly once our daughter, Lauren, was born, always the first to hear her cry in the night and comfort her. Our son, Sam, followed quickly, eighteen months later, as if he could see the precarious future that awaited us, a future that might make his arrival, if delayed, uncertain. My life was filled with nappy changing and bottles, and I was delighted by it: I had someone to share it all with.

Amber grew to be taller than me, pretty, with a pale complexion and brown hair that twinkled with copper in the sunlight. She always had a happy disposition. On the odd occasion she was sad it never lasted long: like a cork held under the water, as soon as you let it go it shoots to the top and bobs happily up and down. She started going out with boys – small, skinny things usually, as if she liked to rescue strays no-one else would have. She left school without taking any exams, and although she went to college she dropped out within a year. Amber had everything – looks, personality, advantage and opportunity – yet she had nothing: no backbone, integrity, ambition or purpose.

Somewhere along the way, my understanding of my daughter disappeared, and the distance between us grew.

Amber

What was it about me? Why was I different? Why was I angry?

It's not that I'd lost something 'cause I never had it in the first place to lose, whatever *it* was. No, it's rather that whatever was missing from my life I didn't deserve to have. Oh, you wouldn't know to look at me, you can't see it from the outside. Anyway, I didn't care. Really, I didn't.

Being the new girl was part of my school life. I was sick of hearing 'This is Amber, she's new, she's going to sit here'. Everyone in class always stared at me – I had to push it all away, all the emotions it brought. It was horrid. I was interesting, for a short space of time, but a new school was never about a new beginning. It was more about hiding – hiding my vulnerabilities. Or did that make them more obvious? I constantly felt the anxiety of school life, that gut-sickening anxiety I carried around with me.

After I was expelled from boarding school, when I was thirteen, Mum sent me to the local school, Weydon, in Surrey. Sitting outside on my first day, the radio playing Bob Marley singing 'No Woman, No Cry' while I stared at the drizzling rain, I didn't want to get out of the car. I thought: if only time could stop and I could sit here forever. My feet made baby steps to the school gate, and when I glanced back Mum was watching me so I couldn't run off.

Most of the trouble I got into was mucking around trying to get the other kids to like me, because no-one did. I never understood why. I wasn't nasty or ugly. There was nothing wrong with me. But it was as if the other kids could always smell the weakness in me and, like the fat girl or the different girl, I was the one bullied and teased.

It was always me in the corner or on the naughty chair, me outside the headmaster's office. I spent hours of my life in the corridor – it became a familiar place for me. There was always an information board there somewhere, and with the pen from my blazer pocket I'd kneel up on a chair and colour in all the round bits from the writing – the o's, e's, a's, q's, p's, d's, b's and g's. It was quite fun to make sure I hadn't missed one and it stopped me from getting bored.

Then Weydon became the different school, the last school, the school I wanted to go to each day, where I didn't care what the other kids said. All because I had found a true friend – what's more magical than that? I met her outside the headmaster's office and in the corridor – she was there as much as me. For the first time ever I felt safe; I knew I wasn't alone. I had someone who would always be there for me, and she never let me down, not once until the day she died. Her name was Leeanne.

Leeanne didn't think she was very feminine. I thought she was strikingly beautiful, but she never quite believed it. Even relaxed, she could be a bit hard-faced, so I started to make her laugh, my jokes usually directed at myself, laughing at my childish ways. We had a connection; our stories were different, but we both loved a father who was absent from our lives. My father left when I was eleven months old and I've only seen him once or twice since then. Her father had died in a car accident a year before. Although she didn't really say, I could tell Leeanne was devastated by his death. He had been a difficult man, a heavy drinker, but she desperately wanted his love and approval, now that love was forever unobtainable.

I was the same. I knew my own father had been violent, that he had hit Mum, but I still wanted his love. And I loved him. It didn't make any sense that I loved him – after all, I hardly knew him – but it was as if carrying fifty per cent of his DNA meant something, gave him that undeserved right to my love. It wasn't a wish or a want: it was just there. I knew I needed the love of both my parents. I absolutely knew.

Leeanne was strong, physically and mentally, and, although I usually felt weak, with her I was self-assured and cocky. We told each other everything; we were united. We always had important matters to debate, or funny stories to recall. We became so in tune that we would say the same thing at the same time. We had several little mottos that we would say in unison, such as 'How boring is that?' but my favourite was 'You and me against the world'.

I started sleeping at Leeanne's house. We slept in the same bed – it was easier. 'Staying at mine?' she would say most weekends. After a while she didn't need to ask, I was always there. I just stopped going home. Opening the double window in her bedroom, we would go twos on a fag, passing it through the outside. Sitting either end of the windowsill in the dark, we talked about growing up, what sort of jobs we would get, what sort of cars we would drive and what sort of blokes we would marry.

We were always sneaking off to do something: taking Mum's Cinzano, making ourselves sick by drinking the lot 'cause it was sweet and sugary, or getting a bit of dope and smoking it in the park. I left school without taking any exams, and although I went to college to study horticulture I dropped out within a year. I got a job at a nursery planting seedlings.

Then Leeanne and I met Jason and Billy. Jason was a lovable rogue, covered in freckles from head to toe and the most beautiful eyes I have ever seen on a man, like cracked shards of coloured glass in vibrant blue. Billy was a 'bad boy'. He had a wild streak I found so attractive, white-blonde hair and eyes like a huge expanse of clear sky on a summer's day. He didn't have a pretty face but he had a lovely physique. Jason always sat next to Leeanne and put his arm around her. I started going out with Billy. Although Billy had this bad boy mentality, when we were alone he wanted to be tender, emotional and soppy. I felt comfortable with him. I could be myself. He was so besotted with me that my physical insecurities just melted away – I never felt self-conscious. Billy pointed out things on my body I didn't know were there – freckles or a tiny birth mark in a private place. Mentally I always knew where Billy was. I never felt a void between us or distance from what he was thinking.

Since Mum had met Tony she hadn't had time for me. I was just there, living in the house, but not part of that intimate bond they shared. I started to stay at Billy's flat all the time. The flat was just an empty shell: no carpets or curtains and only a dirty brown sofa and a mattress on the floor in the bedroom. Once the morning sun came in through the bedroom window, I could never get back to sleep. I would lie with my face under the duvet until the alarm went off.

Billy made promises to me: that he would make the flat a home and that he wanted us to have a baby one day. Months went by but nothing changed. Although we both had full-time jobs and could afford to buy things for the flat, we just sat in our empty shell. We had a routine: Leeanne and Jason came round and the four of us got stoned on dope. We thought there was nothing more interesting to do.

Billy was soon taking things to a different level. He had to be wrecked all the time. Getting home late from work one evening, I found him out of his face on the sofa. I threw my bag on the chair and bent over to take a closer look. He had something on his lap, a piece of foil. I thought: he's smoked all the weed and then eaten all the KitKats. I elbowed him in the ribs. 'Wake up!'

He was surprised, like I'd caught him at something, but then he sank back, relaxed.

'What's that?' I pointed to the foil.

'Liquid dope,' he replied with a fat smile.

'Give over, there's no such thing.'

'Yeah there is, try it. If you like dope, you're gonna fuckin' love this.'

He did a line in front of me, heating underneath the foil with his lighter and then drawing up the smoke with a tube also made from foil. I was fascinated.

There was a knock at the door. I glanced through the frosted glass panel and saw that it was Leeanne. I took the door off the catch and sat back down without looking. Leeanne and I didn't need niceties.

'What you doing?' she asked.

'Billy's saying I should smoke a bit of this.' I held up the foil to show her.

She studied it for a moment. 'Yeah, go on. I will if you will.'

'I dunno,' I said.

'What is it, then?' she glanced at Billy.

'It's liquid dope,' he replied.

'Is it fuck!' Leeanne and I stared each other out. 'Go on,' she said. There always was a hard attitude between us, an energy. 'Go on then,' she said again.

I did it first. Leeanne straight after. Immediately we were both being sick out of the sitting room window. We couldn't even make it to the bathroom. Being sick wasn't the painful, frightening experience it usually was – with heroin in my blood, I couldn't feel a thing. I can't remember anything else about that evening. It just smeared into a blur.

That night I slept like a baby. When I woke the next morning I knew I was going to smoke heroin again. Everything that day was enjoyable: sitting on the bus, working all day – it all felt good. It was the best day of my life.

I nagged Billy to get me some more and when he finally did I made sure Leeanne was there. After that it was a regular thing. My natural state of feeling was so shitty and heavy, like carrying a huge weight, that sometimes I didn't know how much longer I could hold up, but when I took drugs it was a release, an escape. Cigarettes and alcohol felt like putting the weight down for a while, but heroin was like I had never had the weight in the first place – a miracle cure for misery. I was in control; I controlled what drugs I took, when I took them and how much I took. It seemed that I had found the key to my emotional freedom. It was such a powerful thing to play with, I couldn't stop myself.

Addictions start slowly but they build up fast.

At first I didn't need that much; a tenner's worth would last three or four days, then I could go without for a few days before I needed it again. If I didn't have much cash I would smoke it alone; if I had money I'd share my gear with Leeanne.

Billy's drug-taking started to spiral into something more sinister than I had expected or could deal with. He was taking hard drugs first thing in the morning and hardly going to work, so I was paying for everything. I'd come home to find nasty people in the flat, people I'd never met and didn't want there. They were so smashed I couldn't even communicate with them, let alone throw them out. Whatever they were doing must have made them all sick because I'd find sick in the bath, sick in the sink and sick in the toilet. Even when I'd cleaned it up, I could still smell the rancid acid of sick everywhere.

Billy spent all our money on drugs I didn't even want. 'What am I supposed to eat, Billy?' I asked him while I looked through the empty kitchen cupboards at the end of a long, hot day, but he was too stoned to understand. I rummaged about the flat for something to smoke and found an old piece of foil with dregs of heroin, just enough to take the edge off.

Waking up in my clothes, the room smelt of stale cigarette smoke. I felt weak. I heard the alarm go off and thought 'fuck it' and went back to sleep. When I arrived at work, my boss looked at his watch. 'If you're late one more time, Amber, I'll have to let you go.' By Friday he'd sacked me.

Before long Billy and I had no food, no shampoo or toilet roll, not even a fag. I couldn't wash my clothes and spots developed all over my face. The reality and despair of my situation were forgotten for a few seconds when I got lost in cartoons. So I took the duvet to the sofa and watched TV all day.

Until Leeanne came round. She had her own car and a job in an office earning a decent salary. As soon as she came inside, I pounced on her. 'Got any fags? Any money?'

'What's going on here?' she stared at my face. I was grey, under-weight and dirty.

'Lost my job,' I replied.

'Billy not at work?'

'He's out getting wrecked.'

She tucked her shiny brown hair behind her ear and looked around the cold, dirty room. 'Amber, do you love him?'

''Course I do.'

'No. Do you really love him? Are you prepared to live this way? Bring a baby into this?' She shook her head. 'You have to go home.'

Leeanne packed my things and drove me home. 'I'm gonna tell Billy in no uncertain terms where he fucked up,' she said. Then she went back to the flat and waited for him.

Living back at Mum's was like checking into a five-star hotel after living rough. Without Billy there was no more gear and I didn't really think about it. I became ill with a fever – it made me sweat the whole time, my arms and legs ached and I felt sick.

Finally Mum said 'You can't go on like this, there must be something wrong with you,' and she took me to the doctors'.

The doctor said he thought it was a possible case of glandular fever and that I should rest. I stayed in bed for two weeks, and then I felt better and got another job.

Once I had my own money I couldn't resist doing gear again. I wasn't addicted, I just enjoyed it. It made me feel as if everything was going to turn out alright.

Two

Christine

I felt the lump again, and then stared at the reflection in the bedroom mirror. 'It's probably nothing,' I said out loud. It wasn't a hard lump but a knot of soft tissue under my right arm. Make-up done, I jammed the mascara wand back in the tube, but the face in the mirror wasn't me, it was someone else – someone shouting 'Worry! Worry! Worry!' inside my head. A wave of overwhelming doom made my knees buckle. I sank back to sit on the bed.

I rang the doctors' surgery. 'Is it an emergency?' the receptionist asked.

I thought for a moment. Is it?

'Well… yes,' I replied. She gave me an appointment for later that day. I wandered about the house, kept looking at the clock, didn't get anything done.

The female doctor was dismissive while she examined me. 'What makes this so important today?'

'I'm really worried.'

'Well don't be,' she said. 'Do you shave under your arms?'

'Yes,' I said, struggling to do up my bra.

'That's your problem, then. It's an ingrown hair that's caused a small swelling. All women get them.'

I felt pretty insignificant and stupid walking out of the surgery.

Throughout the summer a nagging voice inside my head came and went but wouldn't permanently go away. Each time I felt the lump again and remembered what the doctor said. I couldn't really be sure that the lump was the cause of this sense of foreboding. I started having a recurring dream in which I was drowning. In the dream, I was looking up at the sunlight sparkling through the surface of water while I struggled for air, choking, all the time sinking to the bottom.

That September Lauren started school and Sam, now three, was old enough for playschool. I had a bit more free time.

Amber was living back at home and had settled into a regular job. Growing up, she had always been chunky and solid, but now in her late teens, she'd lost weight and became withdrawn. Now and then, I'd ask myself if she was taking hard drugs. But each time I thought that no, I would know if she was doing anything like that. I dismissed the questions, thinking that it was just the odd joint and maybe some ecstasy pills when she went to a rave or out clubbing. It wasn't serious and she would tire of it naturally. As long as she came home a few nights a week, I accepted it.

By late November I had to listen to my instincts and go back to the doctor. I felt braver – what was the point in worrying? I had private medical insurance and would insist on a referral. This time I saw a different doctor. He was plump with a dark moustache, his face glistened with a light sweat. He smelt of old-fashioned cologne. He pushed the lump and ran his fingers over it several times.

'I don't think it's anything to worry about.' He smiled. 'But if you were my wife I'd want you to get it checked out properly. I'll send you for a mammogram.'

Picking up a pen from his desk, he started writing. 'Give the hospital a ring and make an appointment,' he said, passing me a slip of paper.

Tony came with me for the mammogram. We sat in a comfortable pink waiting room and read the newspapers. He made a cappuccino from the machine. The nurse's hands were round and warm as she squeezed my breasts into the X-ray machine. 'Take a seat back in the waiting room and I'll show these to Dr Wainwright,' she said. I got dressed and returned to my newspaper – I didn't want to look at the frightened faces of the other patients.

A few minutes later the nurse poked her head around the door. 'All okay, Mrs Lewry. You can go now,' she said with a smile. 'Doctor says there's nothing there.'

'What about the lump?'

'Just a harmless cyst.'

Tony smiled and took my hand. Although I felt relieved, the feeling didn't go all the way down, just seemed to settle half way, in my stomach.

A week later, on a Thursday morning, when I was at home alone, the hospital rang. 'Mrs Lewry, there's nothing to be concerned about, but Dr Wainwright reviewed your mammogram before filing away your case notes and has seen something on your left side. We'd been looking for signs of cancer on the right side, your right breast, where you have the lump. Could you come back this morning? It's just routine; the doctor wants to enlarge the area on the left side.'

The hospital did another mammogram, enlarging the area where the doctor had seen the cluster of cells. 'Doctor wants to do an ultrasound,' the nurse with the warm hands said.

I lay on a narrow bed while Dr Wainwright squeezed cool gel on my chest and ran the ultrasound probe over it. The room was dark apart from the faint glow from her computer. Shadows fell on the walls like ghosts in the night.

'There,' she pointed to a haze of white on the screen. 'I'll do a biopsy, then we'll organise a taxi to take it to the lab.'

'What now?'

'It won't hurt.' She opened her drawer and selected a needle, felt again for the lump in my breast and drew out some tissue. 'You'll have the result tomorrow. I'll ring you. Will you be at home?'

Walking back to my car, an unintelligible buzzing started in my head. It seemed obvious to me that I had cancer. It felt weird to have found the cause of the bad feeling. Maybe there was some solace in that.

Tony stayed home with me until the hospital rang. 'Very sorry, Mrs Lewry, but you have breast cancer.' The words sounded so trivial and yet so profound and life changing. The rest of the day I tried to stay positive: it had been caught early, the lump was fairly small. Anyway, what could I do? Break down? Scream? I had to hold on tight to the belief that I was going to be alright.

The surgeon performing my operation was tall and distinguished. His skin was the colour of pale coffee, as if he spent his winters in the sun. 'I'll just remove the lump and the surrounding tissue. No need to have a full mastectomy or remove the lymph nodes, and after the operation you won't need any more treatment. You can go back to leading a normal life,' he said. 'Christmas Eve is the first available date for the surgery, but we can wait until after Christmas if you'd rather.'

I couldn't wait.

The morning of my operation, Dr Wainwright and the

surgeon gathered around my bed. 'We're going to do a larger operation than we originally planned,' Dr Wainwright said, looking down at the clipboard in her hands. 'We've decided to take the lymph nodes from under your left arm, in addition to the lumpectomy. The lymph nodes are used to diagnose whether the cancer has spread outside the lump.'

'You'll be in a bit more pain – this means we have to cut through the muscle,' the surgeon said. I signed the form, leaving it to them to do whatever they thought might save me.

Christmas was bleak. I had done enough shopping to make sure Lauren and Sam each got a stocking on Christmas morning. It must have seemed strange to them to open their presents without Mummy being there. Amber had Christmas lunch with my mother, while Tony, Lauren and Sam spent the afternoon in hospital with me. The kids were fidgety and wouldn't settle, getting on and off my bed and running down the corridor. Tony kept calling them back.

On Boxing Day my surgeon came to see me. He smoothed out the starched sheet and sat on my bed. 'I've got the results of the biopsy. I'm afraid it's bad news,' he said as he laid a perfectly manicured hand on my shoulder. 'Of the twelve lymph nodes I removed, six have cancer. I'll arrange for you to see an oncologist. I expect he'll recommend chemotherapy.'

This wasn't the way it was supposed to turn out. 'You said the operation would be all the treatment I would need!'

'I know,' he said, 'I'm sorry.'

I turned over and stared at the wall, waiting for Tony to arrive. My life was slipping away, like grains of sand falling through my fingers. The thought that I had cancer spreading through my body was terrifying. What if I died leaving Lauren and Sam without a mother? They were so young that there would come a time when they wouldn't even remember me. I would be that photograph smiling back from the mantelpiece, a sad remnant of a woman who died long ago, never moved or put away since she left. 'What was my mummy like?' my children would ask their father.

The hospital discharged me with a drain hanging out of my chest. It filled a bottle strapped to a belt around my waist. I felt like I had aged twenty years overnight. I was weak and it hurt to walk around the house or do the simplest task. After a few days looking after me Tony had to go back to work.

'Amber been home?' Tony asked one evening.

I shuffled over to lower myself onto the sofa. 'Haven't seen her for days.'

'Doesn't she ever come home and help you? Sit with you?' He leant down to scoop up Sam before he could pull a decoration off the Christmas tree. I hadn't had the strength to put it away yet.

I shrugged my shoulders. 'She's always been the same, Tone. Sometimes I think she only cares about herself.'

I wondered why Amber didn't love me. Why didn't she care that I was ill and want to come and see me? I wasn't going to say anything to Tony – if he knew how upset I was he might judge her even more. I tensed my shoulder and moved my arm back and forth to stretch the stitches. When the pain kicked in, I winced.

'Why don't you go and lay down,' Tony said.

Upstairs in bed I let myself cry.

Tony held my hand while we waited in silence outside the oncologist's office. A silver name plate on the door read 'Dr Marshall'. His office was a calming shade of blue, and he was younger than I expected: he had a boyish fringe, green eyes and a pale face. I tried to press him for reassurance about my prognosis, but he couldn't give me any. He talked in percentages and statistics, about improvements in life expectancy of five or ten years, his voice set in a monotone devoid of hope or compassion. I expect it stopped him from getting emotionally involved with dying patients. What bloody good was five or ten years? I wanted to live, not wait it out. I wasn't going to take on his fear or negativity.

'Chemotherapy for five months and then six weeks of radiotherapy,' Dr Marshall said while flicking through my notes. 'Cut your hair before we start,' he looked up at me. 'Makes it easier when it falls out, seems like less on the pillow if it's short.'

I got my hair cut. I watched it fall on the pale, limed floorboards of the hairdresser's salon. Lauren bounded into our bedroom the next morning to climb into her usual place in bed next to me. Staring thoughtfully at my short hair and studying my face, she said, 'Doesn't look very nice Mummy, does it?'

As the appointment for my chemotherapy drew closer, I became increasingly afraid – probably the result of me watching TV programmes where cancer patients lay on the bathroom floor being sick. The chemo did make me feel sick. I tasted its bitterness in the delicate lining of my nose and at the back of my throat. It made me feel like every cell in my body had been poisoned and that I had the most dreadful hangover, yet I hadn't even had a glass of wine.

Mentally I had to pace myself. Six times, once every three weeks. I could manage that. I counted them off. After the first time, I felt sick as soon as Tony parked the car outside the hospital. After the third time, my veins seized up and they couldn't get a line in. But I settled into a pattern I could cope with. Tuesday was chemo day: Tony came with me to the hospital and when he brought me home I stayed in bed. Wednesday I made it downstairs to sit on the sofa. On the Friday after my chemo Tony took me to see a healer, and on the Monday I went back to work. Going to work made me feel normal – there I was someone other than a cancer patient. People asked about budgets, I had contracts to sign off, I had a role.

It was hard for me when all the hair on the top of my head fell out despite the torture of the cold caps. I always did care too much about my appearance.

'Do you love me?' I asked Tony whilst having the pinky-red chemotherapy dripped into my veins. The anti-sickness medication made me constipated for days and I became frail and weak. The more ill I became, the more I thought that if I died he might find a new wife; someone younger, thinner, better than me.

Sometimes at night I would wake with night terrors. I imagined I was a warrior, standing on a dark cliff in the pounding rain, a sword in my hand ready to face my foe. I looked around me to see who stood at my side. Tony was there, but not my eldest daughter.

When my treatment finished, I was cast adrift. All the time I had been having hospital appointments, chemotherapy or radiotherapy I had been doing something positive to fight the disease. Now I floated about, waiting to see whether I would sink or swim.

One day, when I got home from work, there was a silver Mercedes two-seater sitting in the drive. 'Life is for living,' Tony said, pulling me towards him for a kiss, 'and you need a treat.'

'I'll never fit the kids in that,' I laughed.

'We'll still keep the Jeep as a family car. This is just for you,' he said.

He opened the door for me to sink down inside the black

leather interior. At the touch of a button the roof slid back and folded itself neatly into the boot. I loved it.

The reactions of my friends when I told them I had cancer had been mixed. Some who I knew only casually stood beside me in the school playground and asked how I was. Others had fear and pity in their eyes and avoided me. Perhaps they were afraid that if they spoke to me I might start to cry, and they wouldn't know what to say or how to comfort me.

I pushed myself to go to the gym. At first I wore a cap, but it made me hot so I stopped wearing it. I wore the cap to walk the children to school and to go shopping, but I couldn't sit in the office all day in a hat, so I got a wig. I thought it looked alright, but when I showed it to Amber on one of her rare visits home she laughed. I went upstairs and took it off.

At the yearly finance meeting in London I had to wear my wig. Most of the committee members pretended not to notice – it was business as usual – but during lunch the chairman singled me out. He was a rare man; he had a presence that emanated kindness.

'I had cancer some years ago,' he said. 'It changed me, made me a better person. I know it's hard Christine, but you'll be glad one day you've been through this; it'll change you too.'

I smiled and I walked away. What good could ever come from thinking you might die?

Sitting on the train travelling out of London, I noticed the rain trickling down the window. The sky was grey and the darkness came on earlier than usual. Lights from shops and offices sped past.

I thought about what the chairman had said, and realised that he was right: cancer had changed me. The whole experience had made me stronger inside, as if I could cope with anything. All those coincidences, those lucky breaks – they must mean I would survive. The money and possessions I had, all the stuff, it meant nothing to me. The only thing that mattered was the people I loved: Tony and my children. I had a feeling that some destiny awaited me; that my life was mapped out in some way.

Amber

I switched off the engine and sat there for a moment in the driveway. Mum's car was not there. The garage door was open and Tony emerged from the back, wiping his hands on a cloth. 'Mum home?' I asked him cheerfully as I got out of the car.

'Haven't seen you for a while, Amber, where've you been?'

'Oh… staying at Leeanne's.' I twisted the links on the white-gold bracelet Mum had bought me last birthday, turning it around on my wrist until the clasp was at the front. 'You couldn't lend me some money, could you? As she's out.'

'You know your mum's fighting for her life, don't you? Ever think about what she's going through? Maybe you could do something for her for a change? Help with your brother and sister?' He nodded his head towards my car. 'She bought you that car you drive around in.'

If Mum died of cancer I would be an orphan. All I could think about was how much I needed her, selfishly worrying about myself instead of her. Mum always coped with things easily – she went back to work when Lauren and Sam were still babies and I never saw her get flustered or cross. I thought that there must be something wrong with me – I was her daughter, yet I found even the easy things hard.

When I was a child, Mum took me to see *Lady and the Tramp*. Mum would have been Lady: feminine and fluffy, with impeccable manners, but underneath she was tough, like at the end of the film when Lady attacks the rat when it gets into the baby's bedroom. That was Mum – hard as steel if you crossed her or threatened someone she loved. But was she strong enough to beat cancer?

'I do work full time, you know. I've been busy, that's all,' I said.

Tony moved his hand round to the back pocket of his jeans and took out a thin wad of notes. Peeling off a ten-pound note from the top with his thumb and forefinger, he flicked it at me. It fluttered slightly in the cool air and then dropped, as if by magic, at my feet.

'Best you go then,' he said coldly, and walked back into the garage.

I bent down and picked up the note. I needed the money to score. The gear couldn't take it away – the fear that Mum might die – but it helped me forget for a while. Throughout my childhood I had felt alone. I had wanted Mum to stay at home with me but she had wanted to be at work. Then, when she met Tony and had Lauren, I became the outsider. And, even now, I wasn't there at home being part of it. But I clung to that pain for protection. Being unwanted sat easier with me; I could cope with it. The thought of her dying was unbearable. So I told myself: they don't want me anyway, I'm just the mistake. Anything but face the reality of what might happen.

I had this nightmare where I was on the edge of a cliff, holding on to Mum with one hand and Lauren and Sam with the other. I knew I couldn't hold both. I had to save her, but when I looked into her face she screamed 'Don't you dare!' It was so selfish of me to want her for myself, yet what *she* wanted was for me to save them, to take care of them. So I let her go, only to wake with an overwhelming feeling of guilt.

Leeanne had a brother, Stephen. Steve and I had similar characters – we both laughed at the same things. He was stocky and muscular, really fit with a cheeky smile. He had a golden glow – something about him just sparkled. For me, he lit up the room when he entered.

It wasn't easy to score gear. Leeanne and I had spent weeks driving around trying to infiltrate the community, the secret society that was drug addiction. Searching in parks for people we recognised: 'Here, mate, can you get us any gear?'

We'd done a lot of hanging around, waiting for blokes who'd said they'd be back in ten minutes.

In desperation, we had gone to find Stephen. Stephen's story was Leeanne's story. He'd scored for us the first time but then wouldn't – didn't want his younger sister and her mate tagging along. But sooner or later he'd given in, and the spider's web of contacts had appeared.

Stephen had a baby with his girlfriend, Michelle, so the council had given them a flat. The flat was massive, but they had nothing in it. If they had a kettle they didn't have any mugs. In the sitting room there was a dirty sofa and chairs that didn't match. A cheap shelving cabinet against the wall was empty except for a Teddy bear, holding a heart that said 'Be Mine.' There was no washing machine, only a fridge that was always empty.

The baby sat in the buggy all day; it never cried.

Michelle liked to gossip – she was always talking about people – but Stephen and I liked to tease each other and be childish. 'Is that a spot on your face Amber? Or you growing a second head?' he joked while I was sitting on their sofa waiting to score. I touched my face to feel how big this spot was when a dealer came round to sort them out some gear. His name was

Dave Jenkins. He was tall but really thin, very cocky, a bit of a geezer. He hesitated when he noticed me, then gawped for a moment. 'You look healthy for a drug addict,' he said.

I cocked my head to one side. 'That's because I'm not a drug addict.'

He smiled. 'Can I take you out to dinner?'

'No,' I crossed my legs and folded my arms. 'You can't afford to take me out to dinner.'

'Why don't I give you my number? Then you can give us a bell when you change your mind.'

'Okay,' I said, thinking he might be useful to score from if I needed to. He wrote his number on my fag packet and winked as he handed it back to me.

I thought about Dave once or twice, remembering his saucy smile, so I rang him, scored some gear from him. He pursued me right from the start. He always took care of me and let me have it on tick if I didn't have any money.

'Don't worry about it, princess,' he'd say. 'You can pay me next time.'

It was easier to score off him for Leeanne and Jason. Then the three of us would smoke our gear together. Dave always told me where to meet him – an alleyway or a street corner. One night, he beckoned me from my car, I got out and when I was close he reached out and drew me towards him for a cuddle. It was the first time we had had any physical contact; he felt very protective, almost paternal. He gave me the three bags I'd ordered and I gave him the cash.

'Call me,' he touched the side of my face, 'if ever you need anything.'

Sliding back into the driver's seat, I put the bags in the tray behind the gear lever, out in the open where the three of us could see them. I had to pay attention to the road, but Leeanne and Jason didn't take their eyes off the bags. Things were always tense before we had a smoke. When we parked up and I turned around to look in the tray, there were only two bags. Maybe Leeanne or Jason had taken one, maybe I dropped one. We argued about it for a bit then decided to mix the two into one and share it between us. We were done in an hour and I dropped them off at home.

It wasn't enough: I needed a bag to myself. I phoned Dave, told him what had happened and made out I was more distressed than I actually was. He told me to come back, made me park somewhere different. He opened the passenger door and leaned inside the car. 'Look Amber, your friends have probably taken it, that's what addicts are like.' He got in the front seat and pressed a bag of gear in my hand. We smoked it together.

After that I began to do my gear with him more often.

We were smoking heroin together one winter's evening when he said, 'You're gorgeous, you are. Do you wanna go to the cinema with me?'

'What, on a proper date?'

'Yes, an official date.'

Dave arrived for our date with fifty quid's worth of crack on him, so we smoked it in the car park before we saw the film. He let me choose what I wanted to watch, and I chose *Charlie's Angels*.

After the film, Dave invited me back to his place. It was a rickety caravan in someone's garden. As I walked from one end to the other, it swayed from side to side and the floor bounced beneath my feet. Dave got out three bags of heroin and we shared them. This time he cooked it up on a spoon and injected it into a vein. I smoked my share and was pretty wrecked. 'Don't think I can drive,' I said.

'Stay the night here, princess,' Dave said.

It was cold in the caravan. We cuddled up together in his bed. The feeling of heat from his body, the rhythm of his heart, the gentle whisper of his breath on my skin; all these things are accentuated by heroin. I pulled him close to me, but there was no sex.

From that night on, Dave and I were inseparable. After I finished work each day, I went to the caravan to smoke gear with him. Soon I was getting up early to go there in the morning and smoke gear before I went to work as well.

The more my habit grew, the less I cared, about myself or anything else – as if I were swimming in the sea and being pulled out by a gentle tide, it happened naturally. I didn't see a problem. I never had to spend any money on heroin. Never had to steal for it. It just came too easily.

The fresh scent of polish filled the air as I added another layer to the counter. I wiped it away while Stacey, the Saturday girl, told me about her antics the previous evening. We both giggled. 'Isn't that your Dave outside?' she asked.

I turned around to see her gazing past me through the large, glass shopfront. Dave was pacing about outside. His head was low, but it moved up and down when he walked, as if he was trying to see in and yet hide. Holding a fag to his mouth, he looked at me to catch my gaze, then quickly looked away.

Something was wrong; he couldn't stand still. 'I'm gonna take my break now, love,' I said to Stacey.

Once I was outside, Dave was at my side in a moment. 'Babe, got a problem, had to hide some gear and it's been dug up by something. I've lost it.' He raised himself up on his heels. 'It's gone.'

I wasn't quite sure how serious this was. 'What? All of it?'

'Can't score. Don't have any cash.'

'I've got a twenty note on me.'

He was flustered and distracted, glancing left then right down the road. 'Do you get paid monthly?' His hands were trembling and he lit another fag as soon as the previous one was finished.

'Yeah.'

'How much?'

'Take home five hundred and fifty.'

He drew hard on his cigarette. 'I'm gonna need more.'

'I've got an overdraft limit of four hundred,' I offered.

'That'll do,' his face changed to a smile. 'I can get an ounce with that.'

I gave Dave my whole wage packet and drew out cash up to my overdraft limit to give him the money to get re-started. Then I waited at home while he drove to London to score. By ten o'clock my body was screaming for heroin – I was clucking and watching out of my bedroom window for his car. I rang his mobile but there was no answer. I rang again, still no answer.

When finally I recognised his car pull up the drive, I ran straight out, slamming the front door behind me and jumping into the front seat as soon as his car stopped. 'You alright? I've been worried, you didn't answer your phone!'

He was shaking. He glanced up into the rear view mirror and then opened the front of his jacket. 'I'm more than alright. I've got the fuckin' gear!'

He had it close to his chest, snuggled up like it was a baby. He pulled it out with one hand and dropped it in my lap.

It was a huge, solid brick, yet it was feather light. It had been wrapped thousands of times in cling film so that it looked shiny-silver right through. I thought about how much a tiny bag cost, a piece so small you wrapped it in a Rizla. How much would this be worth when broken down into bags?

I felt the power radiating from it, warm, like it was radioactive.

Three

Christine

I looked at my watch. Amber and Dave were an hour late and Sunday lunch was ready.

'Where are they?' Tony said as he opened the oven to a gush of vapour. 'Potatoes are done, we can't wait any longer.'

Lunch was on the table and smelled delicious, butter melting on the vegetables and steam rising from a jug of gravy. Everyone had started eating when Amber and Dave finally arrived – breezing in, all smiles and excuses. Somehow they were always late for family gatherings and could never stay very long. There was usually a compelling reason why they had to leave early. I wouldn't let myself get upset today.

'Would you like a glass of wine or a beer, Dave?' I asked as he settled in at the table.

'No thanks, I'm driving, but I'll have a nice cup of tea.'

I sighed. 'I'll make one when lunch is finished.'

My own mother said, 'He's such a nice boy – doesn't drink and drive, does he?' Then she peered down the table and smiled at him.

'Do you still need to borrow some money from me this month, Amber?' I asked.

Amber opened her mouth to speak, but Dave butted in: 'Don't worry Mum, I've sorted it.'

I blinked; I'm not his mother. Then he gave me this cheesy smile.

'Oh okay, if you're sure,' I said.

When Amber first met Dave I thought he was a decent lad, a steady influence on her. Everyone liked him. But, as their relationship grew, I could see how dependent Amber was on him. Dave was friendly and cheerful around us, but I suspected he had a dark side. I wondered what she saw in him. Amber had this beautiful speaking voice, whereas Dave sounded common and talked in slang. I didn't like myself for being disappointed in my daughter's choice, but I couldn't help it.

A few weeks later, waiting outside Dr Marshall's office for my check-up, I flicked through the pages of a crumpled magazine. By now I knew how the appointment would go: he would ask me if I had any symptoms or pain, and then he'd examine me and I would leave. It was a ten-minute slot every three months during which I would speak about my fears – I was searching for symptoms all the time.

My knee had started to hurt after I did my step class each week, so I told Dr Marshall. He organised a blood test for me, to look for 'markers', whatever they are. Then he decided I needed a bone scan. Both tests came back normal, so he said it was just me getting older. One day, I had a dreadful pain in my head while I was doing a complicated spreadsheet at work. Alone in my car at the end of the day, I couldn't stop the tears welling up in my eyes. I cried, convinced I had a brain tumour and only months left to live. By the time I got home, I had imagined my own death and organised my funeral. I took some aspirin and went to bed. The next day the pain was gone.

Sometimes, when I was alone, I took off my bra and studied my body in the mirror, asking myself whether I was still attractive. My left breast was deformed, but not that badly. I asked Tony what he thought, and he said he only fancied women who had one bigger than the other, which was lucky.

I started to feel different inside – stronger, in a way that only the inward me could feel. I became less afraid of dying one day, and determined that when that day came my life wouldn't have been a disappointment. I didn't want wealth or fame, but something less tangible – the sense that, however simple my life had been, I had been true to myself and done the right thing. I came to see having cancer as a catalyst for positive change in my life, the start of a more spiritual me.

The chemotherapy gave me an early menopause, but six months later my periods returned. At my next appointment, Dr Marshall recommended I had my ovaries removed. 'Breast cancer feeds on hormones. A year down the line we might regret it if you don't.'

I would have it done – I told him I would – but I wanted something to look forward to first. I wanted to take Lauren and Sam to Disneyland.

Arriving home, holiday brochures in my hand, Amber opened the door for me. 'Been out shopping again?' she asked.

'No. I've been for my check-up.' I didn't tell her everything. I kept my fear inside. Because when the panic surfaced there was no-one inside my head to share it – no-one who could feel the terror with me. I was alone.

'Oh,' she said thoughtfully, as if she'd just remembered about the cancer. 'What did the doctor say? Has he given you the all clear?'

'They can't tell if it's spread. You just have to wait and see.'

'Hair's growing back nicely though.'

'Yeah, it's a bit curly.' I ran my fingers through it. 'I'm glad you're home. Tony and I are going to take the kids on holiday for a couple of weeks. You'll be alright here won't you? I want to do things now, in case I get ill again.'

'I'll be fine. You go, have a good time.'

Although it was winter at home, I had been expecting Florida to live up to its nickname as the Sunshine State. The sun did shine, but it was minus six degrees. We were so cold the kids had to wear everything in their suitcase at once. The only shopping we did was to buy winter clothes. The five days in the Disney park were great, watching the parade and going on the rides. The second part of our holiday was a week on the beach. Sitting on my sunbed in a fleece, two towels wrapped around my legs, I noticed Tony shivering.

'Let's change the flights and go home early,' I said.

He smiled. 'Be nice to have a few days at home before I go back to work.'

'Shall I ring Amber and tell her?'

'No, let's just surprise her.'

Landing at Gatwick, there was a light layer of early-morning snow on the ground, with more in shady areas. But by the time we had collected our car and driven home, it had all melted. Pulling up the drive, I noticed the back door was open. Tony noticed it too, but put his key in the lock and went through the front door.

Amber appeared from the kitchen. She was blood red in the face and I could see she was frightened, like she was hiding something. 'Why's the back door open?' Tony demanded.

'Just having a quick fag in the utility room. I opened it to let the smoke out.' Amber's little hands were shaking. 'It's too cold to stand outside.'

'You're not allowed to smoke in the house. Wear your coat if it's cold.'

Tony was pretty pissed off. I felt sorry for Amber – the house was okay, she was only having a fag. Tony walked around looking in all the rooms, checking things, and then I heard him go outside. The kids had hardly slept during the flight back, so I packed them into their beds, drawing all the curtains upstairs to try and make it dark.

Downstairs Dave was standing at the front door. A Onestop carrier bag was in his hand with a roll of tin foil sticking out the top. What were they planning to cook in my house with a roll of foil?

'Back early from your hols?' Dave asked.

'Yeah, weather wasn't too good. What are you doing here?' I asked him.

'Been up the shop, come to get Amber.' They left in his car.

Tony came back into the house holding a piece of tin foil. 'What's this?' He showed it to me – it had lines of brown burn marks down it. 'I found it on the path hidden behind a bush.'

'Do you think they use it to smoke dope or something?'

'I think it's more than dope. She's up to something, I know it.'

Tony was right. Perhaps I should have asked Amber what she'd been doing, confronted her. What was it that stopped me? Maybe there was something I didn't want to see.

The next time I saw Amber I started to question her about the foil. She changed the subject, told me she was moving in with Dave. 'We're getting a bedsit together,' she said.

'What? Have you found something already?'

'Yep, we're moving in next weekend.'

Before I had cancer, when the kids were small, we used to

36

spend time together, the four of us. Amber always made them laugh. She loved having a brother and sister – I think it finally gave her a family. I wanted Amber and me to be close, go shopping together for make-up and clothes, but she never gave me that intimacy. She only allowed me access to the surface of her life. She showed me what she wanted me to see, and I accepted it as the truth.

It was easier for me that way, and it was easier for me not to have her living at home.

Amber

Dave laid out the newspaper on the table. 'Don't want to live in Aldershot,' he said, folding the page over at 'Properties to Let'. 'The police in town know me; if I'm seen, they might start to watch me, follow me.'

We found a bedsit in Farnborough, a town about four miles away. The landlord was foreign and accepted cash, which was good because Dave didn't have a bank account.

The place was a bit dodgy. It wasn't very clean, just a big downstairs room in a shared house with a huge fireplace in the middle of one wall, like you were living in someone's front room. We wandered around while the landlord stood by the door. I was thinking how I could fix it up, make it a home for us. I moved over to where Dave was standing by one of the large windows. Taking his hand in mine, I whispered, 'Do you like it?' Dave didn't look at me, just kept staring out of the window to the ground below.

'Yeah. Could jump that if I had to.'

The other people who lived in the house were foreign. Some

of them were illegal immigrants – we didn't care, it suited us. The landlord had all sorts of cars parked on some waste land at the side of the house. Most of them were old and rusty, as if they hadn't been used in years, but there was space for both Dave and me to park off the road. Best thing was that we could afford the place – we settled in nicely.

I started giving Leeanne free gear – well, sharing my gear with her – so I would ask Dave for more, sooner. But then he put a stop to that. I was never cross with Leeanne for asking. I knew I would have done the same, if things had been the other way round. Leeanne would never beg someone for drugs, but she couldn't afford the habit she'd grown. I began to get distressed phone calls from her late at night, when a boyfriend dumped her or she'd lost another job. I'd drive somewhere to pick her up, as it was an emergency Dave would sort her out some gear and she'd sleep in our bed, me in the middle.

Dave stayed home while I went to work. He played games on his computer and watched TV all day. His mobile rang constantly with business.

'You'll never guess what I've done today, princess?' Dave said one evening when I got in. He was rather pleased with himself. Stubbing the last of his fag in the ashtray, he said, 'I've booked us a holiday.'

'A holiday!' I never questioned Dave's plans. He must have thought this through. 'What about the gear?'

'I'll worry about that. We're going skiing.'

'That's wonderful, babe.' I sat on his knee and flung my arms around his neck. 'Can I get a ski suit and boots?'

'Yep.' He laid his hand on my waist.

'Oh, we're gonna need flight bags and those little travel kits with wash stuff in them.'

'Anything you want, princess,' he winked at me. 'Anything.'

Dave usually bought an ounce of heroin at a time, which cost him between six hundred and eight hundred pounds. He cut the ounce into smaller amounts and sold them on to dealers who knocked out bags. Dealers who worked for Dave were 'laid on' by him. They came to him with no money and he gave them an amount of gear. 'I want eighty quid for that,' he'd say. When the guy had sold it on in smaller amounts for whatever he could make, he came back to Dave and paid him the eighty pounds in exchange for more gear.

The week before we went away, I noticed Dave was giving them double amounts. 'I don't normally do this, right. Make it last. I ain't gonna be here,' I heard him say.

I told Leeanne we were going away. 'You'll have to score your gear somewhere else while we're gone,' I said.

I let Dave take care of our supply of heroin for the trip. I'd never have upset him or challenged him. What would I have done if he'd turned around and told me to piss off? I'd have been screwed. He made two packets of heroin, one for him to carry and one for me. He wrapped them in layers of cling film and burnt it on, to seal it. His he pushed up his arse. Thoughtfully, he made mine in a tampon shape with a string.

Everything about the journey seemed to take longer than anticipated. We had to be at the airport hours before our flight took off, and we had to wait ages for our bags in France. I made sure the driver put our cases in the luggage compartment and then got on the coach, making my way to the back to find a double seat for Dave and me. He was agitated, settling in beside me.

'Not much longer, babe,' I said. Back home it would have been usual for Dave to have a hit every two hours. The driver started the coach and the throb of the diesel engine rattled away as we pulled out of the airport.

The snow on the slopes that week was fresh and thick. Although it was bitterly cold, the sun shone from a cloudless sky, giving the frozen landscape a beautiful brilliance and making it sparkle. We started to have a nice holiday. We skied down the runs without fear. The only thing that bothered us was the exertion of side-stepping back up the hill – we were knackered before we got very far. In the evenings, we went out for a drink and a meal we hardly ate. We went to bed early. We did heroin – lots of it.

It wasn't long before our supply looked a bit sparse. We'd taken loads with us, more than enough for a normal week. But if junkies have gear they can't stop themselves – they do it. We had to evaluate how much gear we had left and how we could make it last until we got home.

Dave phoned his mum, Linda, every couple of days. The day before we were due to come home, I heard him speaking to her on the phone. 'You'll have to bring some when you pick us up from the airport.' He rested his mobile under his ear. 'I've run out. I'll need it. You know where to get it. Make sure you've got it with you.'

Linda must have told him that our bedsit had been burgled.

'Do you know what's been taken? Who called the police? Did the landlord come out?' He questioned her for ages.

Dave said goodbye and threw the phone on the bed. He was worked up and worried, and told me what had happened at home. He needed a hit and we hardly had any gear left.

'Why don't I have a hit babe, instead of a smoke,' I said.

'What?'

'Don't get cross. I'll only need a fraction if I do.'

His face changed. 'You alright with that, princess?'

I wanted to try a hit, wanted to recreate that first rush. I was tired of watching him pass out after banging up, his eyes rolling in his head while I smoked on and on, these days only getting a tingle. 'I'd do it for you.'

He smiled. 'Come here.' I moved over to encircle my arms around his waist. My head rested on his chest. He squeezed me tight and kissed the top of my head.

Dave got out his kit and the remaining gear. He found a vein on the top of my hand – it came up easily under his expert technique. He drew some blood to make sure it was in correctly, then pushed the needle home. The effect was different from smoking a boot – immediate, strong, yet with a softer buzz. It didn't feel so sickly. The injection gave me a sudden wave of good feeling, whereas with a boot it would build up slowly.

We stayed in our room the afternoon and evening before our journey home. We had to wait as long as we could before taking our last hit. Watching TV in our bed, we held on to each other in the semi-darkness. By one o'clock in the morning, we couldn't wait any longer and injected the last of our gear.

Early next morning, we were waiting at the bus stop for the coach before it arrived. Dave was already looking ill. 'You gonna make it back okay?' I asked him.

'Gonna try and sleep,' he said.

At the airport, Dave got our cases while I went inside to find out where to check in. The information board came in and out of focus. I had to concentrate hard to find our flight number. The sweat trickled down my back, yet despite wearing my ski jacket I was cold. A wave of dizziness came over me and I thought I was going to faint. Dave came in, leaning on the luggage trolley. The desperation on his face was unreal. The departure lounge was busy. There were no seats and the only place to sit was on the floor. The time passed slowly.

'Flight should have been called by now,' Dave said, and got up to check the screen. He sat back down for a few minutes before getting up again to hang around the information desk, annoying the airport staff and constantly asking what was happening. Forty-five minutes passed. Nothing.

Then our flight flashed on the screen as 'boarding'. A wave of passengers got up instantly to go to the gate. Dave grabbed me and our stuff, pushing past everyone. We both looked pretty bad. Almost everyone stepped out of our way. You could see the thunder on Dave's face. I heard one guy mutter 'You know what, mate? I'm just gonna let you go past.'

At the head of the queue for security, which was located at the entrance to the gate, Dave shoved himself directly in front of a woman with big bosoms wearing a beige knitted cardigan buttoned up to her neck. 'You won't get there any quicker, you know,' she said in a schoolteacher voice.

Dave swivelled around to face her with lighting speed, like a rabid dog foaming at the mouth. He put his face close to hers and shouted: 'Fucking… watch… me!'

He slammed his bag on the conveyor belt and walked through the metal detector. He was confident; he wasn't carrying drugs this time.

The security guard stopped him. 'What? What?' Dave looked around, opening his hands in a gesture of innocence. The beeper had not gone off.

'No. No. You must go back… shoes. You must take off your shoes,' the guard replied, pointing at Dave's feet.

Dave marched back. He pulled off his shoes and hurled them at the conveyor belt. One of them bounced up high and then fell back into the queue of people we had pushed past. They stared silently. After a few moments, the shoe was passed back down the queue to be replaced on the belt.

Dave had a last fag and we walked out to board the plane.

In the baggage hall back at Gatwick, I pulled a trolley out from the rows stacked up against the wall, placed my hand luggage on the top and rested against it for support. I felt dizzy again and my legs were wobbly. The sweat was running down my forehead and my back felt completely wet. I lay down on the cool tiled floor and looked across the large hall. Everyone was milling around impatiently. I closed my eyes.

The conveyor belt came to life with a whine and a creak. One or two suitcases emerged. Dave saw our bags. It was as if someone had put a rocket up his arse: suddenly he had loads of energy. He grabbed our suitcases, fast, and marched us through 'Nothing to Declare'.

To people standing in the crowd by the passenger exit waiting to collect friends or relatives from flights, Dave looked like a long-lost son who hadn't seen his mother for ten years. He dived straight under the barrier and embraced her. It wasn't a violent embrace – there was nothing nasty or scary about it – but he had a firm grip of her. He put his hands under her armpits and scooped her up to face him, like a praying mantis staring at its meal. I hurried along to stand beside him.

'Tell me,' he whispered in her ear, 'you've fuckin' got it.'

'But... but Dave.'

'No,' he interrupted her coldly, 'just tell me... you've fuckin' got it!'

Linda didn't have it.

'The night you were burgled someone called the police. The

landlord came out to let them into the bedsit. He told the coppers you were on holiday. One of them recognised you, Dave, from a photo on the mantelpiece. The police might be watching me, waiting for me to collect you from the airport. That's why I didn't bring it.'

Dave released his grip.

'The police wouldn't fuckin' bother to pick me up on the way back. Even they would know I wouldn't have any drugs on the way back. They're not fuckin' stupid! They'd wait for me to get home and go and deal some fuckin' drugs!'

When we got to the car he had to have the keys, to drive, to control the journey back. All the time shouting at his mother. We drove out of the airport car park, past the twenty-four-hour service station, on to the motorway. Dave glanced at the dashboard for the first time.

He screamed a high-pitched scream, like a girl. 'You haven't even got enough fuckin' petrol to get me home!' He banged his hands up and down on the steering wheel and stamped his feet on the floor. 'How fuckin' useless are you woman?'

'Oh, yeah,' Linda said and sank back in her seat. 'I meant to get some on the way here.' A few moments passed. She leaned down and picked up her bag from the floor, found her mobile phone and called her husband. 'Hi honey, bit of an emergency here, we need to know where the petrol stations are on the way home from the airport.'

Dave let out the high-pitched, girlie scream. 'I know where the fuckin' petrol stations are!'

'Oh, it's okay. We know where the petrol stations are,' she said and hung up.

We stopped, quickly got some petrol and were back on the motorway again when I felt sick. I'm not sure whether it was the smell of petrol or Dave's erratic driving as he swerved from lane to lane, overtaking anywhere he could.

'I'm going to be sick,' I said with my hand over my mouth.

Dave screeched to a halt on the hard shoulder. He jumped out of the driver's seat, came round to the back where I was sitting and opened the door. I thought: how kind and caring he is, to come and see if I'm okay. With one arm around my body, he lifted me out of the car with a surprising amount of strength and opened the door to the front seat where Linda was sitting. 'Drive home as quickly as you can.'

She climbed over to sit in the driver's seat. 'But Amber's being sick.'

Dave sat in the passenger seat and pulled me up between his legs with my back to his chest, like a rag doll. He pressed the button on the door and the electric window went down. Taking hold of my long hair, he pulled it behind my head and shoved my face out of the window.

'Then she can be sick while we're going.'

We drove the rest of the way while I puked out of the window.

When we reached the outskirts of Aldershot, Dave phoned a dealer on his mobile. 'Are you in? Get cooking.'

We pulled up outside the house. 'You,' he said to his mum, 'wait here.'

'But Dave, I need to…' He slammed the car door shut.

I couldn't walk. I don't know how I managed to get inside. First I knelt on the floor and then I lay down, unable to control the shaking. Dave sat on the guy's bed and took his hit. 'Get your foil out, smoke your boot,' he said.

'I can't, Dave. I can't do it. Hit me again this one time? Do it for me, just this once.'

'Put that idea out of your head, it's not an option. Smoke it or go without. Come on, sit up and sort yourself out while I go and stick the kettle on.' A smile appeared on his face. 'I fancy a nice cup of tea.'

Four

Amber

Sinking back into the bath, I let the warm, soapy water wash away the sweat and dirt of our journey home. Dave's family lived in a Victorian terraced house. It had little rooms with tall ceilings, but the bathroom was large, with varnished floorboards and an old-fashioned bath standing on brass paws. It was big enough for Dave and me to sit in together.

'We can't go back to the bedsit. Now the police know we're there it's dangerous. I'll tell the landlord you're too upset at the thought of someone breaking in to live there any more,' he said.

'How long can we stay here?' I asked him.

'They've already said we can only stay one night.'

'Where can I have a boot?'

'In the shed. Don't worry, princess, I'll show you.'

Dave took me around the back of the house to the garden. It was quite a small garden with quite a large shed. Inside, it had the sleepy smell of rotting wood and damp earth. It seemed to be set up perfectly for Dave. There was a comfortable chair and a bench, just at the right height for him to lay his arm on while he banged up. It had electricity and even a kettle. Dave was right at home doing his gear in the shed, as if he had done it in there many times before.

Before our holiday, Dave had placed the rest of his gear in a tin with some coffee beans, to hide the smell from police dogs, and then taped it to the underside of one of the landlord's old cars that was parked beneath our bedsit window. Linda and I went inside to pack up all our possessions while Dave disappeared outside to retrieve his gear.

Linda saw his head go past the window. 'What are you doing, Dave?' she called.

Although she knew he was an addict, he still lied to her. 'Just checking out this broken window.' Dave stopped as if he had spotted something on the top of the car. He hesitated, then climbed up to have a closer look.

'Amber,' he called through the window, beckoning me with his hand, 'pass us one of your shoes.'

'Why do you want my shoe?'

'I'm gonna measure this footprint, see what size it is. Whoever tried to break in climbed up here.' Dave had a puzzled expression. 'It's a woman's footprint,' he said.

After that first night at his mum's, Dave and I stayed in cheap hotels. He walked into the reception of the Travelodge in Aldershot dressed in baggy tracksuit bottoms, a sports top and trainers, a heavy gold chain around his neck and a large gold hoop through his ear. I followed him, with my small overnight bag.

'We're here on business, mate, we're not from this area,' he said to the receptionist. 'Need a room for a couple of nights.'

'Okay sir.' The guy managed to keep his face expressionless. 'Let me see what I have available.'

'I'm gonna need a bathroom.'

'All our rooms have en-suite bathrooms, sir.'

'I'm gonna need a kettle.'

'All our rooms have tea- and coffee-making facilities. Would you like a smoking or non-smoking room?'

'Smoking. And I'm gonna need that on the ground floor.'

The guy looked up from his computer. 'I'm not sure I know which rooms are on the ground floor.'

'Well, I have a phobia of heights and… and vertigo.'

I held my lips in a tight line and studied my feet. The guy went off to check which rooms were on the ground floor and came back smiling. He gave us a room around the back of the hotel, with a large grass area under our window facing onto a busy road. Perfect.

Dave dealt drugs out of our hotel window that night. Having been away for a week, he did a lot of business. Some of the dealers got lost, trying to work out which window to knock at. A squeal came from two women in the room next to ours as a druggie tapped on their window late that night. 'Is there someone outside?' one of them asked. Then I heard muddy footsteps scuttle away in the wrong direction.

I had to go back to work the next day. Dave was waiting for me when I finished. He was shaking. 'We're not staying at the Travelodge in Aldershot any more; I've packed your stuff.'

'Where're we going to stay, then?'

'How do you fancy the Travelodge in Farnborough?'

He didn't tell me why we had left so suddenly. When we checked into our new room and I unpacked my things, I realised he'd left one of my gold earrings behind.

'I think I'll ring the hotel, ask if they found it when they cleaned our room.'

'Don't fuckin' bother.'

'But I like these ones, Dave.'

'I said no! I'll buy you some more fuckin' earrings!'

Dave had been on edge since he'd got a phone call a few days ago from someone he didn't know asking for a bag of heroin, although all the caller had said was 'Have you got any bags?' A bag is a draw of heroin worth ten pounds wrapped in a Rizla. Dave didn't sell bags any more and hadn't done for at least a year. It was well known on the street; if Dave had gear, other dealers had bags, so there was no need to bother Dave. So when he got the call asking for bags he felt certain it was the police.

'What sort of bags, mate? Shopping bags? Paper bags? Might have a few plastic bags under the sink.'

'No,' the caller protested. 'I want to buy drugs.'

Junkies call heroin 'gear' not 'drugs'. Dave laughed. 'I never touch drugs mate. Who are you? How'd you get my number?'

The caller hung up.

Dave switched off his phone. We knew that if the police had his number they might be listening to his calls, trying to get evidence against him. 'I'll have to use your phone now for business,' he said.

Dave and I had to move hotels every couple of days and it was proving more difficult to get a room on the ground floor. One of the hotels we tried recommended a nearby pub where all the rooms were on the ground floor. Dave booked us in. The landlady liked Dave. She made lovely food each night and after dinner Dave liked to sit in the bar drinking cups of tea. He met drug dealers there. He dealt drugs from our room.

'You know what, princess?' Dave said when I was searching through the papers for somewhere more permanent for us to stay. 'I can afford a house now, all to ourselves.'

'Really? Oh Dave, I've always wanted a home of my own.'

It took me a week to find something Dave was happy with. I showed him the ad and he rang the landlord. Luckily, the landlord was happy to accept cash and didn't seem bothered about a reference. We met him at the house the next day to look around. He had a tenancy agreement for us to fill in.

'Gonna stick it in the girlfriend's name; got a couple of CCJs,' Dave said.

The landlord didn't seem phased and gave the form to me.

'Got some cash here, for the deposit,' Dave said.

'Lovely, mate.' The landlord counted it out and slipped it in his back pocket. Dave arranged for everything to be in my name: gas, electricity, council tax, everything. 'Safer that way, princess.' It suited Dave that I was working. It gave our life credibility.

We were busy shifting boxes from my car the day we moved in when my mobile rang. Dave answered. 'Who is it?' I whispered.

'Dunno,' he passed me the phone.

It was Michelle, Stephen's girlfriend. 'Here mate, thought you'd wanna know, your best friend's sitting in my flat right now, saying you're banging up.'

I didn't know what to say. Why would Leeanne say that? I'm not a dirty drug addict injecting gear. I only smoke it – I'm in control and it's just a bit of fun. I denied it.

'Yeah, thought you'd wanna know. Left the baby and everything, come up the phone box to tell you.' Michelle was a stirrer, but she got me wound up with this one.

I spent the evening moaning to Dave about Leeanne. He listened to me ranting and raving. Finally, he said, 'I think it was Leeanne that broke into the bedsit.'

'Don't be ridiculous!' I snapped.

'Think about it, Amber. She's the only addict who knew where we were living. The only person you told we were away and might be desperate enough to try and break in. The only cunt that would fuckin' steal off us!'

'Don't be so bloody stupid. She wouldn't do it. She wouldn't steal off me.'

'It doesn't matter anyway.' He turned away, as if talking to himself, and muttered into the doorway. 'I'll get my revenge.'

Christine

Shaking open a black dustbin bag, letting out a strong smell of cheap plastic, I gazed around Amber's room. Opening up the drawers and cupboards, I slowly collected all the things she had left, things that she hadn't had room for in the bedsit: clothes she had hardly worn, cuddly toys from her childhood and some old photographs. I sat down on the bed and looked through them.

'We're getting a house now, Mum. Can you bring my stuff over?' she'd said when she phoned to tell me about their holiday. I was glad they'd had a nice time.

I glanced at the time. I needed to be back from their house before the kids finished school. The address Amber had given me was on a large council estate. It was all grey, each house the same. Built in the seventies during an explosion of badly designed cheap housing. The garden was an oblong piece of dried brown grass with a muddy path down the middle where people had taken a direct route to the back door and the grass underneath had lost the will to live. There was rubbish in the garden – I hoped they were going to take it away.

Inside, the house smelt musty and old, as if someone had died in there. There were no radiators and it felt damp. The old-fashioned kitchen had a few free-standing cupboards and a sink. I looked inside the larder. Old jars of spices were left at the back. Layers of dust had fallen on them over the years like gentle snow that had hardened now into a layer of black filth. I shut the door. 'It's a bit dirty, Amber.'

Amber's face dropped. 'I know, Mum, but I'm gonna clean it up and make it nice.' I leaned back against the wall. Okay, I supposed that they had to start at the bottom, make the best of things. Amber pulled on some yellow rubber gloves and started to clean the sink. 'I'm ready for this. We'll get married one day and have a baby,' she said.

Why did I have a sense of unease? Was it her? My daughter had been beautiful before she met Dave, but she had become so un-groomed, never wearing make-up or painting her nails any more. Her hair had got really long but she never had it cut or styled. Every time I saw her she was thinner, as if she was fading away.

'Is this what you want?' I asked her. 'Are you happy, Amber?'

'I'm different now, I've changed.'

I walked around upstairs. The toilet was dark brown beneath the water line, I was glad I didn't have to go to the loo in there. In the bedroom lots of clothes were hanging on coat hangers, on the back of the door and on hooks in the wall.

'Where did you get the money for all these clothes?'

Amber stood in the doorway watching me. 'I have a uniform allowance from work, and if I want anything else I get a discount.'

I wandered past her into the spare bedroom; her eyes followed me. It was a big house for the two of them. 'Are you sure you can afford this?'

'Dave's got more work on now.'

'You haven't got a bank loan or credit cards, have you?'

Amber was becoming irritated. 'No, Mum! Dave's working, that's why he's not here.'

I wrap my arms around myself. 'You're not lying, are you?'

'Why would I lie to you? What reason do I have to lie? Where else do you think we got the money?'

'You've lied to me before.'

'Dave works with his father. We go to church with them every Sunday. They know we've got this house. How could he go to church with them yet lie?'

She was right, I was being stupid. What could they be doing? It's not like they could have robbed a bank or something. I told myself that I'd already had my share of bad luck and that everything was fine.

I paused for a moment. 'You know… if you wanted to, you could just come home.' I was surprised when I heard myself say it – it was like the words just popped out.

Amber hesitated and gazed into the room. For a moment I thought she was going to say 'okay I will.'

'My room will always be there, won't it, Mum? It'll always be *my* room?'

A door slammed downstairs and she became agitated and jumped out of her daydream. 'I know you think Dave's not good enough for me! You're right he's not that good looking. Doesn't have the body of a god! But he makes me feel secure. Don't judge him, Mum! He's sweet to me and good natured. I feel safe with him… like nothing can touch me.'

I never had understood her. Although I couldn't accept less, maybe she could. And why did I always want her to come up to my standards? Why couldn't I just be happy for her? Part of me was glad she had said no – what would I have said to Tony? I should have been grateful Dave was taking care of her.

I helped her to unpack her things and left, taking with me all my hopes of ever being proud, of telling everyone how well she was doing, of how I had struggled at times when she was young to bring her up on my own but had done a good job. And I buried all thoughts of us ever being truly close. This was her life; it was what she wanted. I couldn't make her into what I wanted her to be.

Amber

In the dim light at the back of the shop, I glanced at one of the mannequins. Although their eyes were fixed in a stare, occasionally I thought I could see them move. It was spooky, like a waxwork museum. I kicked a pile of cardboard out of my way and moved nearer to the security system. Fibres and dust floated into the air, scratching at my nostrils. It smelt industrial, sterile and new.

I pressed the buttons on the numbered keypad. Beep, beep, beep, then nothing. The other members of staff waited by the front door. My mind had gone blank.

'Can we go yet, Amber?' someone shouted.

'Hang on.' Beep, beep, beep. I was sure that was the right number. Had I written it down somewhere? I tried it the other way round. Beep, beep, beep, then a low, dull, continuous tone. That was it. 'Yeah, let's go.'

The early evening was overcast and dull. Although it wasn't cold, I felt a chill breeze blow around my legs. I shivered and pulled my coat tight at the neck.

Dave was hanging around the back door waiting for me when I got home – he was always right where I left him. He was a bit more alert than normal, shifting his weight from one foot to the other.

'Something ain't right,' he said, and pushed his hands deep into the pockets of his trackies. 'I can feel it.'

'Uh huh,' I said and strolled past him into the kitchen. I never got too excited about Dave's strange feelings. 'Cup of tea?' I unbuttoned my coat and slung it on the side.

I prodded the tea bags in the hot water while he stood beside me.

'Yeah.' He stared past me through the window. 'I reckon they're out there, watching us.'

I wandered into the sitting room and crashed in the chair; I didn't bother to change out of my work clothes. He followed me in with his tea, sparked a fag and drew hard, making the butt wet and flat. 'Can you feel it, princess?' He blew the cigarette smoke curling into the room.

'Yeah, suppose I can.' Slipping off my shoes, I tucked up my feet, switched on the TV and gazed at the screen.

Dave drifted back to the kitchen. He stood at the window, looking out at our back garden. I heard him muttering 'Shall I hide it? What if I lose it? What if they follow me and then they find it?'

He decided to go out, not in the car but walking. He reckoned it was easier to lose a tail on foot down the paths and alleyways that linked the estate where we lived. He sorted me a boot of heroin before he went out. I was glad to enjoy it in peace.

Within an hour he was back. 'I'm definitely being followed,' he said.

'Are you, babe?'

'Yeah, did you see them at the bottom of our road, trying to look like workmen?' His eyes darted from side to side. 'They've been there for two days, right, but they ain't even dug the road. I thought they're odd them blokes, they're wearing new hard hats and fluorescent jackets. It ain't right, I know it.'

From my chair I watched him through the open back door. He wheeled his push bike out of the shed, turned the wheel with his foot then rode it out of the gate.

He was only gone fifteen minutes. 'It's no good, I gotta bad feeling,' he said when he got back.

'If you're not going out to bury it, then hide it at home. You decide, Dave.'

If he did bury it, out in the woods away from the house, there was always the risk of losing it. Dave had buried drugs before. When a few days had passed and he hadn't been raided, he'd relaxed again and, thinking things were okay, he'd gone back to get the stash only to find it had been dug up by a dog or a fox. Animals always know where the ground has recently been disturbed and are attracted to it.

Hiding drugs is like asking someone to bury three grand in the woods and then find it again when they're smashed out of their face.

Dave didn't go out again. He decided to hide the heroin in the house. There was a ventilation shaft beneath the airing cupboard, like a chimney, and once you took out the floorboards you could access this hollow shaft. Dave often hid things down there: drugs, cash and a gun.

'Feel better now.' He brushed the dust off his sleeve. 'Think I'll cook up another hit.' So we both got even more wrecked.

I smiled, letting the wave of good feelings sweep over me.

Dave was invincible – there was no way the police would ever catch him. Heroin induces a state of mind, a serenity, a sleepiness, and on the nod I went to bed.

I woke to the sound of our front door shattering against the banister. It ruptured the night like a rifle shot. I opened my eyes and looked at Dave. He was wide awake. 'It's the Old Bill,' he whispered.

'Shouldn't we run?' I lay still, listening to heavy footsteps pounding up the stairs, shouts of 'Police! Police!'

'Won't make any difference now.'

Part Two

Realising Reality

Five

Amber

Navy blue uniforms burst into our bedroom. They fill the room like water through flood gates, moving around, crowding the space.

'Is there anybody else in the house?' A policewoman leans down and shouts in my face. 'Is there anyone else in the house? Any children? Any dogs?' I look at her silently. I feel no adrenaline rush. No fear. 'Answer me! Is there anybody else in the house?'

'No, no-one,' I say.

'David Jenkins, get up and sit on the bed. We have a warrant to search the premises. Get dressed, now!'

Dave is submissive. He gets up and finds some clothes, and the male officers surround him and take him into the spare bedroom.

'We know there are drugs in the house.' The policewoman stares at me. She folds her arms and leans back. 'You don't want to be an accessory to this. He doesn't have to know you've told us. If you tell us where they are it'll make the whole process a lot quicker, be easier for you.'

Still stoned on smack from the night before, I feel I'm

protected by bubble wrap. Reality is distorted and distant. The situation is bad, I know that, but it's as if it's happening to someone else and it's not quite close enough to touch me. The policewoman's lips are moving and I recognise some of the words she's saying but can't quite understand the whole sentence. She narrows her eyes. 'What clothes do you want to wear?' I point to some jeans and a tee shirt hanging over the back of the chair. She searches the pockets thoroughly before handing them to me. 'Underwear?'

'In that drawer.'

'Which ones do you want?'

I raise my shoulders. 'Any.' She takes a pair of knickers out of the drawer and puts her fingers inside the cotton gusset, probing for anything I might have hidden there. Satisfied, she gives them to me.

A police dog trainer brings two Alsatian dogs into the bedroom. 'Oh, nice doggie.' I reach out my hand to stroke one of them. It snarls slightly and curls its top lip.

The door opens and Dave is brought back into the room. He holds my gaze before looking away. 'Put your hands out,' a police officer says to us both. One of the dogs has a really good sniff. It tickles my fingers. The other dog does the same to Dave. The trainer gives the dogs a verbal command and a hand signal. Immediately they start to sniff the floor, the walls, everywhere.

Dave and I recently bought some new carpet for our bedroom, but, being stoned the whole time, we hadn't measured it properly. Later, when we tried to fit the carpet, it was too big and there was an overlap around the edge where about two inches stood up against the wall. While Dave was out last night, I'd taken a Stanley knife and tried to trim it off, but after a short time I'd got bored and only one corner of the room had been done. The dog that sniffed my hands goes straight to this corner and sniffs all over it, then scratches the floor three times and stares at the trainer.

One of the coppers lets out a cry of delight. Another one rips up the carpet where the dog is standing and then starts to remove the floorboards. The dog has told them what they asked it to – where my hands last were – but this information won't necessarily give them the answer they were hoping for.

A plain-clothes detective enters the room. He's tall and bald, and his face is dominated by a large nose; he could smoke a fag in the shower and it wouldn't get wet. 'Where's the rest of it, Dave?' He shows Dave a piece of mirror from downstairs. 'Come on, you know I'm gonna find it. There's enough heroin on this mirror to hold you both for questioning.' He looks across at me and smirks. 'Make it a lot easier on you and the girlfriend if you tell us now.'

Dave says nothing.

They cuff us then, wrists parallel behind our backs. It makes my shoulder blades pull together. There's a hard bar between the cuffs, preventing any movement.

'You've got thin arms,' the policewoman says as she adjusts the lock. 'Never had to use the tightest setting before. May have to get the child cuffs out for you.'

Once the cuffs are on, I submit, my head drops down, I know I can't escape.

The policewoman marches me down the stairs, pushing me every third or fourth step. The front door is lying on the ground in splinters. Police are all over the house like ants, opening drawers and cupboards, searching through my things. My home is being ransacked and my possessions are strewn all over the floor.

Dave climbs into the back of the police van and slumps in the corner. I sit beside him and lay my head on his chest. Dave whispers into my hair, 'Don't worry, princess, the police won't find it. We'll be out in a few hours, back at home, feet up, cup of tea and a boot on the go.'

Living with Dave, I've always had an easy supply of heroin. The thought of what a long, enforced withdrawal might be like flits across my mind. I dismiss it – he's right, I'll be okay and we'll soon be home. 'Sleep as much as you can, it'll help slow the cluck. The more you move around, the more it'll hurt,' he says.

The journey to the station doesn't take long. The police van pulls up into an under-cover, concrete courtyard. A policewoman unlocks the barred door of the van and swings it open. We step down, straight into a frigid, stark cage.

'Out you come,' the custody sergeant says as he opens the door from inside the station. He points at me. 'You first.' I follow him to his desk. He has a two-page questionnaire to fill in about me. When he reaches the end he says, 'Do you need to see the doctor?'

I lift my chin. My eyes settle on his face. 'No. I'm not a drug addict.'

'Okay,' he marks it on the paperwork. 'If you say so.'

In my cell there is no mattress or pillow, only a scratchy old blanket. I pick it up and shake out the dust. It smells of old men and greasy hair, like it's never been washed. I lay the blanket on the wooden bench and use my coat to cover me.

The mental itch for heroin creeps over me. I close my eyes and try to sleep, turning on my left side and then my right. The fake-fur collar of my coat makes my nose itch so I push it away. I take off my shoes then decide my feet are cold, so I put them back on.

It's been ages. I ring the bell on the wall of my cell. The empty echo of the policeman walking down the corridor gets closer. He pulls back the slat in the door.

'What is it?'

'Can I have a cup of tea?'

'Only after you've been here an hour. I've got too much to do.'

'Well, I've been here an hour.'

'Fifteen minutes actually.' The slat slams shut.

Fifteen minutes! He's having a laugh! Panic rises up inside me. I must get a grip of myself, stop the uncontrollable shaking. The itch is getting stronger and I have no idea how long the police can keep me here.

Pacing up and down the small room, I notice the heavy door is scuffed excessively on the inside, as though most of the previous inmates have leant their weight against it and kicked it continuously. One of the walls is painted yellow, the colour of sick, and the other three are brick. The floor is cold concrete and there's a stainless steel toilet in the corner that smells of bleach. I lie down, telling myself to relax and stay still.

A heavy key turns in the door and someone opens it. A cup of tea is placed inside. My hand shakes as I take a small sip from the white plastic cup. It squashes in and I think it'll spill over the top. The tea is tepid, not hot, and tastes of metal like it's come out of a machine, weak with no sugar.

Later, a copper comes in and asks if I want something to eat. 'What can I have?' I ask.

'Microwave sausage hotpot, microwave spaghetti bolognaise or microwave chicken curry.' The meal choices don't change for breakfast, lunch or dinner. I order sausage hotpot but when it's brought in the smell of overcooked onions makes me feel sick. I poke at it with the plastic fork but can't eat it.

I ring the bell. 'I want to make a phone call.'

This time the custody sergeant unlocks my cell. He's a big bloke – his forearms protrude from a white, short-sleeved shirt, revealing a selection of tattoos. I follow him to his desk.

I think for a moment. Who can I ring? I phone Dave's mother.

'Hello darling,' she says. 'I know where you are. I've been to the house. Haven't heard from Dave yet – hope he's okay.' She chats on, but I'm not listening. I put the phone down. Speaking to her has left me feeling even more alone, without any comfort or reassurance about what's going to happen to me. She's not my mother. I need to know everything's going to be alright, and I need to hear it from someone I trust.

The custody sergeant stoops down to my eye level. He has a kind, round face. 'Would you like to ring someone else? You could ring your own mum.'

'No thanks,' I reply. 'Why would I?'

He can see right through my pretence. 'I have a daughter your age. I'd like to think she'd call me if ever she was in this much trouble.'

I consider for a moment, allowing myself to feel the glimmer of hope his words have given me. Time seems to slow, and for those few moments he's not just a copper but a wise man, an angel from God.

Why would my well-spoken, wealthy mother accept a heroin addict for a daughter? Mum knows nothing of my drug addiction, or of Dave's career. How do I even begin that conversation? 'Hi Mum, how are you? Good, yeah, great. By the way, I'm a drug addict and I'm in jail. Sorry to ruin your day.'

I'm in a bad way trying to survive the heroin withdrawal. I

can't cope with being shouted at or made to feel bad. Even if she didn't shout, she'd be disappointed and worried about me. I can't deal with that right now. Anyway, what can the police charge me with? I haven't done anything. I'm just a drug addict – you don't go to prison for that. I'll say nothing – keep everything sweet at home and my family will never know a thing.

So I say, 'You don't know my mum.'

I've been walking up and down the limited space in my cell for most of the day. The windowsill has hundreds of messages, names and poems scored into the wood. I read them all, running my fingers over the surface as if it's Braille. Do I know any of the people who have been here before me? Are they addicts? Dave's punters?

The pain in my arms and legs is excruciating; I can't stand it any longer. I'm starving hungry yet sick to my stomach. Freezing cold and shivering, but when I touch my skin it's burning and wet with sweat. I'd do anything now, anything to stop the unscratchable itch for heroin.

I ring the bell again. 'I'd like to see the doctor.'

The policeman looks at his watch. 'Sorry love, too late for the doctor to come out tonight. You'll have to wait until the morning.'

'But I can't wait till then. Please.' My mind is frantic, searching for some reason I could give him to make the doctor come out.

'Did the custody sergeant offer you the doctor when he signed you in?'

'Yes, but you don't understand…'

'Then you should have said "yes" when he asked you.' He shut the slat.

I sit on the cold floor and rest my head between my knees, waiting to see whether I'll puke. The blood in my ears is roaring. The ache of withdrawal has taken over. I'm exhausted, but my speeding brain prevents me from sleeping. The pain comes like a hard punch, as if I'm a boxer in the ring being beaten, but even a boxer gets a thirty-second break between rounds. I clench my fists and knead them hard into my guts as a wave of agony flows over me. The worst part is knowing that if I just had a little gear all this pain would go away.

I want to go outside into the small courtyard, classed as the exercise yard – anything just to get out of my cell. The same custody sergeant comes to let me out. He's a monster of a man, naturally large. I'm a petite, frail female – I'm no threat to him. Outside, I'm cold and want to come back in. I keep asking him to let me in and out the whole time. My loneliness and boredom make me start to chat to him.

'Oh, is that a wedding ring you're wearing?' He looks at me and smiles but says nothing. 'How long have you been married?' I point to one of his tattoos. 'What does that say?'

He sighs and pauses at his desk. 'Do you want a book, Amber?'

'Oh, yes please.'

He opens a drawer and passes me a paperback. It has crumpled corners and some of the curling pages stick out further than the others where they've fallen out and been stuck back in.

I take it back to my cell, it's a fiction book by Tom Clancy. I try staring at the words on the page, but my eyes can't focus. It's nice to hold the book, though – it feels warm in my hands. Looking at the words makes me feel the person who has written them is there with me and I'm not completely alone.

After an hour with the book, I ask to go outside again.

Passing his desk, the custody sergeant says, 'You can sit there for a while.' He points to a chair in front of the counter. 'At least I can keep an eye on you.' I'm happier sitting there with him, holding my book.

In the morning I'm taken to see the doctor. He's particularly short, which is made more noticeable by the tall policeman who stands beside him. The top of the doctor's head is completely bald and the hair at the sides sticks out in an uncontrollable frizz. He shines a torch into my eyes, making me blink.

'Are you pregnant?' I shake my head. 'When did you last eat? You need to eat something.' The doctor takes my blood pressure, then listens to my chest; satisfied I'm in no danger, he writes out a prescription for two DF118s every eight hours. They're some sort of morphine-based painkiller used to treat heroin addicts.

Every single cell in my body is screaming *where is my heroin?*

'Please, I'm in an awful lot of pain, I really need something stronger.' But it's as if he doesn't hear me. I bet the coppers like it that way; the more pain I'm in, the more likely I am to talk, tell them what they want to know.

A plain-clothes detective collects me and takes me to an interview room; his name is DS Thompson. I recognise him from the raid at our house. Inside the room there is another police officer and a solicitor. The solicitor sits down beside me. He's a guy Dave has used before.

DS Thompson starts the tape recorder, reads me my rights and cautions me. He leans back in his chair. 'Do you and Dave deal heroin, Amber?'

'No, certainly not,' I reply.

'So this ounce of heroin we found at your property, what's that for then?'

'I've never seen it before, don't know what you mean.'

'Do you have a lot of visitors to the house? Regular visitors, people that come every week?'

'Umm, a few, maybe.'

DS Thompson pushes a piece of paper on the desk, moving it forward an inch with his finger. 'Alright. We have evidence that you and Dave have an awful lot of regular visitors.'

'We do? Err, sometimes we do, it depends, we have a few friends round sometimes.' My mind starts to race. Why is he asking me these stupid questions about regular visitors?

'Amber, do you know Mark Walton?'

'Never heard of him.'

'He's a known drug dealer, might be a friend of Dave's? Might come to the house?'

'No, I'm sure, don't know him.' Under the glare of the fluorescent light, I start to feel sick.

'Okay, for the purpose of the tape, I'm passing Amber photograph A1.' He slides a photo across the table. It shows Mark Walton coming into our house. The date on the right-hand corner is four days ago.

'I think he must come to the house when I'm at work. I don't know him.' I slide the photo back. What should I say? Dave never told me what to say.

'Okay, so how do you explain this? For the purpose of the tape, I'm passing Amber photograph A2.' This photograph shows Mark Walton talking to me in the car park. It's taken the same day as the first photograph. I study it carefully. There are loud sounds in the background of my mind, like an echo. I can't think.

'Do you have a problem with remembering people, Amber? People you've seen a few days ago.'

'I do have problems, yeah. At the moment, I've got one huge fuckin' problem.'

'We can prove Dave's dealing heroin. You're living outside your means, Amber. We've found your wage slips – we know how much you take home.'

'I have money my father gives me.'

'So your dad is regularly giving you large amounts of cash?'

'He never sees me, so he gives me money instead.' Let them prove he doesn't.

'Not the man who is married to your mum, then?'

'No. My real dad.'

'Where does he live, Amber. You got an address for him? I'll need to check that out.'

'He lives in Scotland, moves around a lot, he contacts me.'

'That's convenient, Amber, but don't worry, I can find him. Write down his full name and date of birth.' DS Thompson passes across a pad and pen. I smile to myself. I knew where he was a few years ago but I can't find him now so I bet they can't. 'Dave sold a car recently?'

'No.'

'You sure, Amber? You would know if he sold a car, right?'

'I'm sure. He hasn't sold a car.'

'Okay, because Dave is saying the cash we found at the house came from the sale of a car, just last week. For the purpose of the tape I'm stopping the interview. Amber, you need your own solicitor. You and Dave are telling different stories.' The chair grates against the floor as he stands up to leave.

The solicitor looks around the room. 'Oh… oh, we ending now, are we?' he says. He picks up his briefcase and places the papers from the desk inside, then nods at DS Thompson before leaving the room.

My custody sergeant is on duty that evening. He trusts me now so he leaves the door to my cell open. I can go in and out to the yard without having to ask him. There are three or four more doors to unlock before getting to the outside world, and he can see me from behind the counter.

Standing in the yard in the early hours of the morning, I stare up at the sky. There are no stars and the night is black. I wrap my arms around my body and listen to Dave being violently sick in his cell. It sounds as if he's bursting blood vessels. There's nothing I can do, even if I could be with him. He's way beyond the point where anything could comfort him. I go back to my cell. I'm lucky I never started to bang up – that my habit, however large, was miniscule compared to Dave's.

In the morning, I'm escorted to an interview room to meet my new solicitor. The room is quite small but has a large table in it, so I have to squeeze in to sit down. While I'm waiting for the solicitor to arrive, I go through in my mind all the things I have to tell them and all the questions I want to ask. How long can I be detained before the police have to charge me? Can I have some clean clothes and a cigarette? And, yeah, I did know Dave was dealing drugs but can they get me off?

The door finally opens and a woman comes into the room. She's wearing a smart, navy blue suit and her hair is styled in a neat bob with a fringe. 'I'm April Williams,' she introduces herself and places a large briefcase on the table.

I jump up. I'm about to explode with everything I need to say.

'Don't speak, Amber,' she raises her hand and stops me. 'I'm going to explain the law to you.'

Isn't she here to listen to me? Not tell me about the law? I sit back down, grip the edge of the table and puff through my nose.

I glance around the room. I know the law.

April searches out my eyes, and when hers meet mine she says 'I *am* going to help you, Amber.' She tells me what is classed as drug dealing and what I can go to prison for. 'I'll only represent you if I believe you're telling the truth, and I won't lie on your behalf,' she says.

Everything I'd been planning to say to my solicitor changes completely in those few moments. I tell her the truth, as much as I can. I'm not going to stitch up Dave, not even for my freedom. 'Dave and I are heroin addicts. We buy drugs and use them together. I go to work each day and I've never dealt drugs.' All of this is true.

April spends hours with me, asking questions and making notes. When we're finished, a copper comes to take me back to my cell.

I've no idea what time of day it is – it's all just one long nightmare.

Christine

The afternoon sun shines in through the window behind me, casting a fuzzy white glare on my computer screen. I draw the blinds at the back of my desk, and then the phone rings. Sinking into my chair, I tilt it backwards as I take the call, one hand on the phone, the other on the mahogany desk. It's Tony. 'Hi, sweetie, how are you?' I say.

'The police have just phoned me.'

As soon as he says the word 'police' I know it will be about Amber, not that the house has been burgled or that my mother has died.

'Amber's in custody at Aldershot police station.'

'What's she done?' I wait, expecting him to say she's been stealing from work or shoplifting.

'It's bad…' a long sigh whistles down the phone. 'That house she's been living in with Dave, it's been raided, they've seized a large amount of heroin, a load of cash and a gun. Apparently they're both drug addicts and have been dealing.'

There it was: the line across my life. Drawn in a moment, it could never be reversed. I could never step back to the other side of the line, back to the place where I didn't know my daughter was a heroin addict.

'Love, you still there?' Tony says, breaking into my thoughts.

'When did this happen? Surely it can't be true?'

'The police must have evidence against them. They've been in custody for two days.'

Two days and she hasn't called me. Am I that bad a mother? My daughter is in trouble and she can't even speak to me. 'Why didn't she ring me herself?'

'You know what Amber's like, she always thinks she can get away with it. They're both being charged with drug dealing, possession of heroin and handling stolen goods. I spoke to a DS Thompson. He said if we agree they'll bail her to our address. I said I'd ring him back when I'd spoken to you.'

'Do you mind if she comes home?'

'What do you think I'm going to do? Turn her away? She's your daughter.'

The chatter outside my office falls to a murmur. I don't want the girls who work for me to hear me say the words 'heroin' or 'drug addict'. 'Thanks Tone.'

'I'll call DS Thompson now, tell him to bring her home tonight.'

I hang up the phone and stare into space. Could Amber really be facing such serious charges? Could she really be a heroin addict? But in my heart I know it is true. All the signs of her addiction have been there, yet somehow I have ignored them all, as if I've been surrounded by a mist and couldn't see through it. Now the mist has lifted and for the first time everything is clear.

'Would you like a coffee, Christine?' my secretary, Jane, pops her head round the door.

'Yeah, that would be nice, thanks.'

'Everything all right at home?'

'Just kids, you know.' The rest of the afternoon I shuffle paper around on my desk. Of all the drugs she could have been doing, why heroin? It's so addictive, so destructive – how could she have been that stupid? I remember a guy I knew when I was a teenager. He was a friend of my sister, really attractive, a brilliant guitar player. He had started using heroin and within a year he wasted away. He died of an overdose just when he was trying hard to quit. Back then it scared me that someone so young could die.

I have to help Amber. There is only one condition: she has to stop using heroin.

Amber

DS Thompson opens the door of my cell. He has a cheeky grin on his face. 'I've spoken to your stepfather,' he says.

Spoken to Tony! How dare he! What right does he have to interfere? At all costs I have to hide it from them, from Mum. 'What did you tell him?'

'I told him what's been going on.'

'Is that all? Thanks a lot,' I say sarcastically.

'He wants you home.'

'What… you told him about the gear and he wants me home?'

'Yep. Ms Williams has arranged for you to be bailed to your parents' address. I'll be back in a couple of hours to take you.'

Alone in my cell, I put my elbows on the windowsill and rest my chin in my hands. I gaze out at the changing light – shadows of people going past are the only thing I can see through the frosted glass squares. Drug addiction is no-one's fault but your own. No-one makes you a heroin addict; it's always your own decision – that's the first thing I have to admit to myself. How do I explain to Mum how I got like this? When she finds out it'll be over between us – she'll never want me.

The door to my cell opens. The past three days I've been desperate to be released, but now I'm frightened to go home. 'Ready to go, Amber?' the custody sergeant asks.

'Yeah, suppose so.' I step out, gaze down the corridor to where Dave's cell is. 'Can I say goodbye to Dave?'

'Well… okay, while I sign your release form you can have two minutes. Just through the slat, mind.'

I pull back the slat. Dave's huddled on the wooden bench. His knees are drawn up to his chin, his body rocking slightly back and forth. The blanket is pulled over his head and, when he hears the slat open, he lifts it up a bit to look at me. His eyes are swollen and bloodshot. His face is wet, as if the pain is so bad he can't stop the tears streaming down his face, but he makes no sound to cry.

'The police are releasing me, Dave, bailing me to my mum's.' I stand up on my toes and put my face close to the small opening in his cell door. 'I love you,' I say and peep at him one last time. 'We're in more trouble than you realise.'

And, although he doesn't speak, the look in his eyes tells me that he knows.

Six

Christine

Bang! Bang! The knock on the front door sounds as if someone is smacking the side of their fist against it. Even though I've been expecting it, I jump.

The vibration settles, and for a moment the house is silent.

I stare at Tony across the kitchen table he gives me a gentle smile. I'm reassured that I'm not in this on my own. He pushes back his chair and gets up to answer the door. 'Okay, you two,' I say to our kids, seven-year-old Lauren and five-year-old Sam. 'Upstairs. Get yourselves ready for bed.'

Two plain-clothes police officers stride into our kitchen. Amber hesitates, holding back in the doorway. She glances at me nervously with an expression somewhere between a smile and a smirk. What can she say? There are no words to span the divide between us; no small apology she can make that means this will be okay.

She looks familiar in the white coat she was wearing the last time I saw her, but her hair and face are dirty now, as if she hasn't washed in days, and when I study her face I can't see who she is any more. Her pupils are large yet motionless, two glass marbles that appear big and bulging in her tiny features. I try to search inside them to see if I can tell what's going on in her head, but the marbles stare back at me and give nothing away.

'I'm DS Thompson,' one of the officers says and places a form on the table. 'Amber's on police bail. She's facing serious charges.' His voice has a charming and likeable tone, as if it belongs to someone else and he's not saying these awful things. 'Her heroin habit has been estimated by us to have a street value of two hundred pounds a day.'

Two hundred pounds a day! How on earth does he think we can manage that? Do the police really believe she'll just stop using heroin now she's been caught? Don't they realise that within the next twelve hours she'll probably have to commit some sort of crime to get her through the night? They must know that we won't understand, that we won't be able to stop her.

DS Thompson doesn't seem to care, and who can blame him? Dirty drug addict – she's not his problem tonight. It probably amuses him to think of us trying to deal with her.

'The conditions of bail are that Amber resides at this address and has no contact with David Jenkins. She must appear before the court at the time and place stated on the bail notice,' DS Thompson says. He looks around our kitchen, his eyes alert. I notice him reading the notes I have written on a calendar. He leans forward on black-rubber-soled shoes. 'You've got some smart cars outside,' he says to Tony.

'What, the Jag and the wife's Mercedes?' Tony replies with a smile.

'What do you do, then, to afford all this? Been dealing drugs as well?' he jokes.

'I run my own business,' Tony replies.

DS Thompson turns away as if he's bored. 'We're going to

drop Amber off to pick up her car, if that's okay with you. I'm sure she'll come straight home,' he says.

'Okay, I suppose so, if you say that's alright,' I say.

'Tell you what, we'll give her an hour. If she's not home by then, ring us.' He passes me a card with his name and number on it. 'We'll send a squad car out to find her.'

Tony doesn't notice the smug look on DS Thompson's face as he shakes his hand and says 'Thanks.' Yeah, thanks for bringing this raging drug addict into our home. Amber is like a cornered animal. She raises one shoulder and turns her head to hide in the collar of her coat. She doesn't speak or look at me, and she leaves with the police officers. Although Tony and the kids are still there, I'm alone.

'I never thought it would be that bad. What on earth are you going to do with her? Won't she have to go through some sort of withdrawal?' Tony asks.

I'm numb. 'I've no idea what I'm going to do.'

Tidying away the plates from tea, I check the clock every few minutes. Picking up the small white card, I turn it over in my hand. How long it will take her to collect her car?

Exactly an hour later, I hear a car pull up. I listen to see whether it belongs to a neighbour, but there's a knock at the front door. The outside light brightly illuminates Amber's face. Her pupils are pin-pricks now. I step back to let her in. Her persona has changed; she's confident this time. 'You're different, Amber. Where've you been?'

'To get my car, you know that.'

'It doesn't take an hour to get to your house and back.'

'Okay,' she shrugs her shoulders, 'you don't believe me.'

I squeeze my hands into the front pockets of my jeans. 'You're my daughter, Amber, and you're welcome home, but you're not going to stay here and use heroin. It has to stop. Sooner or later you're going to have to come to terms with that. Don't do drugs in this house and don't bring your druggie friends round here. I've got Tony and the kids to consider.'

'Alright,' she looks down. 'Can I go to bed?'

'Yeah, go on.' I want to talk to her, to find out everything that has happened and why she started taking heroin, but I can see she's not interested. Nothing matters to her tonight – not me and her family, not her freedom, not her health. Amber will come to me when the time is right, when she's hit rock bottom. I hope it won't take long.

Tony shuts the bedroom curtains and then walks around to his side of the bed and climbs in. He pushes his head into his pillows. 'People don't give up drugs just like that, even celebrities with loads of money. They go into rehab but then start taking drugs again after a short space of time,' he says.

'I don't know anything about drug addiction.'

I lean over and switch off the bedside lamp. I stare into the darkness. I feel like a doctor, trying to understand a sick person's disease before deciding how to treat it. At this moment I can't begin to fathom it. I only know one thing. 'If Amber's going to live at home, as part of our family, she has to be clean, no half measures,' I say to Tony. 'Either you're a drug addict or you're not. She'll have to find a way to quit. I'm not about to let her carry on.'

I'm wiping breakfast yogurt off otherwise clean navy-blue school jumpers, checking lunches are made and gathering up reading books to be packed before walking Lauren and Sam to school. I'll talk to Amber this morning – once Tony's left for work it'll be quiet and we'll be alone. On my way back from school I rehearse what I'll say, how she has to want this for herself, how I can't do it for her. Giving up heroin would be the hardest thing she has ever done, but I would be with her all the way.

Hanging my coat over the banister, I slip off my shoes and push them under the radiator, then climb the stairs to Amber's room. I knock gently; no answer. I open the door.

Her bed is empty.

Years of her bad behaviour, lying and shutting me out come back to me all at once. Where was she when I had cancer? When I needed her? Now she's in trouble I still want to help her, yet she's sneaked off and can't face me as usual.

I feel the need to clean the house, to be constantly busy with some mundane task, in an attempt to make the day seem manageable. I wipe all the kitchen worktops and cupboard doors and then start loading the dishwasher, all the time thinking about Amber, wondering where she is. Is she out somewhere using heroin?

The telephone rings. 'It's DS Thompson. I've a few questions I'd like to ask you about Amber. Shall I come to the house?'

I've no wish to speak to him. Besides, he might ask why Amber's not home. And I don't want a police car parked on the drive. What if the neighbours start asking questions?

'I'm not going to be much help. I didn't even know she was taking drugs,' I protest.

'It's a formality. May need to take a statement from you – won't take long. You can always come down to the station if you prefer.'

I lean against the wall. 'I suppose you'd better come here.'

Hanging up the phone, I'm flooded with emotions I feel ill trying to contain. A thought pops into my head: maybe they'll be able to reassure me, to tell me it's Dave they're really after, that they've seen Amber for what she is, a rather childlike girl who's been taken in, got involved with a dealer and now has a heroin habit. Perhaps they can tell me they're pretty sure she won't be going to jail.

Looking through the dining-room window every few minutes, I'm expecting a striped panda car to pull up, but the officers arrive in a rather old green Vauxhall. They offer me their IDs at the door and wait. I notice DS Thompson is carrying a smart La Senza carrier bag, holding on to the neat cord handles. I wonder if it has those nice scented beads in it.

At the entrance to the sitting room, they step cautiously onto the pale beige carpet. Glancing around the room, DS Thompson picks up a photograph from the sideboard. It's of Amber as a child. In the picture she's on the beach playing in the sand. He studies it carefully and puts it back down.

'Please, have a seat,' I say. They sit together on one sofa and I cross the room to sit on the other, glad somehow of the distance; they are not my friends, just good at making out they are on my side.

'Amber's been feeding us a lot of confusing stories about her real father.' DS Thompson takes out a notepad and flips over the pages. 'Can you tell us where we can contact him?'

'Sorry, I can't. Haven't spoken to him… oh, for years.'

'Amber says he lives in Scotland. Is that right?'

'Last time I knew, he was living in Edinburgh somewhere.'

'Do you think it's possible he's been giving Amber large sums of money? Say six hundred pounds?'

'I doubt it, he's never given her anything her whole life.'

'She's made a signed statement saying her father regularly gave her cash. You know Dave doesn't work, don't you? Where did you think they got all their money from?'

'Well, I knew he didn't have a regular job. Amber said he

worked for his father and was a bit of a whiz with computers, so that when he did work he got paid really well.'

'Do you buy her clothes? Underwear maybe?'

'No, she buys her own clothes.'

'Can she usually afford to buy matching underwear? Because we found these at the house.' He reaches into the carrier bag and takes out a beautiful fine lace beige bra and matching thong.

Of all the stolen goods they removed from the house, it seems out of proportion to be worrying about underwear, considering the scheme of things. 'Umm, I'm not sure.'

'There's a receipt in the bag to show that she paid cash for them the day before the raid. Where do you think she got the money from?' The corner of his mouth curls into a smirk as he puts the underwear back in the bag.

'I guess Dave must have given them to her.'

'We've been watching them for a while. The bedsit where they were living was burgled – apparently they were away skiing at the time. Did you give Amber money for that holiday?'

'No, she said Dave booked it last minute on the internet, got a really good deal.'

'So, what do you think it cost? Two people skiing for a week. Five hundred? More? Less?'

'I suppose about five hundred, maybe a bit more.'

'We recovered documents at the house showing he paid nine hundred and thirty-six pounds in cash for it. Do you think Dave can afford that? Seems a lot for someone who's not working all the time.' DS Thompson stares across at me. His eyes squint a little. 'Do you see where I'm coming from?'

I fiddle with the back of my hair. 'I didn't really think about it.' My cheeks are hot; why didn't I question her about the money at the time?

'Right, okay.' He turns the page of his notebook. It seems to contain a list of topics. 'There's a lot of expensive stuff in their house; money, mobile phones, all the latest electronic gadgetry. Any of it belong to you?'

'No, only personal things we've given Amber, on her birthday or for Christmas.'

'We've taken what we need for the case against them. It's impossible to find all the owners of the property we believe is stolen. Amber says you give her money, is that right?'

'I know she doesn't earn much and she has a lot of time off sick, so I do give her money sometimes, and I pay for her car and things.'

'We believe she's been living off Dave's illegal earnings. We also want to prove he's been giving her drugs; domestic supply. Did you know he was a heroin addict when your daughter started going out with him?'

'No, I had no idea.'

'He's well known to us. Last time he got sent down after we prosecuted him for dealing. We're always picking him up for drug offences. He's a cocky bastard.'

'Surely the case is against Dave, not Amber. She was out at work all day. I can't believe she ever dealt drugs.'

'Well, she's an addict. You wouldn't understand. They do anything they can to fund the habit – we see it all the time. Anyway, Dave is pleading not guilty so we have to press the case against Amber. 'Course, if he put his hand up to it, we'd go easy on her, reduce the charges against her.'

'Is he likely to do that? To protect her from going to jail?'

'Dave Jenkins? No, he's not.'

'But she was just living with him.'

'No,' he points his pen at me. 'It's more complicated than

that; we have every reason to believe they were doing it together. Watching someone deal drugs and not informing the police is a crime, as is living off the proceeds.'

I lean back into the cushions on the sofa and cross my legs. I'm not going to say anything else. I don't know what Amber's been doing. I haven't even had a chance to talk to her.

The silence sits in the room. After a few moments, the other officer says, 'We're looking for a car Dave said he sold recently. According to him that's where the cash we found at the house came from – and the money to buy the heroin. We ran both their names through the police computer and came up with a BMW 3 series registered in Amber's name, insurance is in her name, it's gunmetal grey. Do you know anything about it?'

'What… do you mean the one parked outside?'

'Here?' They both lean forward and glance towards the door as if they might see it through the wall. 'At this house?'

'Didn't you notice it when you pulled up? Dave asked us if he could leave it here for a while, said the road tax had run out.'

'What, it's been here the whole time? It was here when we came last night?' DS Thompson asks.

'Well yes, like I said, it's parked outside.'

They look at each other and smile, then leap up from the sofa and walk out. The car is parked in front of them, opposite the house in the overflow parking. They peer in the windows, cupping their hands around the sides of their faces to cut out the glare. DS Thompson bends down on one knee to examine underneath, then he tries the doors and the boot.

'Do you want the keys?' I ask him.

'Have you got them?'

'I told Dave we'd need them in case the alarm went off, or we had to move it.'

'Thanks very much.' He extends his hand to take them from me. 'Mrs Lewry, we're seizing this car as evidence in the case against David Jenkins and Amber Cameron.' He presses the key fob – the car yaps and the indicators flash. Opening the driver's door, he slides into the seat. The other officer walks back to the green Vauxhall.

They drive away. The thought that Amber might go to prison stays in my mind. Where is she now? Why isn't she doing something to try and sort this out? How will this ever, ever, be alright? I'm angry now. It sears down my veins and sparks through my fingertips.

I walk to the school to collect the children at three o'clock. They're happy to see me and chat about their day. I smile and appear to listen. When we get home, Amber's still not there.

Making the children a sandwich in the kitchen, I hear her stumble in. I throw down the slice of bread instantly and am in the hallway. She tries to get up the stairs before I can catch her. She's stoned out of her head. Nervous energy seems to seep out of every pore of her skin. Her hair is greasy and pulled back tightly. Her face is pale, drawn, as if all the moisture has been sucked out of it and her ageing process has been accelerated.

'Where've you been all day, Amber?' I scan her up and down.

'Just out.'

I breathe deeply, trying to control myself. 'I know you've been doing heroin again. I'm not stupid.'

'Whatever.' She starts up the stairs.

'Amber, I do understand you can't just stop. You can talk to me, you know.'

She hesitates, without turning round. 'I know.'

'Where are you getting it from? Dave's mates supplying you

now he's inside, are they? Think they're helping you out?'

'Leave it, Mum, you don't understand.'

'What are you going to do for money? I'm not giving you money for drugs so you can forget that. You'll have to get a job. You can't live here for free.'

At the top of the stairs she stops and looks at me. 'I'll sort it. I want to give up, okay?'

'The police were here today. I'm not going to lie for you. They've taken Dave's car – it's registered in your name, Amber. Have you even thought you could end up in prison?' She carries on to her room. I'm shaking. I shout after her, 'How long do you think it can go on? You can't take heroin while you're living here!'

Lauren calls out from the sitting room. She's still in her school uniform, watching TV. 'Mummy, is Amber going to prison?'

I lower my voice. 'No sweetie, but she's been a naughty girl and the police have told her off.' I sit beside her on the sofa and pull her close to me. Her soft hair tickles my cheek. I rearrange the clips holding back her fringe.

'Is Dave still her boyfriend? Is he in prison?'

'Yes, he's in prison and I hope he'll stay there until Amber's better and doesn't like him any more.'

'Why's he in prison?'

'Well, do you know what it means to take drugs?'

'Yes… I think so.'

'Taking drugs is breaking the law and you can go to prison for it.'

'Has Amber been taking drugs?'

'Yes, she has, but she's going to stop now.'

'Why isn't she in prison, then?'

'Dave has to stay in prison because he's been selling drugs to other people as well as taking them himself.'

'Did he sell them to Amber?'

'No, he gave them to her.'

'Did she want to take them?'

'Yes she did, he didn't make her.'

'I'm never going to take drugs. Then I won't have to go to prison, will I Mummy?'

'No you won't baby, now give us a cuddle.'

Lauren throws her arms around my neck and squeezes me tight, and then she goes back to watching cartoons.

I stare straight ahead. Does Amber want to give up heroin? Or is she just saying that to please me? She has always done a lot of lying to get herself out of trouble. When she was a child I had the upper hand, able to convince her to tell me the truth or admit what she had done. Over the years her lying has become more skilled. She'll find it easy now to tell me whatever I want to hear, so she can stay at home while she finds a way to carry on her addiction. Maybe she'll find another dealer she can sleep with who'll pay for her habit. She can play me if she chooses to. She knows I'll stand by her, accept what she says, because I am desperate to believe she will stop taking drugs.

Seven

Christine

Tony opens the back door. Wiping his feet on the deep brush mat, he says 'There's a dodgy bloke hanging around outside, looks like a nasty bastard.'

'What! What nasty bastard? Outside here?'

'I'm outside cutting the grass and I noticed an old red banger drive up – no reason to pull in here unless you're coming to one of the houses. When he saw me he turned around, drove away. He's done it twice now.'

'Who do you think he is?'

'Bet Amber knows him. She can put herself in danger, that's up to her, but not you and the kids; it's not fair. I don't want blokes like that round here or knowing where we live.'

'Amber!' I call up the stairs to her bedroom. 'Get down here now! Get rid of your druggie friend.'

She leans over the banister. 'What druggie friend?'

'Bloke in a red car, don't act the innocent with me!'

'Why do you always assume it's something to do with me?'

'Just go and tell him not to come round here again.' Amber takes her old, green parker coat from the downstairs rail and goes out. I watch from the window as she pulls the hood up, walks down the drive and turns the corner into the road.

Shoving another load of washing into the machine, I find Amber's nightie tangled up with Lauren's pyjamas. I must have picked it up from the bathroom floor. It's pale blue with sheep on. Scrunching it into a ball, I hold it to my face. I sink down on my knees. I have to believe that the real Amber, the daughter I love, is still there and that once the drugs that have taken over her body are gone she will pop out again and show her little smiley face.

I pass Tony in the hallway and he stops and draws me towards him. 'What's the matter, love?' I press my head into his jumper. He smells of everything I know and trust, of the most intimate part of my life.

A tear comes to my eye. 'She's a full-blown addict, Tone. She can't control her behaviour, but when I try to talk to her about it she lies and wriggles away. She's been doing it for years – what did I think she'd been doing?'

'You can't worry about her all the time. She got herself into this,' he says. He kisses my forehead. 'It's our weekend; the kids are bored, I'll take them down the park, get them out for a bit.'

I glance at the clock. Where is she? Why doesn't she come back? Who was that guy? Does she owe him money?

Watching the ten o'clock news, I notice Amber slipping past the sitting-room door to avoid us. Tony turns to me and rests his hand on my leg. 'When are you going to speak to her about the seriousness of it?'

'I'll do it soon.'

'We can't go on like this.'

'Tomorrow, I'll do it tomorrow. We're going to close up the house she shared with Dave.'

I throw my mobile on the bed, watch it bounce slightly on the thick duvet. Standing at the window, I stare down the road. Seven times I've rung that number with no answer; the bastard is avoiding me.

Dealers that worked for Dave owe me, and I've been collecting from them, but that's running out now. They've stopped answering their phones and always manage to be out when I call round. I'm alone with this huge addiction and I don't know what to do or how to satisfy it. I'm a fish out of water, struggling not for water to breathe but for the heroin I believe I need just as much.

With Dave gone, I have to score my own gear, pay for it and smoke it away from the house, although I do have my car. I'm not uncomfortable at home. I was a heroin addict before I moved out. I know the rhythm of the house – which days Mum's at work, what time Tony comes home and what time everyone goes to bed. Most nights I sit outside in the car until their bedroom light goes out, then I creep, unseen, upstairs to my room.

I pull on my jeans and an old sweatshirt, study myself in the mirror and brush my hair into a ponytail. I'm going back to my house today – the thought of it gives me a lovely warm feeling. There are things in the house I need, but Dave's mum has my key so I haven't been able to get in until now. The day we moved in the landlord was keen to take Dave's cash, but now he wants me and all our stuff out. He's already had to pay for the front door to be repaired. He came round to Mum's house asking for the money and, when I said I didn't have it, he said 'I'll get it back one way or another.' I was scared. He only left when Tony came out and asked who was at the door. I hope he doesn't come back.

Downstairs I pour myself some orange juice and sit beside Mum at the kitchen table. She picks up a knife and spreads some more jam on her toast. 'What time do you want to go?' she asks.

'Look, Mum, you don't need to come. I'm sure you've got better things to do today. I'm only grabbing my things. Linda's gonna be there, we can manage.'

'I'm not stupid,' she says, taking a sip of her coffee. 'Anyway, I want to see what you're bringing back to my house.'

I leave in my car and Mum follows me. I check my rear-view mirror to make sure she's still behind me. She's only been there once before, when we first moved in – after that I made excuses not to invite her. Driving into the car park I notice all the usual neighbours' cars are there – life goes on the same for everyone but me. I walk along with Mum. It's quicker to go through the alleyway, into the back garden. It's a dark alley with overgrown hedges at either side. Litter and fag ends are strewn on the narrow pathway. A group of children hang around, watching us. They make me feel intimidated.

The back door is open. Inside the house are the remnants of my life. It feels surreal, everything as we left it when we went to bed the night of the raid. Plates with the remains of food from our dinner are still in the kitchen, tea cups on the side and washing up in the sink. I feel a rush of painful emotion, but I pull it back. I've had to put up a tall wall around my feelings, so I don't have to believe it's all really happening. It's a lot for my mind to cope with.

Linda's kneeling on the kitchen floor with her head in a cupboard. Her coarse, dark curls stop at the nape of her neck.

She's wearing jeans and a tee shirt as usual. Different jeans and sometimes different tee shirts, but always the same outfit, same jewellery too. Lots of rings and a gold rope chain. She keeps them on all the time, wears them to bed, in and out of the bath.

Dave doesn't look like his mum, so I've always assumed he must look like his dad, although I've never seen his dad or heard his name mentioned. I think Linda must still be in love with him because of the way she treats Dave. She can't do enough for Dave and she's always making excuses for him. She doesn't bring anything to Dave but he brings something to her – something she needs, as if he's that man who broke her heart all those years ago.

Dave plays on it. I heard Linda say to her husband once, 'Leave Dave alone, you don't know what he's been through!' I remember thinking 'He doesn't see his dad, I don't see my dad – what's he been through that's so special?' Although she'd re-married she'd never had any more children, just focused on Dave.

Hearing me come in, Linda turns around and pushes herself up. 'How you doing, Amber?' She studies my face, places her hand on my lower back and gives it a rub.

I close my eyes and nod my head. 'Not too bad.'

'You alright? You know, at your mum's?'

'Yeah, I'll be alright.' Linda turns back to the cupboard where she's packing my tins of food and washing powder into a large cardboard box. Then she moves along to open the next cupboard. 'I'm taking all the plates and cutlery, saving them for Dave when he gets out. Some of this stuff is nearly new.'

I know that. My house, my things. I chose those plates only a couple of weeks ago. It's all being torn apart, as if my life had been pretend and, now the play has ended, they're packing away the set. I'm a ghost, not really here.

'You don't need them, do you?' Linda asks me.

I'm not sure what to say. I want to tell her they're mine. I look through the door to where Mum's standing in the hall. She shakes her head and her long, blonde hair swings to the side. 'I don't want any of it,' she says and turns away.

'Well, Dave did pay for all this,' Linda says.

Mum stiffens and stares at Linda. 'Yeah, with dirty money. If he were my son I'd take it all out on the front lawn and burn the lot. I'm only here to collect Amber's personal things.'

Linda picks up the cardboard box with a huff, carries it out to her car.

'Don't be nasty to Linda. It won't help anything and it's not her fault,' I say.

'I'll be civil, Amber, but I'm not her friend nor will I ever be. She knew what her son was doing and said nothing to me. She should see him for what he is.'

I leave the kitchen and go into the sitting room. Mum bought me a beautiful fig with a plaited stem for a house-warming present. It stands alone in the corner. All the shiny green leaves have dropped on the carpet, leaving a few stragglers hanging on the pale branches. It looks as if it's had a fright. Mum's studying Dave's kit on the floor: needle, surgical wipes and a tourniquet. I move away. Having your mum search through your druggie house is every addict's worst nightmare. I'm not up to discussing it with her. I'm searching for dregs of heroin on tin foil.

After heroin is smoked through a foil tube, the tube is discarded. As it cools, the liquid solidifies and the tube then has leftover heroin smeared all over it. I wouldn't bother with it normally – it's a bit like smoking a fag butt – but it's okay now, I'm desperate.

Tubes are left all over the house – in drawers, bags and fag packets. The ones in fag packets are the best: I chuck the packets in my bag and no-one watching gives it a second thought. These amounts of gear are trivial stuff, what's classed as 'paraphernalia': the police don't need them for evidence. They're mine, I'm entitled to them and Mum won't have a clue I've got them.

Dave's a hoarder, a squirrel, who hid stashes of cash all over the house. He doesn't like to go short and holds on to it for emergencies. I was never sure what sort of emergencies might crop up and I didn't need the cash then, so I never paid attention. Now that I'm clucking, my mind is sharp – it has a clarity that gives me the ability to re-play in my mind all those times he hid things; where he was standing, which drawer he opened.

Striding upstairs two at a time, I call out to Mum, 'I'm just going up to the bathroom to get my make-up.' The bathroom shelf is stuffed with cosmetics and toiletries Dave bought me. Before packing them, I lift the lid of the wicker washing basket. It creaks and wobbles as I search through the pockets of Dave's jeans. I find twenty quid and a bag of gear. I glance up at the open doorway. Seeing that there's no-one there, I slide them into my pocket.

The week before the raid, Dave bought a pine four-poster bed with cream chiffon curtains to hang from the beams. It fills the room. Linda's going to take it apart and put it into storage. The sheets and pillows are pulled back, the way we left them that morning. I want to get back in and lie down, to see if Dave's pillow smells of him. I imagine myself lying there with him. It brings him closer to me and I worry about how he's coping in prison and when I'll be able to see him.

I place the large sports bag I borrowed from Tony on the

bed and then start to pack my clothes. Dave kept eighty quid in a pair of socks in his drawer; I know which pair it is, give them a quick squeeze and feel the crunch of cash. I don't bother to take the money out, just throw the socks in with my stuff.

'What's left in here, Amber?' Linda asks. For a moment I hadn't noticed her come in behind me. She stretches her tee shirt down over her tummy and sits on the bed.

'Why don't you pack his clothes from the wardrobe?' I suggest.

She hauls herself up from the bed and opens the doors. 'Oh, he's got some nice stuff in here.'

I bend my knees, keeping my body straight, and slide my hand under the mattress, feeling for the money I know is there. I take it.

My bag of clothes is full and ready to go to the car. On the way I notice Mum in the kitchen. 'What are you doing?' I ask her. She stops, seemingly at a loss for words.

'I found these bottles in the fridge. What did you and Dave want with other people's methadone? I'm pouring it down the sink. It must be illegal, Amber, to keep prescriptions made out to someone else.'

Thanks, Mum, tip it all away. I could have used that or sold it. How useful you are. There are moments when I want to confide in her, ask her to help me. I don't have anyone else. Then she does something like this and I realise just how little she understands my addiction. How could she ever help me?

Christine

The first thing that strikes me when I step inside the house is the smell. It's not a smell I recognise. It's like a vile chemical mixed with strong tobacco smoke. The magnolia walls seem to be covered in a thin layer of brown resin. I run my finger along the sitting-room wall and it leaves a white mark.

A large black leather armchair sits alone in the middle of the room. In front of it is a huge TV with surround sound, the latest Xbox (which has only been out a few weeks), a PlayStation, a DVD player, a video player and a computer with the internet – everything you would need if you stayed home all day sitting in a chair. Wall-to-wall bookcases are full of DVDs, whole series of every show I could ever think of – *ER*, *Friends*, *The Simpsons* – plus hundreds of films and expensive games.

Dirty needles lie on the floor around the chair. It makes me feel sick seeing it in reality for the first time. I imagine their life together, Amber watching Dave inject heroin into his veins.

I am not going to take the easy way out any more. I want to know everything about what Amber's been doing and what went on here. That way it will be harder for her to lie to me. I can't hide from it any more. She has to look at this existence and see it for what it is. The first step in Amber's recovery is for her to come to terms with the fact that her old life with Dave is over and she can't get it back.

The spare bedroom is filled with all sorts of odd things, packed tight from floor to ceiling, lots of it boxed and carefully labelled with what's inside. Golf clubs, car radios, gym equipment, things that have been stolen by addicts and exchanged for heroin. Stolen goods that are someone else's misery. All this unhappiness piled into one house. Amber didn't have any nastiness in her – how could she have watched it all going on?

Linda wants everything. Everything is to be saved for her

boy when he gets out of jail. She seems to know every single thing in the house and where to find it. I just can't see why anyone would want twenty-seven stolen car radios.

I'm careful to watch my step as I make my way down the stairs, glancing over the side of the large cardboard box in my arms. Amber and Linda are chatting in the hallway. They stop when they see me and Linda walks away. Why is Amber being so nice to her? Sucking up to her? Why can't she choose? Come back to her family and leave all this behind.

Amber is really skittish, like a nervous young horse ready to bolt at the first opportunity. If I make her choose now I might lose her. I'll wait, think about what I want in the long run and how my actions now will best achieve it. I'll play along until I've thought things through.

I take the box out to my car. Passing the kitchen on the way back I spot Amber searching through drawers. I notice a quiet smile appear on her face. There's heroin in this house and she knows it. She licks her bottom lip slightly, like a snake, as if she can taste it in the air.

I accept it. I don't have a choice.

I have to watch her sneaking off to find a dirty place where she can be alone with her heroin. She's waited patiently all day – now she is so close, I sense she can hold back no longer before tasting that sweet, sickly poison.

Amber

I count up the few remaining boxes. One more trip to the car should do it. I catch Linda in the hallway. 'You wouldn't believe what a hard time I'm having at home.' I take a long breath and sigh. 'My mum doesn't understand me, she's thinks you can just stop doing gear. She doesn't know how hard it is. 'Course, you understand, you know what I'm going through. Can I stay the night with you? Give myself a bit of a break.'

'Sure you can, you don't need to ask.' Linda takes her fags out of her pocket and offers me one. I don't light it – Mum doesn't like the smell. I hold it in my hand with my lighter and go into the sitting room, where she's sitting on the floor packing the last DVDs.

I'm feeling quite weak but I'm thinking about the gear in my pocket. I'm calm – I know I have it, so I know I'll get stoned. It's the same every time you're clucking badly: once you score and get that gear in your hand, the sweating and stomach cramps stop, before you've even taken the hit.

There is only one thing on my mind, the only thing I can cope with. I'm not thinking about the future, next week or next month, only today: how I'm going to get enough heroin for today.

'You go on when you're done, Mum. I'm going home with Linda tonight, gonna have some dinner with them and stay the night. I'll be home in the morning.'

Mum stops what she's doing and looks up at me, hard in the face.

'I know what you're thinking,' I say. I cross my legs and sit down on the floor beside her. 'I'm not going to do drugs. Dave's family know what to watch out for, they've seen it all before. They're not about to let me take drugs at their house, are they? Besides, you know I haven't any money.' I lay my hand on her knee. 'I need a break. I want to spend some time with them.'

'I've had enough, then,' Mum says, and stands up to leave.

Result. I don't tell Linda I'm going. I hang back in the alleyway, wait till I hear Mum's car pull away. I know which way she'll turn to go home. I turn in the opposite direction, don't want to get stuck behind her.

I'm going to one of the quiet, out-of-the-way places I've been to before to smoke heroin. A car park down a long, unmade road where people walk their dogs during the day but no-one goes at night.

Daylight is fading when I drive in. The trees are silhouetted black and cold against the pink-red sky. I put the car in reverse and push hard on the throttle, bumping over potholes and puddles. I stop ten yards up a path off the side of the road, under the black trees, so you can't see the car from the road. I switch off the engine, open the sunroof and lock the doors, settling back in my seat.

Cars are designed to do gear in. The dashboard is just the right height to lay out the foil and, as I lean forward to smoke the heroin, anyone looking in won't have a clue what I'm doing. If someone comes along, I simply drive away.

I take the gear and dregs from my bag. No-one can stop me. My hands are shaking while I make the foil tube. The lighter flicks once, twice, then sparks into a flame. I smoke the heroin.

My head starts to tingle. This wonderful feeling spreads through my body, waves of pulsing calm. It's more than okay. I know, I just know, that everything's going to be fine.

The night descends into total blackness; it enfolds the car like a thick blanket. The complete silence of the woods is punctuated by the hoot of an owl in the distance.

I'm not afraid to spend the night out here alone. The only thing that frightens me is being caught by the police and having my gear taken away from me. I'm not scared of a face appearing at my window, a hand trying one of the car doors, or a werewolf jumping down from the trees.

I have my heroin to protect me – it's company, my close friend, so I'm not alone.

Eight

Christine

The postman whistles as he walks up the path and I hear him push the post through the door. Tony gets up to collect it. The letterbox snaps like a mousetrap.

'He's got cheek.' He tosses a yellow envelope on the side, spinning it across the worktop until it hits the tile. 'That bastard gets her on drugs then writes her love letters.'

It is a condition of Amber's bail that she has no contact with Dave, but somehow he manages to send her cards and letters. The first one came via Linda, but now he blatantly sends them to our house. I see Dave as the danger. If they weren't together, I think I could reach her. 'I reckon she's still in love with him,' I say.

'I'm surprised she hasn't finished with him already. What's she waiting for?'

'I don't know, I just need a bit more time to get through to her.'

I expect to be treated badly by Amber: deceived. It's early days in a completely new situation. I want her to be honest, and, when she eventually is, I'm going to have to try and understand. I have to find the strength to come out from behind the cloud where I have been hiding and stand at my daughter's side.

'When are they going to court? Has she seen a solicitor yet? Has she told you?'

'She doesn't tell me anything.'

'Now it's all out in the open, she'll have to face what she's done.'

I am quiet for a moment. Tony leans towards me, tilts my chin and kisses me. 'I'm going to work.' He pulls on his jacket and leaves.

I envy him. I know that after a few minutes he can put this pain and worry aside – he doesn't have to carry it, yet I can't let it go.

Pulling into the early-morning traffic at the top of the road, I realise I have forgotten my phone. I must go back for it – Amber might need to contact me. This is going to make me late for work. I am flustered and rushed when I get there.

'You alright, Christine? You look tired,' Jane asks.

There's no way I am telling her what is really going on at home. I am not going to let everyone at work judge me on this. I haven't failed as a parent. It is none of their business. 'I'm fine, didn't sleep that well last night.'

'You work too hard.'

I hang my coat on the back of my office door. Jane follows me in. 'When's the next management meeting? I haven't missed it, have I?' I ask her.

'It's next Wednesday. John was asking if you had the budgets for his department yet.'

'I'll do them today. Make me a coffee, would you?' I sort through the pile of stuff in front of me: work I haven't done, post unread. I open my emails to find fifty waiting in my inbox.

I can only concentrate on the things I can't afford to postpone.

I am not achieving anything, just waiting to get away. At four o'clock I decide to go.

The house is silent when I open the front door. I tread on the wooden hall floor, glance up the stairs and wait a moment. Silence. Amber's not here. I want to know what's going on between her and Dave. What sort of hold he has over her.

The curtains are shut in her room. I don't want to disturb things by opening them. I switch on the light. The room has a faint acrid smell I hadn't noticed before. It's coming from plastic see-through storage boxes filled with the things she took from her house, seeping out like poison.

There is a large picture of Dave and her on the dressing table. He's on display as if he's someone to be proud of. I want to cover it up or hide it away somewhere.

Making my way further into the room, I step over a spare pair of curtains lying on the floor. Her room is rammed with junk. Why did I let her bring it all back? Why is she hanging on to all this? I don't know how she can function in here. A pile of letters tied with a pink ribbon lies by her bed. I pick them up. Taking out one at a time, I read them.

Hello my princess, the day that we'll be together grows closer. Holding you for the first time when I'm released will be like holding you on our wedding day.

She must be on drugs to believe all this crap. I can see how Dave provides a safety net for her mentally, a cop out in the future if she needs it. Perhaps she is only waiting for him to be released.

The sound of a car engine makes me stop and listen. It sounds like Amber's car. I peep under the curtain and, seeing it's her, I slide the letters back. She won't notice if they are out of place, she's always stoned.

I'm ready for her when I hear her key in the door. 'Ah, you're home,' I say. 'How about a drink? I'm just making one.'

She hesitates. 'No, I'm alright.'

'Well, I want a word with you anyway. Come and sit down.' She follows me into the sitting room and slumps down on the sofa with a huff. 'So… how are you coping?'

'How do you think?'

'Police said your heroin habit was two hundred pounds a day, so what have you been doing?'

'Little stint in jail halved that.'

'Maybe there's some scope to reduce it some more?'

'I'm trying.'

'As long as you're doing less today than yesterday, less this week than last, surely you can wean yourself off the stuff?'

'Look, don't pressure me – it's not going to help. I've got it under control. My habit's only twenty or thirty pound a day now, it's not that bad.'

'Thirty pounds a day! Where're you getting that? How can you think that's okay?' I pause. 'Give me your car keys.'

'What?'

'You heard. Give me the keys!' I shove my hand towards her. 'I'm making this too easy for you. I pay for the car, give me the keys!'

She searches my face. A look of panic flashes in her eyes, then she bites her bottom lip and lets a shallow breath out of her nose. Fiddling in her pocket, she takes out her car keys and gives them to me.

In my bedroom I sit down on the bed and search around for somewhere to hide them. My jewellery box? No, that's not the brightest idea – don't want her looking in there. Sliding open a drawer where I keep jumpers, I put the keys at the bottom.

Should I hide my jewellery as well? Am I being paranoid now?

Amber eats dinner with us, pushing her food around and picking at it, then goes to her room. I am still angry, but I can't solve it by pushing her away. I go to the bottom of the stairs, shout up to her bedroom door. 'Amber! Come and sit with us, there's a good film on, we want you to be part of the family.'

She appears in her dressing gown and huddles up on the other sofa, choosing to sit the furthest distance away from us. We watch TV in silence. When I think she won't notice, I glance over at her. She is so thin.

I'm dozing off, lulled into a dreamless half-sleep, when Amber says 'Why don't you go to bed, Mum? You're exhausted.'

'Yeah, you're right, I'm knackered.'

After a moment she comes across and shoves my shoulder. 'Oh. Was I asleep again?'

'Yes. Now go to bed.'

I make my way upstairs and climb into bed. I hear Tony in the bathroom and after a few minutes he gets in beside me. I'm about to fall into a deep sleep when something brings me back. At first I think there's an unfamiliar noise in the house, then I realise it's in my head. 'Go and move your car, Christine,' the voice tells me. I turn over, cuddle into the duvet. It smells fresh and sweet. Why would I move the car? The voice won't go away. 'Move your car. You might regret it.' My mind switches; I can't afford to regret anything.

I swing my legs over the side of the bed. There's a shaft of brightness under the bedroom door, so I don't switch the light on. I float down the stairs, my hand resting lightly on the banister. The brightness of the kitchen surprises me for a moment, then I remember what I'm doing. 'Where are you going, Mum?' Amber calls out. She's alone, still watching TV.

'I'm moving my car.'

'Moving it? Where? It's late, you're in your pyjamas. Go back to bed.'

'I'm moving the car.' I search around for my keys.

'No, Mum. Why?' Amber is standing in the doorway. 'Please… don't.'

I reverse the Jeep out of the driveway, swing it into the overflow parking, pull up a fraction behind the bumper of Amber's car. I would struggle to be that accurate if fully awake. I turn the engine off, glance around. There's a brick wall on the other side – no way she can get her car out. I go back into the house and climb the stairs to bed.

In the morning, I wake and remember what I've done. I feel rather foolish. Drawing back the curtain, I stare out of my bedroom window. Amber's car is jammed in sideways, nearly in the hedge. I check the drawer for her car keys. The neatly folded jumpers are a bit of a mess but her keys are still there.

For the first time, Amber is up before me, already dressed and in the kitchen. I lean past her to put the kettle on. Her face is clammy and milky white, and she seems tense.

'Struggle to get your car out last night?' I ask.

'Don't know what you mean,' she says.

'So, you never took the keys out of my drawer and put them back? That never happened?'

I notice a fresh bead of sweat appear on her forehead and trickle slowly down her face.

'Not feeling too good? 'Course, it's not that bad, is it? You've got it all under control, haven't you?'

She turns to me with a look of hostility. 'Still in your dressing gown, Mum? You'll be late for work if you don't hurry.'

'Not going to work today. I'm staying home so we can

spend all day together talking about your problems.'

I smile to myself. I am glad I moved my car last night. I think there's an angel somewhere helping me to keep Amber safe. Perhaps she might have done something if she'd gone out, something that would have been a turning point for her – she might have taken a step too far and not been able to come back to me.

'I'm going to see if Lauren and Sam are up for school, then I'm coming straight back.'

When I reach the top of the stairs the front door closes with a cutting click. She's slipped away from me again.

Nine

Amber

Pigeons peck for crumbs on the pavement beneath an overcast grey sky. They speed away when I'm close, their thin legs jogging under fat bodies, then they slow down to peck again once they're at a safe distance.

I wander in and out of shops. Mums with children in buggies are the only customers. Harsh lights sway in front of my eyes. I try to appear normal, check where the cameras are, where the tills are. I'm looking for a blind spot. It's difficult to know what I can steal. I've shoplifted before, when I was a teenager. I only ever took small things – a lip gloss or body spray; it was easy. Now I need something valuable, something I can get money for. The trouble is I'm not sure I know anyone who will buy stolen goods from me.

The heroin itch is intense today; it's crawling over my skin and through my mind. My skin is cloying, damp. Heroin addiction is my way of life – it's what I do. I've never thought about getting clean. I don't believe anyone who's been doing it as long as me could stop. I couldn't do it alone – I would need help, and who's going to help me? Mum? I'm a past mistake she can't shake off.

I'm in shock Mum still wants me in the house after the police told her everything. I've got no desire to please the Old Bill, nothing to care about – they're the faceless authority of the system. But home touches me emotionally. I want to fix it – that's why I lie so much, anything but see the disgust on their faces.

The money and the gear I took from the house soon dried up. I've sold everything I own – first the gold jewellery Dave gave me and then my DVD player, stereo, even clothes and perfume; anything to get ten quid together. I thought about stealing from Mum, but she's totally clued up. I've watched her check the money in her purse and she's locked her jewellery away.

My habit didn't grow as a result of my ability to steal or scam; although I'm in very deep, I don't have the guts for it like some addicts.

Stephen and Michelle live nearby. We used to share our gear sometimes; maybe they'll share with me now. The pavement moves from side to side as I walk along. I feel disorientated. I knock at their door but there's no answer. Standing under the front window, I peer in through the curtains to see if there's any movement inside. They might be too wrecked to come to the door. I wait in the street. Where can they be? I walk to the end of the road and back, but they don't show.

I can't think of anyone else. I'm running out of options. I don't know if I'll make it home. There's a park opposite, with an empty wooden bench on the edge. Wiping away a patch of rain with my hand, I sit down and rest.

After a few moments I lift my head a little to see a short, black skirt and skin-coloured tights. I glance up to see a girl I vaguely recognise. She's wearing black ankle boots that are clumpy and cheap-looking – they're covered in scuffs like a child's school shoes.

'Amber, ain't it?' She sits down beside me. 'Donna, remember? Used to score off Dave.' Donna, yes, I remember her now.

Donna is naturally blonde with pale blue eyes, and when I study her face I can see she was pretty once. The huge dark circles under her eyes make it look like they're sinking into the back of her head. She's wearing far too much make-up and is constantly scratching her nose; it's red raw.

Heroin addicts often think they have ants or something running underneath their skin, crawling like parasites. Heroin addicts don't feel pain. They know the pain is there, but it's a distant pain, a memory, they don't *feel* it, so they scratch in an obsessive, inhuman way.

'You and Dave been raided, ain't you? Yeah, Johnny told me.' She moves a long fingernail to the end of her nose and scratches it viciously, making her problem much worse. 'What you doing now then? He's banged up, ain't he? He'll be away for a while.'

'I'm out on bail, living at my mum's. I've been round Aldershot trying to nick something.' I clutch my belly as another cramp grips me. 'I'm clucking my tits off; really need a boot.'

Donna laughs. 'I give up thieving a while back.'

'How do you pay for your gear, then?'

'Tell you what,' she places her face close to mine. 'I'll sort you out with a smoke, then I'll show you – it's easy.' Donna stands up and pushes her hands into the pockets of her jacket, then turns and walks away.

What could she be doing to get easy gear? But the promise of a boot makes it impossible for me to draw back from her now. I tag along behind, my body bent over. I'm holding my stomach with my head down, lifting my face up every few paces to check she's still in front of me. Donna stops at the door of a terraced house and turns around. She waits for a moment while I try to catch up. Then she places her key in the lock and I follow her inside.

The house is dirty and smells of heroin and cigarette smoke, as if the windows have never been opened. She slumps down on the sofa in a downstairs room, and I'm grateful to sink in beside her. Everything is old and worn out. Manky curtains hang loose at the window, casting a tea-stained light. As the warm sun briefly shines through, it heightens the stale smell. The coffee table by our knees is covered in dirty ashtrays and half-filled mugs of tea and coffee; some of them have mould on.

Donna gets out her gear. She lays it out on the table, smokes a line and then offers it to me. I'm relieved. The cramps and sweating stop immediately and I feel normal, good. The gear hits me harder because I've been clucking – it gives me a heady buzz but also a feeling of calm. Everything's okay now.

A pale girl shuffles in wearing skimpy bright red shorts and a sparkly, low-cut top. 'Got a light?' She picks up a Bic lighter from the table. Her top falls open at the front; I can see her tits. She shuffles out again.

I look at Donna primly and she lets out a short laugh. 'Well, she's working, ain't she?'

'Working? What do you mean, working?'

Donna rests her hand on my shoulder. 'It's a working house, ain't it?'

All of a sudden I very badly don't want to be there, but it seems foolish and rude to leave now, now she's shared her gear with me.

I flinch at a loud knock on the front door. Donna jumps up to answer it. From the sofa I lean forward to see a wealthy-looking man standing in the doorway. He's in his mid-forties, wearing a dark grey suit. Through the glass door, I notice there's now a smart car sitting outside.

'Alright?' Donna greets him. Her head tilts up to his and she kisses him on the cheek. 'Come in, meet Sapphire; she's new.'

She hangs on his arm, staring into his face for a reaction.

He's not ugly or unattractive but he has a forceful presence. I can tell he's not a drug addict. I understand addicts, know how their minds work. My sense of danger is heightened despite the gear I've had. Instantly I'm sober and experience a huge adrenaline rush. Donna takes his hand and leads him upstairs.

'Come on, you.' She beckons me to follow.

My feet feel like heavy weights. Dragging them one at a time I go as slowly as I can. I can't believe how stupid I've been to get myself in this situation. I feel sick and, deep inside, I know I have to find a way out.

I follow them into a bedroom. It's clean and has an en-suite bathroom. The walls are plain white and the décor is simple, stark. The man takes a coat hanger from the back of the door and arranges his jacket on it. He undoes his belt with soft, flabby hands and, sliding it out of his trousers, places it carefully on a chair. I notice he's wearing a wedding ring. He is meticulous in the way he folds his clothes and leaves them in a neat pile. He's a fairly big man and his figure has been softened by years of good living. He bends over to remove loose-fitting, white underpants, whipping them off without hesitation. Standing there fully nude, he isn't the slightest bit bothered; it's as if he's just come home. He turns around and steps into the shower.

Donna sits down beside me on the bed. I can hear my heart

beating in my head, thudding at my temples as if I have a huge hangover.

'Don't be scared.' Donna rolls her eyes at me. 'It's easy. He'll wear something, won't he? It'll be over in no time. Let him shag you. We'll get some more gear, and some white.' She pats my leg, 'I've been giving it away for years, 'bout time I got something back.'

'I can't do it.' I close my eyes. 'He's gross.'

The water is welling up inside me, but I'm desperate not to let her see me cry. I can feel myself starting to shake.

'First time's always the worst.' She leans in close to me. I can smell the light perfume of her make-up. 'You'll get used to it. Anyway, you owe me, I sorted you out.'

There's menace in her tone now, like she owns me, can control me. In that moment I know I hate her. I thought she wanted to help me.

I'm on the edge of a slope and about to slide into a dark place. The world of drugs has always given me acceptance and security, but now it's turned on me. As if I've been seduced by a hundred-year-old vampire who appeared to be young and handsome and made me love him, but now I'm infected is showing me his true form. Now I have to pay. He wants something back from me, something I've never agreed to, something more than I'm prepared to give.

The man opens the door of the shower. He steps out with his large penis dangling between his legs. A breeze of damp air follows him. He reaches for a small towel and ties it around his waist.

His eyes widen as if he's undressing me, removing my simple jeans and baggy jumper. 'I'll see you in a minute,' he says, grabbing my wrist and squeezing it hard, hurting me. He takes a long breath and his nostrils dilate. 'Make sure you don't go anywhere. You're my seconds.'

In my mind a picture appears of him on top of me, thrusting himself inside me. My stomach turns and I have to clench my bum; I'm petrified.

Donna scratches her nose and smiles, then leans her shoulder against mine. 'Go to my room and get into some of my stuff, put some make-up on. Oh, and get some lube if you need it,' she whispers.

My toes are on the line, and if I cross the line, do something sordid, gear is the only thing that will ever, ever, make me feel okay again. I think about Mum. Fuck it! I'm getting out!

Stepping out onto the landing, my heart is pumping in my chest. I shut the door behind me and inhale deeply, look down at the dark red carpet; it's dirty with fag burns and there's fluff all over it. I place my ear closer to the door and listen. There is a sloppy sound of them kissing. I must get out without them knowing. I wait. The adrenaline is rising like a fire. It takes all my control not to run. I tell myself to wait, I must wait. I rest my hand against the cool wall.

The bed creaks as they lie on it. Slowly, with my back to the wall, I move down the stairs, one at a time. When I reach the bottom I hear the headboard banging against the bedroom wall.

I glance into the room where Donna and I got stoned. There's a small amount of gear left on the tin foil; it's still there among the ashtrays and mugs. I want it as much as I want to get away. I can't stop myself. I steal the last of her gear.

The front door clicks as it fits into the catch and I run.

I run till my chest hurts but I don't care. I run till I'm gasping for air, the tears coming fast now, blown off my face by the wind before they have time to make my cheeks wet. Stopping at the bottom of the path to my mum's house, I bend my head down, panting to regain control of my breathing.

I'm scared of the thought of withdrawal; I think it might kill me. But I'd rather die than stay in the hell I'm living in.

Christine

My bare feet tucked up beside me on the sofa, I've drifted into a kind of daze, staring through the patio doors at the familiar outlook; like me the garden seems to wait, still and hesitant.

I allow my mind to rest, to think things over without getting upset, not wanting to disturb the calm I briefly feel.

I'm tired of the nights I now lie awake, expecting to hear Amber sneak out. Staring into the dark, one hand under my pillow, I play out scenarios in my head, how I am going to help her quit. I have considered spending thousands of pounds on professional therapy, have investigated hospitals nearby that offer this type of help.

If Amber had a serious illness, I would be relating the circumstances to every family member and well-meaning friends. As it is, I hide it inside, the knowledge that she's an addict, as if I'm the only one allowed to know.

My brief respite is broken by the click of a key in the front door. Amber rushes in. Her face is wet with tears.

'What's the matter, Amber? You've been crying,' I say as she drops down beside me.

She steadies herself and lifts her face to mine. 'I can't do this any more,' she says, and a couple of loud sobs burst out of her. 'You've got to help me. Please.' Wiping the tears from her cheeks with her sleeve, her shoulders shake violently.

This is the breakthrough I've been waiting for. I'm relieved. 'You know I'll help you. Just tell me. I'll pay for rehab if you'll go. If it'll help you.'

Like when she was a child, I want to make it alright, take away all the pain with a kiss and a sticking plaster. 'Are you in more trouble? Is that why you're crying?'

'I can't wait for rehab, Mum. I need help now.'

'You'll have to be honest with me, about your addiction. How much you're using. You've got to start talking to me about it.'

'I've been doing a lot. I can't get clean at home. I have to get away.'

For the first time in a long time, I put my arms around her. I feel her body stiffen as I hold her, then she relaxes into me. I stroke the back of her tangled hair. She might wriggle and squirm but I have to believe she will give up heroin. I am her mother, I can be strong enough for both of us.

'We could go somewhere, spend a few days together, just the two of us?'

'It's gonna be hard staying off it once I'm clean, Mum. I don't know if I can do it.' She tightens her hold on me. The back of her throat clicks several times and she lets out a long breath, then breathes in again quickly.

'Of course you'll do it. I told you it can't go on. I'm surprised it's taken you this long to realise.'

I pull out two or three tissues from the box in the kitchen and give them to her. 'I'm going to help you, Amber. I'll do anything I have to.'

Amber

Listening to the sound of voices talking downstairs, my chest begins to heave and I turn over in bed. I try not to look inwards at my darkest fears, try to believe I can face the days ahead.

I'm not worried about bumping into Donna again. I didn't agree to anything. She can start on me if she wants to – I'm bigger than her. It's him I'm afraid of and all the men like him; I'm afraid I'll be tempted to sell myself for drug money.

I hear the TV being switched off and footsteps on the stairs.

I've been trying to get to sleep for hours. I glance at the clock beside my bed. I know that without Mum I'll be walking the streets again tomorrow, and next time I won't be so lucky. Donna will spread it around that I've stolen from her. Next time, she'll make me do it first – shag someone before I get the gear. If I go back to her, I'll have to work off what I've stolen.

I'm hot and the bottom sheet is starting to feel damp. My eyes are wide open, staring at the ceiling. On the dark, smooth surface I see flashbacks from my past, from my childhood, even of my father. I throw off the covers. I know what I need.

Sitting on the floor in the silent darkness, I search through my bag, feeling for the piece of gear I took from Donna. I creep downstairs.

Outside, I glance up at Mum's bedroom window before sneaking across to my car. Everyone else is asleep.

I want to give up. I do. But sitting here, smoking the gear, the itch from my mind and my body are gone. I feel that warm, golden glow again; it edges right through me, fills me up. I'm calm, content, euphoric.

Maybe I'm not ready to say I will never use heroin again, ever.

I can't face that right now; to live the rest of my life without that emotional release. It's too big a job. I don't know if I can do it.

But that's tomorrow, so I just won't think about it.

Ten

Christine

My feet feel the outline of slippers in the early morning light. I watch the gentle rise and fall of Tony's shoulders for a moment before pulling on my dressing gown. The house is still. Things have changed and I feel a sense of hope. I've broken through her barrier. Our talk yesterday about her addiction, about her options for recovery, was a turning point for us both. I am eager to get started, energetic; my battery is full.

I open the door to her room and sit on her bed. 'You awake?'

'Mmm, yeah.' She opens her eyes.

'I've got a meeting in London today. I can't get out of it, but after that I'm going to stay home with you, until we sort this out.'

She turns towards me. 'What are we going to do?'

'What do other people in this situation do? I know you don't want to go into rehab, and I respect that, but we need some help. What about Acorn and organisations like that? What do they do?'

'They just prescribe methadone. I've seen more addicts die from it than heroin. I'm over twenty-one so I'll have to wait three months for an appointment. I told you; I can't wait.'

'Alright, let's just do it together. I've spoken to Tone, he's going to take care of the kids. We'll go away tomorrow, spend two nights in a hotel, then I'll ask Nanny if you can stay there Friday night. That'll give you an extra day and I can be home for the weekend.'

'I still have to get through today and tonight. You're at work and I'm here alone. I can't manage a whole day on my own without something.'

I lean towards her. 'What do you want, Amber? Money? Where've you been getting it from so far? What makes today different?'

'I haven't stolen anything if that's what you mean. I really want this to work, but if you leave me vulnerable I'm in danger of doing something we both might regret.'

She's right. I can't afford for anything to go wrong now. I have to go with my instincts. 'Okay,' I pause, 'I'll give you money for heroin.'

I search about downstairs for my handbag, take ten pounds out of my purse. Back in her room I pass her the note. 'This is the one and only time.'

'Thanks, Mum, I didn't think you understood.'

'I'm trying. It's not easy for me.'

I drive to the station to get the train to London. The platform is crowded with people. I am staring at posters for shows I'll never see. I can't stop thinking about Amber. Where will she buy heroin? Will she use it near the house?

The train appears in the distance and then slows to a gentle halt beside me. I press the entry button and the doors hiss open. Once the train has pulled out of the station, the repetitive movement sedates me slightly. Rows of houses speed past, their gardens a never-ending pattern of squares. Some are overgrown and neglected, others neatly cared for. I take the papers for the meeting out of my briefcase and stare at them, then put them away without having read a line. The train arrives at Waterloo station. I know I must concentrate on my job; I will be part of this emotionally draining mess again soon enough.

'The Chairman's been looking for you, Christine,' the managing director's secretary is waiting for me in the hotel foyer. 'He's in a panic about the meeting, wants to see the projection for next year before you present it to the board.'

'I'll go and see him now.' I've prepared the figures; I hope I haven't missed anything. I thought there might be a chance to go over them one more time.

The committee accept the financial report, and once that part of the agenda is over I am not listening. I draw a complicated doodle on the top of my papers, remembering to glance up every few minutes at whoever is talking, nodding my head with feigned interest. Thankfully no-one asks any difficult questions and the meeting finishes on time.

The sun is shining through the clouds and the spring air is warm on my back as I walk along the river to the station. I notice some homeless people, alcoholics and addicts, lying on the grass enjoying the weather. Vacant eyes stare out at the people passing by. I view them differently now, with more compassion: each one is someone's lost child, and they don't choose to live this way. I can't let that happen to Amber.

On the train I ring Jane. 'I won't be in for the rest of the week.'

'You and Tony going away?'

'No. I'm spending some quality time with Amber. She's a bit delicate, got boyfriend trouble, needs her mum.'

'They're never too old to need their mum.'

I open the front door at home to find Amber waiting for me. She's agitated and tetchy. 'I'm probably gonna need another tenner to get through the night, so we can start tomorrow.'

'No.'

Her eyes search out mine, pleading. 'But…'

'Start now.'

She slumps down on the bottom stair.

'This could be a good thing – we can start earlier. You may as well accept it.'

Emotionally, she's a child looking to her mother for comfort and reassurance. She seems to be filled with a superstitious terror of what lies ahead. I have to be strong with her, to do what I know she can't do herself. 'I'm locking you in tonight.'

After dinner I sit in the study surfing the internet. Amber's been following me from room to room all evening; now she sits on the floor, watching. I am hunting for information about heroin addiction and where I can get help. I don't know what to expect with her withdrawal, don't really know what I am doing.

When I type 'Help for heroin withdrawal' into Google it comes up with some information about a drug called naltrexone. It blocks the euphoric effects of heroin by coating the opioid receptors in the brain. Taken orally, as a daily dose, once you have it in your system you can use heroin but you can't get high. I just have to find a way to get Amber a prescription for it.

'This could work,' I show her the website. She stands up and peers over my shoulder. 'It's the answer to our problem; it will give us more of a chance.'

'Err… what does it do?'

I explain it to her.

'Really?' she looks surprised.

I register at a medical website to obtain a private prescription for the naltrexone, the sort of site where men get Viagra. After paying a fee with my credit card, I send an email request. I'll have to pay for it at the chemist but at least I don't need to answer any difficult questions or see a doctor. I have no real knowledge of the side effects of this naltrexone, but I'm so desperate to stop Amber using heroin I'm going to make her take it anyway. It seems like the lesser of two evils.

When I tell her I've ordered it, she grunts at me.

I'm a bit more upbeat and, on a roll, I find the strength to call my mother. I am not sure what I want her to say; it's just good to get it out in the open. I tell her about the raid, about Dave's drug dealing and that Amber's a heroin addict. 'What on earth are you going to do with her?' she says.

'Amber's going to quit – that's it, end of story. She needs to get away for three or four days to get clean. I've booked us into a hotel for two nights but I can't leave the children any longer than that. I need someone to care for her for one more night. Will you do it for me?'

'Well… if you think she'll be alright with me.'

'Just one night. Feed her and be sure to lock her in, that's all I ask.'

Before going to bed, I lock down the house. Every window and every door are locked and bolted. Then I unplug all the house phones, take Amber's mobile and hide them all in our room. Tony watches me. 'Is she really that desperate already?' he asks.

'She's uncomfortable. It's not that bad yet, but I'm not taking any chances.'

Tony looks at me and raises his eyebrows but says nothing more.

In the morning I open my eyes to the sound of Amber

retching in the downstairs loo. She has a long way to go over the next few days. This is day one; today and tomorrow will be the worst. If she sees a crack in my belief, it will fester in her mind and grow into our reality. I have to believe she can do it. I won't accept any other outcome. When I open the toilet door she's on her knees. 'You okay?' I ask her.

'Help me up.' She's pallid and clammy. 'I need something extra Mum, sleeping pills or Valium. I can't do it with nothing.'

'I'll ring the doctors, get you an emergency appointment.'

The thought of having to explain this to my GP fills me with a dread I haven't felt since chemotherapy. Which would I rather do: this or chemo? This. I settle down, put on my parental persona and carry on.

I make the call and return to find Amber sitting on the sofa biting the skin around her nails. 'You'd better get dressed, our appointment's at ten,' I say.

At the surgery we check in with the receptionist and wait. A few out-of-date magazines can't distract me from my churning stomach. In my mind I rehearse my little speech; there's no easy way to say 'my daughter's a heroin addict' so I may as well just spit it out.

The doctor's room is cramped and cluttered. As we walk in he's staring at the computer screen on his desk; he turns to look at us. He is a large man in his sixties and has a Latin appearance. 'What seems to be the problem?' he smiles.

'This is my daughter. She's a heroin addict.' I cross my legs and shuffle in my chair. 'She's been brought home by the police on bail. She's desperate to give up. From today she's going cold turkey. I wondered if you could help us. She's already in a bad way; we need a few sleeping pills to get her through the next few days.'

He raises his glasses from his nose and peers at me. 'I don't deal with drug addicts. Go to Acorn, get some methadone.'

Amber groans and drops her chin towards her chest. I know she appears to be just another hopeless addict, but she's different, she's my daughter. I take a deep breath. I must get some help for her. I can't walk out with nothing. 'I'm asking you to help us, please, to prescribe a few sleeping tablets.'

'Why should I prescribe sleeping pills? So she can sell them for drugs? That's what addicts do, you know.'

Stupid man. I am trying to help someone quit a dangerous addiction and all he can do is judge me and all addicts. I can understand how someone who has dedicated his life to helping people get well could get pretty fed up dealing with all the self-inflicted harm drug addicts do to themselves. But I won't allow myself to get angry.

'I'll keep custody of the pills. I'll make sure she only has one a night, and she won't sell them.'

He stares at me for a few moments. 'Ten. I'll give you ten.' He waves his hand at me dismissively. 'I'm not getting involved after that. Don't come back asking me for another prescription when she's back on the heroin in a few weeks.' I see from his expression that he doesn't think she'll make it past that.

The doctor types up some notes on his computer and the printer springs to life as the prescription is printed. What did he write in her medical records? Will she be viewed with suspicion every time she goes to see a doctor? We leave the surgery, my self-respect only just still intact.

Amber takes my arm to steady herself. 'What will you do, Mum, if I can't bear it? If the pain gives me a heart attack or something?' She's gulping for air and wheezing, then takes in a few short, rasping breaths and manages to control herself. 'What will you do?'

'Don't worry, sweetie.' I give her hand a rub. 'If things get too bad, I'll take you to casualty. They'll look after you.'

But I won't. I'll make her put up with it unless I really think it might kill her. I have no idea what heroin withdrawal is like, but I know if I fuss too much, give her too much sympathy now, I'll have nothing to add when things are at their peak.

'We've got the sleeping tablets but I need some Valium. I know where I can get some.'

'What, from a dealer?'

'Yeah, but I only need a few, a tenner should do it. You'll need to take me, wait outside.'

Seeing the eagerness in her eyes, I wonder if I am being a fool. Am I making this all too easy? On balance, I decide to chance it. I can't leave her to suffer like this.

'Okay. Let's get them now.' Before I change my mind or have to explain myself to Tony. I look at her beside me in the car and smile. 'Tell me where the dealer lives, then.'

Amber gives me the directions and I pull up outside a normal semi-detached house down a leafy road. I wonder where the people who live there get Valium to sell on.

I wait in the car while Amber goes inside. She emerges from the house a few minutes later, gets in the front and slams the door hard. 'Don't do that, Amber! It's my car, not a taxi.' Her mood seems to have changed.

'I'm scared, alright?'

'Look, I know it's hard, but you can do this.'

'Can I?'

'Yes.' I sigh. 'You can.'

She folds her arms and stares out of the window.

'Well, did you get them?' She nods her head. I count the Valium in my hand: ten. Does that seems right, a pound each? I suppose so. 'Right, let's collect the prescription for the sleeping pills and go.'

Back at home, Amber puts our bags on the parcel shelf in my Mercedes and sinks into the passenger seat beside me. I turn the ignition and the engine purrs with a deep, throaty rattle. The car is close to the ground; the vibration of the engine goes through my body and I drive away. From behind a bank of cloud the sun appears, warming my face through the windscreen. I pull into a lay-by and put the top down and the heated seats on. The breeze whips around my ears and I wish I'd brought a scarf. 'We could be Thelma and Louise,' I say.

'Who?'

'It's a film. They're two rebels who drive off in their car and never come back.'

'Yeah, I like the sound of that.'

This trip is a new start for us. Our relationship as mother and daughter is the missing piece in my life. We'll come back, but I have a feeling we'll be different.

'It's going to be alright. Concentrate on what you can do today rather than think about the withdrawal. Tell yourself you can do anything, as long as it's not heroin.'

I tuck my hair behind my ear, trying to wrestle control back from the wind. I put my foot down and we burn up some miles on the motorway.

The hotel room is modest, just two single beds and a bathroom, but it's clean and smells of paint and new carpet. Amber gets into bed with her clothes on. She wraps the duvet around her body. 'You wouldn't run me a bath, would you?'

The en-suite bathroom has white-tiled walls that shine with a harsh, clinical light. I run the hot water and glance around for some complimentary bubble bath. Staring at my reflection, I wonder whether it's my imagination or whether I look older than I did a month ago. The strain of this is taking something out of me.

When the bath's ready, I leave her to soak.

I go back into the bedroom and check the window by Amber's bed to see how far it will open and whether the gap's wide enough for a person to climb out. The long drop into a narrow yard is too far to jump and the plastic double-glazed window won't open more than a couple of inches.

'Mum!' Amber calls. 'Can you help me? Don't think I can get out.'

I pull back the thin shower curtain to find her struggling to raise herself out of the water. Putting my hands under her armpits, I take her weight to help her to stand. There's a large mirror that runs the length of the bath and up to the ceiling. As she reaches across for a towel, I glance up at her reflection. I haven't seen her naked since she was a child.

She's emaciated – her arms and legs are stick thin. Her skin is the palest white, with large blue veins showing through her chest and down her legs. Where her ribs stick out, the skin is even whiter, stretched over her bones. The whirl of the extractor fan seems to increase, making my head spin. My eyes are stinging. I turn my face away, put the lid of the toilet down. 'You sit there and get into your nightie, then into bed.'

Sinking into a chair in the other room, I rest my head in my hands. I let a few tears fall before wiping them away. How could Dave have let her get like this? Wasn't he supposed to love her? I make myself a promise – whatever happens, I won't give up on her, ever.

Amber takes a Valium and a couple of her sleeping pills and we settle down for the night. I lock the door to our room and put the key under my pillow. I keep waking up, checking to make sure Amber's still there and still breathing. She turns and mumbles; at times she seems delirious, but eventually the night passes.

In the morning she's finally sleeping peacefully. Rather than disturb her, I lock the door behind me and go down for breakfast in the hotel alone. I bring her back some toast, yogurt and fruit, but she screws up her face. 'Not hungry?' I ask.

'I feel sick.'

'Try and drink some water and eat a piece of dry toast.'

She shakes her head and snuggles back down in her bed. 'I can't eat anything.'

I try to think of something nice, give her something to look forward to. 'When this is over, I'll take you on holiday.'

'Where will we go?'

'Somewhere hot.'

I use room service and watch TV all day, dishing out the sleeping tablets and Valium to keep her sedated. The second night passes like the first, Amber tranquillised and delirious, while I watch. My ignorance has worked in my favour because I wasn't afraid of the withdrawal, didn't know what to expect. I didn't allow her to panic or give in.

When we check out of the room on the second morning she's different, as if something evil has left her body. 'How're you today?' I ask her.

'Well, I hurt all over, even my clothes hurt. I can feel every stitch and button cutting into my skin. Alcohol, fags and sleeping pills are about all I can manage.'

'Can't be as bad as when you were in jail.'

'There was something final about being in jail. It was easier when I knew I couldn't get any gear, and I had the doctor's prescription.'

'Let's go to the nearest town; we could look round the shops,' I say.

She shrugs her shoulders. 'Whatever.'

Later the sun begins to fade and a chilly breeze blows up. Amber starts to shake uncontrollably. 'You cold?' I ask.

She wraps her coat tighter around herself and shivers. 'Feels as if I've got ice bolts shooting through my body. It helps when I'm in the car, it takes my mind off it.'

'We'll drive down to the coast and take in the sea air, then start the journey back.'

I glance out to the ocean as we drive along the seafront. People walk along the wide expanse of pavement. The weather's mild and bright and the sun sparkles on the water like a thousand diamonds laid upon a grey sheet.

'How many hours has it been since I last had a boot?' She yawns and stretches back in the front seat of the car. I think she's starting to believe she can get clean. That's what been lacking: belief.

'About seventy-two. We're nearly there, sweetheart; another twenty-four hours should do it.'

She leans over and puts her hand gently on top of mine as it rests on the middle console.

I leave it as long as I can before dropping her off at my mother's house, balancing the time I have left with her against my need to get back to Lauren and Sam.

'You'll be alright here; it's only one night,' I say. Amber's lip trembles briefly, then she gets out of the car. I wait with the engine running until my mother opens the door, then I wave and smile at her as Amber steps inside.

The prescription for the naltrexone has arrived in the post while I've been away. I go to the chemist to collect it.

'It'll be ten minutes,' the girl behind the counter tells me. There is a display of make-up to one side of the till: cheap lipsticks, in shiny pinks and reds. I take out several testers and try them on the top of my hand.

The pharmacist comes out from her office. 'Is the prescription for you?' she asks me.

'No, it's for my daughter.'

'She's a heroin addict?'

My throat tightens. 'Yes,' my face starts to flush, 'but she's clean now.'

'Okay. She needs to be at least seventy-two hours completely free of opiates, otherwise there are some nasty side effects. Has she taken anything else with opiates in it?'

I let out a long breath. 'No, I've been with her the last three days.'

'Good luck, then.' She passes me a white paper bag with the prescription inside.

I pick up some groceries on my way home and have already started dinner when Tony gets home from work.

'How did it go with Amber?' he asks.

'So far so good. I'm exhausted mentally and physically. Thank God Dave's in prison, otherwise it would have been impossible.'

He draws me into his arms. Whispering into his neck, I say, 'Difficult bit over, let's hope things start to get back to normal.'

He pulls back and looks into my face. 'Love, this is just the start. Even if she stays off the stuff, what about all the charges against her? What if she gets a prison sentence? Who's going to employ her with a prison record? You can't support her forever.'

We spend the evening cuddled up on the sofa. I don't

mention Amber again and he doesn't ask any more questions. I'm glad to get an early night.

The ring of my mobile wakes me and I glance at the time before answering. 'Mum, it's me. Come and get me,' Amber says.

'Is something wrong? It's five in the morning.'

'I'm cold. I'm lonely.'

'Okay, if I have to. I'll leave now.'

I shake Tony's shoulder, tell him where I'm going. 'I'll be back before the kids are up,' I say. I pick up his fleece from the hall and put it on. It feels cosy and warm.

It's still half dark. I put the headlights on and swing the car out of the driveway; the windscreen wipers clear the condensation that has settled in the cold night air. The roads are empty as I drive the distance to my mother's house. Everything is in darkness when I pull up. Amber opens the front door. She's dressed and ready to go. 'Hiya,' she lowers herself into the front seat.

'Wasn't the door locked?'

'Not from the inside.'

'I told Nanny to be sure to lock you in.'

She shrugs her shoulders. 'I want to be in my own bed, in my own home. It's you I need.'

I tidy up the kitchen from last night and take Tony up an early cup of tea. Instead of taking her coat off, Amber puts another one on top. She has a security blanket from when she was a child; it's been carefully washed and mended ever since. She wraps it around her neck like a scarf. I make her some hot chocolate. When Tony's left for work I ask 'Are you ready to take the naltrexone?'

'Let's do it in your room,' she says.

We sit on my bed together. I read the information leaflet

out loud. It explains the side effects you can get if you have heroin in your system. We count up how many hours it's been since her last hit. As I take the tablet out of the packet her head sinks back, like a tortoise hiding in its shell.

'Now I'm clean, I think I'll be alright without it,' she says.

'No, Amber. You must take it.'

She breathes heavily through her nose and then pops the tablet in her mouth and swallows it down with a sip of her drink. We sit there holding hands, looking at each other, waiting for unusual symptoms or pain. But it's alright, nothing bad happens.

I haven't really thought about what will happen now. She should slowly get well. She wants to be clean – we planned this together and worked hard for it. I'll give her the pill each day and watch her swallow it, so we're pretty sure to be okay.

Amber

'Alright, mate? It's Amber. You at home? Is it worth me popping round?' I ask the dealer.

If the dealer's got nothing he'll say 'No, ain't worth popping round yet.' But I'm in luck; he says 'Yeah, I'll stick the kettle on.'

While I've been away with Mum, I've held on without heroin, but nothing's changed. I'm still an addict. I still think about gear all the time. I'm desperate and frustrated and there's nothing I can do about it. My body is frail and worn out. I'm exhausted and battered as if from a long fight. I want a day off from my life.

My desire for heroin is strong. Strong as an overwhelming love, a romantic love, it has changed my perception of reality, altered my mind. I'm used to being able to change my emotions with drugs, like when you get a headache and you control the pain by taking a painkiller. Suddenly, I have the worst migraine of my life and I can't take anything to control it.

I'm okay taking the naltrexone. I am. It's what Mum wants, what we both want. But I have to see if I can lean on this blocker, if it can give me the strength I don't have on my own.

I blag some money off Mum, drive to the dealer as quickly as I can. I'm annoyed and agitated as I walk up the harsh concrete steps to his flat. I want to quit. I do. But right now I'm afraid to, so I have to get stoned first. Maybe I'll need to use more than normal. The blocker might dilute the effect.

The dealer opens the door. 'Alright?' he says. 'Just a bag, then?'

'Yeah,' I say and step inside.

I heat the foil. The smoke gives off a vicious, acid smell, filling my lungs. It brings bile to the back of my throat. Can I feel it? Can I? Do I feel a buzz? Is it working?

I get another twenty quid's worth, getting it on tick I'll have to pay back.

Slamming the dealer's door on my way out, I storm down the path to my car. How the bloody hell did she come up with this blocker idea? I've smoked loads more than I would normally need to get stoned.

I haven't felt a thing, not even a tingle.

Part Three

Relapsing

Eleven

Amber

The magistrates' court is square and bleak. In the front are stupid little hills and flowerbeds that remind me of Teletubbie land. A lorry passes close to the curb and the backdraught lifts my hair and blows a puff of warm air into my face. Exhaust fumes fill my nostrils. Mum puts a ticket inside the car windscreen and hurries along the path towards me.

My mouth is dry and my tongue is sticking to the top of my mouth. I'm starting to sweat. Now I've been taking the blocker for three weeks I can't even smoke a boot before the hearing. I've never had to face my emotions head on before.

If Mum wasn't here with me, I would be somewhere now smoking a boot, laughing that I should be court. But her caring that I do the right thing makes me want to do the right thing, so she'll think I'm worth saving.

Sometimes I watch Mum care for Lauren and wonder why she didn't care for me like that. Lauren's not better than me, yet she has a daddy and she has a mum who wants to be a mother. Why wasn't I good enough as a child to make Mum happy?

My solicitor, April, is waiting in the reception area for us. She has a flat fringe and pointed nose. From the side she reminds me of a robin, round apart from her head and legs. But she looks well groomed in her stylish business suit, the colour of her blouse picked out to match her pointy-toed shoes. At least I've got her on my side. She brings that exact neatness to her work: always has every piece of evidence and argument she needs for my case.

My Nike Airs squeak on the shiny floor as we walk down the corridor leading to the courtroom; it smells of polish and creaks beneath my feet. The walls inside the court are covered in wood panelling and the high ceiling gives me the feeling I'm in a church – that same emptiness in my stomach. We sit at the front and wait in silence. I feel different from everyone else as if they're all thinking 'We're okay. We behave but you don't.' Like I'm an exhibit.

Dave's pleading 'not guilty' to the charge of dealing. He's saying the amount of heroin the police found at our house was for his personal use.

DS Thompson saunters in. I know he's using me as leverage against Dave, leaning on him with the threat that I'll go to jail. That's why we're being charged together: without linking me to Dave they've got nothing on me and yet I'm being used as a pawn. It would be easier for the police if Dave pleaded guilty to the charges. When DS Thompson was interviewing me at the station, he asked me why I was lying for Dave, protecting him. 'You think he loves you, don't you? We'll see how much he cares before I'm through,' he'd said.

At the start of our relationship Dave told me you can't deal drugs forever. He said it would be a short trip, a rollercoaster, but still I stepped on the ride with him, believing that we'd get away with it, that this would never happen.

Two security officers bring Dave in, flanking him. His shoes shuffle along the parquet floor and his hands are cuffed behind his back. They place him in a glass booth at the front of the court. He looks ill and gaunt.

It's the first time I've seen him since I was bailed; it gives me a rush of butterflies. The longing in my chest starts to grow. I want to climb over the barrier that separates us and hold him. How can they keep us apart? I study the back of his head, the shape of his neck and shoulders. He doesn't even turn round; doesn't he want to see me?

Linda and Dave's step-dad arrive. Linda gives me a condescending smile. They sit in the gallery, looking down on the proceedings. When Dave catches sight of them, at the edge of his vision, his head drops further. I feel his shame. Yet I'm gutted that they got that slight movement, that recognition, and I got nothing.

Everyone stands when the magistrate enters. He settles into his position in the centre of the bench and glances up at the people in court. The magistrate leans towards Dave; he seems concerned. 'Would you like a chair?' he asks, and then motions to an attendant to fetch one.

The hearing only takes ten minutes. It's standard stuff: reading out the charges and transferring the case to the Crown Court. Once it's finished the guards escort Dave out. Watching him walk away, I know things are never going to be the same again. My fairy-tale life is peeling away.

Dave looks so ill that you'd think he'd consider getting clean while he has a chance to in jail. But heroin controls you, gets inside your mind, talks to you in a voice you think is your own; it tells you it's not the heroin that's bad, it's being without it. You must make sure you're never without it again, then you won't need to go through this pain. Even if you steal from your mother or your baby brother, you'll do anything you have to. Normal people see things the other way round. They say, 'I'd never let that drug have power over me, so I'd do whatever I had to do to get myself clean.'

But drug addicts don't think like that.

Christine

April picks up her briefcase and walks beside Amber and me into the lobby. I'm impressed with the way she handled herself in court. She's professional yet compassionate. I like her.

'Everything went as I expected,' April says.

Linda appears and muscles in beside Amber. Is that her husband standing next to her? He's wearing a prominent gold cross that sits on the knot of his tie, like a badge to let everyone know how superior he is because he's a devout Christian.

'How *is* the case looking?' I ask April.

'The police seized a large amount of heroin,' she starts to explain. 'Amber's in a lot of trouble.'

Linda butts in: 'I've seen more gear than that before. That's only a few days' worth for my Dave. 'Course Thompson could tell you that.' Linda looks across at DS Thompson, who's standing on the other side of the lobby, then she smiles at him and he becomes flustered and looks away. Am I mistaken or did those two just share a moment? I reckon Linda's husband is deluded at how far she is involved and how much she knew about what was going on. I think she plays at being the godly wife.

'We wait now, until we get a date for Crown Court,' April continues. 'We've got a lot of work to do before then to prepare our case. My secretary will ring you with an appointment for next week, Amber.' April turns to me. 'Mrs Lewry, can I have a word?'

She steers me to one side and places her expensive leather briefcase on the floor. 'If you have any resources you can use to get her some help I advise you to do it. I see drug addiction a lot; it's so destructive.'

'Amber's clean. I've got her taking this heroin blocker called naltrexone.'

'I'm glad,' April says, and gives my arm a squeeze. 'Amber's a sweet girl and I'm going to do my best to keep her out of prison. Let's hope she stays away from Dave when he gets out. I think she's protecting him. It's so frustrating.'

I step out of the building and into the sunlight. Amber is standing by the metal fence rummaging about in her bag; she takes out a packet of cigarettes and lights one. Her face is childlike, frightened. Listening to the proceedings in court, the reality that she might go to prison has sunk in. How would she cope in prison? Amber has never known violence. When she was young she was picked on at school and it made her ill. Why can't Dave just admit to what he's done?

'What did she say? Did she say anything about me talking to Dave? Does she know about the letters from him?' Amber asks me.

'She asked if you're still using heroin, told me how dangerous the addiction is. I told her you're clean.'

'Anything else?'

'Not from April, but I do have something to say, Amber.'

I stop on the path and turn towards her.

'I'm standing by you through all this. The court case. The heroin. You not working for a while. But if you think when Dave gets out of prison I'll let him back into your life again, you're wrong. I'll do everything I can to stop it. I'm not interested in promises of how he's changed or that he won't take drugs again, so don't waste your time trying to convince me. I'm just not playing this game, Amber, so wake up: I've had enough.'

I pause. I know I've flipped into critical parent mode; my face has changed.

'All the time he's in jail, you can write to him and realise in your own time he's no good for you. But because I won't go on about it or mention it again, don't be naïve enough to believe I'll change my mind one day. I won't. When he gets out, it's me or him.'

I don't wait for her to answer; I just walk on to the car. I know she still holds this romantic notion about him and I can't convince her to see him differently, but Amber's weak. The longer he's in jail, the more she'll lose interest in him. I'll wait.

Amber

The phone rings constantly while I wait on the sofa by reception. April's secretary comes down to get me; her name's Kelly. She's pretty, with expensive highlights in her straight, blonde hair and carefully applied make-up. She's wearing heels that she's confident in.

'You can come up now, Amber. April's ready to see you.' I follow her up the stairs. 'Would you like a cup of tea or coffee?' she says.

'Tea, thanks.' I'm feeling nervous already and wish I could smoke in April's office.

'Coffee for you, April?' Kelly asks and shuts the door on her way out.

The office is cramped. It smells woody; boxes of papers fill all the space on the floor and the walls are lined with bookcases containing every sort of legal encyclopaedia. 'How are things, Amber?' she says. 'Have you got the references I asked for?'

'I've got one from my next-door neighbour and one from a previous employer who's an old friend of my mum's. I know a drug counsellor I can get one from; he used to visit me and Dave. He's a registered Acorn worker, I just need to contact him.' I pass the letters across the desk.

April scans down the pages. 'These are good, Amber. I'll put them forward to the judge before the case. We need the drug counsellor as well. Your mum said you're clean, is that true?'

'She's got me on this heroin blocker, so I am, yeah.'

'If you can get this counsellor to drug test you at home, we can use the results to press your case for leniency. It's important to prove you're not taking heroin any more. Is your mum coming with you to court?'

'Yeah, it'll be the two of us.' I've been trying not to think about the court or what might happen.

'That's good. The judge needs to know you have the support of your family. Do you have anything else to say about Dave?'

Kelly returns with the drinks. She places my tea on a mat on the desk in front of me. April waits until she's gone before continuing.

'The police have a good case against you and Dave.' She takes a sip of her coffee. 'They've been building the evidence for some time. With a suspected drug dealer they can afford to wait, hold back until they obtain enough to convict; they know he's not going to stop. Everything to do with the house that you shared with Dave is in your name, Amber, implicating you deeply. Now the police have recovered the car, Dave's story about where he got the money from has fallen apart.'

I lean forward to pick up my tea, but my hand is shaking so much I'm afraid I'll spill it so I put it back down.

'DS Thompson is evoking the criminal asset recovery law to try and stop the BMW and the cash they found ever being returned to Dave. Anything the judge decides has been gained through criminal activities can be seized by the court.'

'I think it's a bit personal with Thompson and Dave.'

'Well, I'm beginning to think it's personal with you too. He's added another charge to your list: possession of diazepam. That makes five charges in total, Amber. Possession of twenty-eight grams of diamorphine, with intent to supply. Possession of methadone, with intent to supply. Two charges of handling stolen goods, namely a Dell colour monitor and a red Wilson golf bag.' She reads from a list she has on her desk; it's covered with files tied neatly with pink legal tape and stacked into piles.

April sighs and leans back in her chair. 'You could get a prison sentence for this, Amber. It's different for Dave. He's done time before, he can handle it. You don't seem to me to be the type of girl who can.'

She clasps her hands together on the desk and leans forward. 'Thompson tried to get you remanded in Holloway for a week when you were arrested; you've got no previous convictions so I soon put a stop to that.'

Shit! My stomach drops down twenty floors. I didn't know the police could do that. I know there is a chance I'll do time for this, but till recently heroin took my fears away.

Clearing a space in the middle of her desk, April puts her pen down and studies my face. 'Off the record, Amber, I'm going to tell you a story about one of my clients. Her name is Tracey Smith. She's a tall girl, heavily built. She's in Holloway for violent assault, but now she's decided she likes it there. Each time her case comes up for review and they take her down for the hearing, she attacks one of the prison officers. She usually manages to give one of them a hiding before they can get her back in her cell. Tracey likes girls, especially new girls. You're pretty and feminine, Amber – she'll like you. I don't think you'll make it out of there the same person.'

April's right; girls can be nasty. I know Tracey Smith. I watched her in Guildford town centre one Saturday afternoon. She made another girl get down on her hands and knees and bark like a dog. I'd probably spend my first three or four months in prison being forced to be her bitch. I clutch my cup of almost cold tea that I didn't really want and now can't drink.

Twelve

Amber

'You don't mind if I hang around with Jason, do you, Mum?' Now I'm clean Mum allows me a bit more freedom.

'Does Jason do drugs, Amber? Heroin?'

'He used to, I won't lie to you, but not any more. Besides, I'm taking the blocker.'

I still have his number, so I ring him. We arrange to go out for a beer.

Jason stopped using heroin on his own. He's resilient, mentally and physically. He can take a lot of pain – I can't explain it, he just can – and he's always completely on my wavelength.

Jason gets into my car making chicken noises. 'Cluck, cluck, cluck.'

'You're not funny,' I say.

'How's the cluck going, then?' Jason laughs.

'Think I'm over the worst of it, but mentally the itch for it is doing my head in.'

Jason flashes me a cheeky smile, showing the dimples in his cheeks. 'Yeah, know what you mean, that bit's the worst. How long you been clean?'

'Six weeks.'

'After about twelve weeks that should wear off a bit.'

'The nights are long; doesn't feel like I'll ever sleep properly again.'

''Course you will, I sleep alright now. It's a matter of time.'

'Really?'

'What about your mum? Does she think you're okay without the gear?'

'She thinks I'm cured, but I'm not. It's not just the desire for it. I miss Dave and the lifestyle.'

'Yeah, but it wasn't reality, was it, Amber? Anyway, you didn't become an addict overnight and it can't be undone overnight. You can't rush it.'

He's right. My addiction built up in stages, steps up a hill, and I have to come back down the other side of that hill in steps. But sometimes I think it's just a dream to be normal one day. Eventually even Mum will realise that.

He buys me a couple of beers in the pub and then I drop him home. I'm still a raging heroin addict, it's just that I'm not using right now.

Christine

'Can't Amber at least pick up the fag butts when she smokes outside?'

Tony's leather shoes make a crisp sound on the kitchen floor as he walks in and puts something in the bin. Amber has a way of dramatising her imposed suffering and doesn't keep to the simple rules around the house.

'She got a job yet?' He stands at the sink and starts to wash his hands.

'No. She'll get one soon, I'm sure.'

I'm moving forward with tunnel vision, focusing on the goal to keep Amber off heroin. Her track record isn't good – she finds it hard to stick at anything. But she *is* clean so it's just a question of time – time to recover and support so she can let the heroin go. Breaking a habit is always hard at first. Like breaking free from the earth's atmosphere, launching takes a lot of energy but after that it's effortless to float around.

'What does she do all day? Has she been helping you around the house?' he leans back against the worktop.

'Not really.'

'What about the Job Centre? Has she signed on?'

'Umm, don't think so.'

'So where does she get the money for fags? You been giving it to her?'

'I do buy her ten sometimes.'

'Is she still taking that blocker?'

'Of course. I make sure she swallows it.'

'Then why can't she stop hanging around all day and get a job?'

'I'll talk to her.'

I wait until Amber and I are alone – I don't want the children listening. They know things at home aren't quite right, but I want to keep them away from it all whenever I can.

The hairdryer is whirring noisily as I dry my hair in the bedroom. I see her go past the door and switch the dryer off. 'Amber,' I call out, 'come and talk to me for a minute.'

She sits on the end of my bed. 'Why haven't you been down the Job Centre yet?'

Her shoulders slump. 'I hate going. There's always junkies

hanging around outside. Things are difficult enough without having it in my face.'

'But what about a job? You need a job.'

'You know what, Mum? A job seems insurmountable to me at the moment. How can I mix with normal people?'

'You'd be fine. It'd do you good, get you out, give you a reason to get out of bed in the mornings.'

'I feel weak without heroin, like I'm recovering from an illness. I don't think I can do it yet. I couldn't keep a job if I got one.'

'I can't support you forever, pay for your phone and your car and buy you cigarettes all the time.'

'Keep the phone, and the car keys. If you fling me out into the real world after only a few weeks I'll go back to what I know, I won't be able to stop. And I've got the worry of the court case on my mind.'

Perhaps I'm being soft, but when she tells me why she can't work yet, I do understand. 'Okay, a few more weeks then.'

'I know this drug counsellor. His name's Graham, he's a really nice guy, used to come to the bedsit to see me and Dave. April said if he takes random drug tests they can be used in court as evidence that I'm not using. Can he come here to see me? Only when you're here.'

'Anything that'll help. Ring him. Why did Dave need a drug counsellor?'

'He used to bring a sin-bin – you know, a plastic box you can't open, has a hole on the top with a sucker in it. You put dirty needles in there. He gave Dave clean needles as well. Graham doesn't judge. He's no stranger to addiction: he used to be an alcoholic.'

We sit in silence for a few moments. Amber gets up and

stands in the doorway. I remind myself how far we have come, how hard she's trying. 'Let's go out today, just you and me,' I say. 'I'll take you shopping and buy you some lunch.'

'Okay,' she says, and her face brightens. 'I'll have a shower and get ready.'

I have to stay positive and not expect too much. I'll smooth over the job issue with Tony – not lie to him, just not tell him everything. Anyway, there's something else I need to ask him.

On Tuesday afternoon Graham comes round. He is about forty, a tall, slim man with red hair. He wears plain jeans with a black belt and a tee shirt tucked into them. His face looks damaged, almost ravaged, as if he's been stuck out in the wind and rain. I can see he's had more than a couple of drinks over the years.

Amber's watching TV in the sitting room when he arrives. 'You're still in the lifestyle, Amber,' he says as he draws the curtains, letting the daylight in. He switches the TV off and sits down on the sofa. 'You've got to stop watching cartoons all day.'

There is something about Graham, how he's so familiar with the signs of addiction, like a specialist doctor. He knows things I don't.

'Her ability to laze about is amazing,' I say, passing him a cup of tea. 'She goes into a stupor for weeks on end. I can't get her out of it.'

'Well, let's do a test, see what she's been up to.'

He takes out a white card with four patches on it. They change colour with the result, like a pregnancy test. There is an example next to each window to show what colour it changes to if the test is positive for that drug.

'I'll ask you to go to the loo with her, just so we all know there's no cheating,' Graham says.

Upstairs in the bathroom, she does a wee on the card. 'Err,

you can take that back to Graham yourself,' I laugh.

Graham studies the card and smiles. 'Well, she's clean of cocaine and dope, which is good – lots of addicts swap one addiction for another – and the marker for heroin is pink, which means there's a residue left in her system. If she was using on a regular basis it'd have come up red.'

'That's good, Amber,' I say. 'You see, we're getting there.'

I leave Graham and Amber to chat in private and after twenty minutes he leaves.

Opening a bottle of cold Sauvignon Blanc, I pour two large glasses. I've made steaks for dinner, pink as Tony likes them. Once I've put the kids to bed, we settle into our usual places on the sofa. Tony and I are going to Portugal in a couple of weeks. Lauren and Sam are excited about a week playing in the pool and I'm looking forward to some sun.

Snuggling up to him, I ask the question I've been putting off. 'What would you say if I wanted to take Amber to Portugal with us?'

'I'd say no.'

I sit up straight. 'What? No discussion, just no?'

'I've had weeks and weeks of her lying around, hanging around. I want a break from it.'

'I don't want to leave her, Tone. I'm afraid she'll start using heroin again. I can't trust her to take the blocker.'

'You can't be with her every second of every day for the rest of her life. She's going to do it if she wants to, with or without you there.'

'But it's too soon. I'll pay for her flight and everything. Why not?'

'Look, I've had a lot on at work. I need a holiday. I don't want it dominated by a drug addict.'

'She's not a drug addict, not any more, she's a recovering addict.'

He stares past me into the distance. The tone of his voice and the way the muscle is set in his jaw tell me he is not going to change his mind. I leave it. I have enough going on without starting a row.

I say to myself that if I ask him again in a couple of days perhaps he'll change his mind. But each time I ask him the answer is the same: no.

Really we are two families, and I am the only person in both. That shared DNA, that closeness, doesn't apply to Tony and Amber. I am not sure whether the distance has always been there or whether it's grown out of her uncontrollable behaviour, but it's there and I don't know how to change it.

I tell Amber we are going away. I've been hoping to find a solution so I wouldn't have to leave her in the house alone. I don't know anywhere else I can send her or anyone I can trust to supervise her, someone I can confide in who would understand a drug addict.

'Don't worry, Mum, you go and have good time. You deserve it,' she says.

The idea that I might want to speak to Amber's father never entered my head before Amber's problems came out. It was hard enough to get away from him. Yet over the past few weeks I've thought about telling him that she's a recovering addict – if things had been different she could have gone to him. Even if I could find him, though, with the sort of man he is it would have been pointless. But I shouldn't stop her from seeing him if she wants to.

'Do you think about your dad sometimes, Amber?'

'Try not to.'

'Was that where your problems started? When you were little and didn't see him?'

'Don't know.'

'Want to see your dad now? I could help you find him; maybe it would help you feel differently about yourself?'

Her head drops and she picks at her nails; her face is thoughtful. 'No.'

'Why?'

'When I saw him when I was little it was okay, but then he disappeared again and I felt down. I'd rather stay down than keep getting up just to be kicked in the face. I'd rather it just stayed the same. That's what I'm used to; him not being there.'

'You've got a family, Lauren and Sam, they love you.'

'I know. And I've got you, Mum; you're the only one I can really trust. When you had cancer I thought I might lose you too.'

'What do you think your dad would say if he knew about the heroin?'

'I think he'd break both my legs.'

The car park is full when I pull in. I am late for work all the time these days. I will have to squeeze into the half space on the end.

'How's Amber and her boyfriend problems?' Jane asks when I get to my office.

I think about it for a moment. They know there's something wrong and I can't keep it up any more; I let my defences down a little.

'He's in trouble with the police: been taking drugs and handling stolen goods to pay for them.'

'Oh, Christine! Is Amber involved?'

'Not really, but she's guilty by association according to the police. He's on remand in prison and she's living back at home at the moment.'

'That must be difficult for you. Has she been taking drugs?'

'She may have done some, nothing serious.'

'Is she still working in Mark One in Aldershot? I went in the other day, couldn't see her.'

'No. She's looking for something else. I'm sorry, I've got a lot of work to do today so I'm going to shut my office door. Anyone asks for me, take a message, tell them I'm busy.' I sink into my chair. Concentrating on work, I lose myself in spreadsheets and printouts so I don't have to think.

My mum comes over to give the children some spending money for their holiday and sweets for the journey. 'Sweetie Nanny' they call her – she always brings too many sweets. She still looks good for her age, wearing just the right amount of make-up. Her blonde hair is cut stylishly short and her nails are painted a perfect red.

Lauren has a friend over for tea. They sit at the kitchen table together making cards and pictures, felt-tip pens and colours are strewn about and several are on the floor.

'I've made this for you, Nanny.' Lauren proudly holds up a drawing of a beach that she has carefully coloured in.

'That's lovely, Lauren. Thank you, darling. I'm going to hang it up at home.' My mum takes the picture and lays it out carefully on the worktop to dry.

'Will you help me with Amber while I'm away, Mum?' I ask.

'You know I will, but I don't live close by, I won't be able to come over.'

'I just want to leave some money with you for her to buy food and cigarettes. I've told her to ring you when she's coming round for it. Don't give her the money unless she takes this.' I pass her a naltrexone tablet in its packet. 'Watch her swallow it.'

'I thought she'd stopped all that drug-taking, Chrissie.'

'Well, she has, it's not that simple. Heroin is a powerful drug; it has a hold on her I can't even begin to understand. This helps her to stay off it.' I open the door of the fridge and rummage about for the salad ingredients.

'What's heroin?' Lauren's school friend asks without lifting her head from the picture she's colouring. Mum stares across at me, says nothing.

I'm not sure what to say. I don't want her going home repeating what I said. 'A heroine is a female hero, like Cinderella or Sleeping Beauty – they're heroines,' I say.

My mum goes over and sits beside the children at the table. 'Draw me a picture of the swimming pool, Lollipop,' she says, using our nickname for Lauren. 'I'll put some birds in the sky.'

The suitcases are locked and waiting in the dining room ready to go out to the car. I switch the contents of my handbag into my hand luggage and go through in my head all the things I might have forgotten. Tony is in charge of money, tickets and passports.

I make Amber take two naltrexone tablets. She swallows them both.

'A week will soon go by. Try to be good until I get back,' I say, searching her eyes for some reassurance.

'Not gonna hold a party in your house, am I?'

'A week. I'm asking you to stay off heroin for one week while I'm away. Now, will you be alright?' I stand there for a few last moments. Tony is in the car waiting with the kids.

'Don't spend your holiday thinking about me. Now go,' she says.

I hug her and walk away, open the car door and slide onto

the seat. Tony frowns. 'Are you worried about her?' It's not really a question. He knows.

'No,' I lie. 'Are you?'

He shakes his head slowly and pulls out of the drive.

Thirteen

Amber

Standing at the window watching Mum and Tony drive away with the kids, her words are still in my head, but I'm not taking the blocker. I'm not going to smoke a boot, I just hate taking the blocker. No-one's home, so I don't have to. It's easier to rest on Mum's desire for me to stay clean rather than find the self-respect to do it alone. Once that authority figure is gone, I turn into a naughty child.

I'm okay watching TV, hanging around the house on my own. Then I get lonely. I didn't want Mum to go away. I knew she had to and I'm not angry at her for going – life just works like that sometimes, I understand. But I wanted us to stay together.

The evenings are light and I feel I should do more with my day. It's a big house to be alone in. I ring Jason. 'Do you wanna go for a drink tonight?'

'Yeah, cushti,' he says.

We sit outside at the pub. The garden has lots of wooden tables and benches rammed in together, and a high fence to shut out the noisy road. The grass is short where the tables are, but all around the edges it's been left long.

The beer I'm drinking doesn't stop my craving for gear. The buzz I get from alcohol can depend on so many factors. Even when I can get nice-drunk, it's only enjoyable for an hour or two and the rest is torture. Sometimes no matter how much I drink, I don't feel the effect until it's too late and my head's spinning. But I always get the right result with gear – it never lets me down.

I feel warm and sweaty, and then a gentle breeze blows past, giving me goose bumps. Without heroin in my blood, just coming to the pub has exhausted me. I'm fed up, anxious and twitchy. 'Do you ever see Leeanne?' I ask Jason.

'Well, no, obviously not. I'm clean.'

'I miss her. She must know about the raid.'

It's starting to get dark as we leave the pub. I'm aware of how much the inside of my Fiesta still reeks of gear. The dashboard glows green and orange. I pass the junction near Leeanne's house. Pulling out onto the large roundabout, I know that there's a split second before I turn into the exit for home when her bedroom window can be seen from the road.

I glance up. 'Her bedroom light's on,' I say, and look across at Jason.

We're both thinking the same thought, waiting to see who'll suggest it first.

It's an achievement to get off the gear, but another thing to stay off it. Like me, Jason thinks he can just have one little tickle, but once that opportunity presents itself you're already a gonner. I can feel I'm going to let myself down; I'm my own worst enemy. The scariness of not being able to trust yourself is huge. Being so weak that you go ahead and do something that you don't really want to do. Like being possessed, why do you do it? I don't know because I wasn't me when I did it.

'Come on then, let's go round,' Jason says.

'Do you think it's a good idea?'

'Oh, for fuck's sake, let's just go.'

I go back around the roundabout again. I'm on autopilot driving to Leeanne's house. It feels comfortable, right, like going home.

Jason and I walk up the path. The low hedges on both sides smell of pollen and dust. The front door is old, painted wood, with a glass arch at the top shaped like segments of an orange.

I knock my special knock, the one I had when we were teenagers so that she'd know it was me. The house is black from the front, but I know she's in. I knock again. It seems a long time before Leeanne opens the door. At first she looks as if to say 'Who's got Amber's knock?' When she sees it's me, she smiles.

'Oh. Hello.' She swings the door open, walks back into the house.

We step inside. Jason shuts the front door and we follow her to the sitting room. Heavy curtains are drawn tight at the window and all the lights are off. The TV is on with the sound turned down; as the picture changes it illuminates the room with a flickering, grey glow.

Leeanne sits down in front of the gas fire and pulls a blanket over her knees. She's clucking a bit – not too bad, but twitching. 'What you been doing, then?' she asks.

I'm about to answer when Jason butts in.

'What's up?' he says. 'Can't score or haven't any money to score?'

Leeanne looks defeated, as if she's spent the whole day trying and now that it's late she has no choice but to give up. 'No money to score.'

'I have,' he says.

They're both stronger than me. Once I know they're going to do it, I know I am. My resistance is fragile, like a whiff of smoke – blow it and it's gone.

Leeanne is up like a shot. 'Jay?'

'Nah,' Jason says.

'John?'

'Definitely not.' Then Jason says 'I might know someone. I'll give him a quick call.' He flicks open his mobile and walks into the hallway. 'Hi mate. It's Jason. Worth me popping round?' He waits for the reply. 'Right, we'll have two.' Jason sticks his head round the door. 'We're on, twenty minutes.'

We pile into my car. We stop at the cash point for Jason to get some cash. Then we park up at the agreed spot and wait.

'Come on, mate. Hurry up,' Leeanne says, breaking the silence.

A figure appears almost from nowhere. He peers in at Jason in the back and gets in the car beside him.

'Drive round the corner,' the dealer says to me. He passes something to Jason and Jason gives him the cash. Then the dealer gets out and we drive off.

'Fuck! Foil!' Leeanne says. We stop quickly at the nearest shop.

I drive to a large trading estate and park in a quiet corner. Leeanne's clucking so she goes first, then Jason 'cause he paid. Leaning forward between the seats, he passes it to me. I struggle to do a line without feeling sick.

'Little green there Amber, are you?' Jason jokes and pushes me in the ribs. 'Bit of a lightweight?'

I smoke another line but feel too queasy to do any more. It's been a couple of months since my last boot. Leeanne and Jason do four lines each. I wind the window down to let the smell out.

The night is black and silent. In the rear-view mirror I see a car driving towards us. I sit there mesmerised as it pulls right up to my bumper and blocks us in. The blue light on the roof rotates sluggishly.

Shit! It's the police! Now I'm completely screwed. If I'm caught in possession of drugs while on bail I won't get out. For Leeanne and Jason it's just a caution. For me, all that hard work with Mum and April is pissed away in one evening. I have to think of something quick.

I'm pretty wasted and feel extremely sick. The bile in my stomach is telling me I won't be able to hold it in much longer. I'm shaking. I get out of the car. I screw up the foil and gear in my hand, press it against a metal lamp post so the police can't see it. It'll just look as if I'm steadying myself. I puke.

Two police officers get out of their car, a man and a woman. The policewoman goes to the driver's door of my car and takes the keys out of the ignition. She sits in the front seat and starts questioning Leeanne and Jason.

The young policeman comes over to me. 'Are you alright?' he sounds concerned. 'What's your name? Have you been taking drugs?' With his thumb he points towards my car. 'Is that why you're parked round here?'

I've no idea what I'm going to say. Then it comes to me.

'No!' I shout, loud enough for Leeanne and Jason to hear. 'No! I work here. We've been into town straight from work. I left my car here.'

I puke again. 'I was going to take my friends home. I feel so ill. I must have eaten something bad. I think I need an ambulance.'

He bends down to look at my face. 'An ambulance? No, you don't look that bad.'

I stare back at him 'Are you sure? You could ring one for me.'

He smiles. 'You don't need an ambulance.' He walks over to my car. He rests his arm on the open door and leans in to speak to the policewoman. I slide down the lamp post, sit on the foil and gear that had been in my hand, then put both hands under my bottom and lean forward.

The policeman comes back over to me. 'I've spoken to your friends. One of them is going to drive you home. You don't need an ambulance. You'll be okay tomorrow.'

'Are you sure? Don't need one, really?'

'Yes, I'm sure.'

They get back in the police car and I watch them drive away.

I stand up, go back to my car and get in the front. Leeanne and Jason are silent. I straighten out the foil in front of them and take a look. 'Yeah, we can rescue that.'

'Oh my God, Amber, I can't believe we got away with that!' Jason says. 'You jammy cow, how do you always think of something to say?'

That night at home I lie in bed thinking about what a lucky escape I've had. I only went out for a beer and could have ended up in jail.

It's a relapse. I'm not back on heroin. I can hide this and Mum will never know. I'll be clean again by the time she comes home.

I sleep in until three o'clock the following afternoon. It's the first time for weeks that I've slept through the night. I feel alright – in fact, I feel good.

Within an hour, I'm clucking. Mum's left me ten quid for fags and petrol and I spend it on gear, sharing it with Leeanne and Jason.

I won't think about Mum, not until I have to, not until she comes home. Druggie mentality is to play today and pay tomorrow, never worry about later, live for now.

There's nothing left to eat in the house the next morning, so I count up the last of my change and walk up to the shop to see what I can get, thinking I might have enough for a tin of beans and a loaf of bread. I bump into Mick, a dealer Dave used to serve up. My first thought is, oh shit. Even Dave was afraid of him. He never let Mick know where we were living but would weigh up Mick's gear and go out somewhere to meet him.

Mick's really tall and, because he's been doing gear for so long, he's very thin. It gives him a strange, stick-like appearance. He has long, greasy hair all the way down over his ears and around his neck and he constantly pushes it to one side. It's so dirty he can bend it around his ear like a pipe cleaner. His eyes are black globes. You can never tell if he's clucking because you can't see his pupils. There's a feeling of menace around Mick, regardless of how frail he appears.

'Alright, Amber?' he says, then smiles his predator smile. He smells like a dog that just got out of a pond.

'Yeah, you?'

'What you doing now, then? Heard you're living at your mum's.'

'No, I'm living with me dad and his brother in Guildford.' He can't know anything personal about me. The idea that I could score from him pops into my head. 'You still working?'

'Yeah, here and there.'

'Give us your number then.'

Walking away with his number, I'm scared that I might actually ring him.

Soon I'm clucking again, only worse this time. The urge is

overwhelming. I can't control my behaviour, even if it means stealing. I'm afraid of myself. I don't want to do it, but I'm doing it anyway. There's nothing I can do to stop myself.

I search the house until I find Mum's cash card. It's simple to forge her signature. I did it a lot when I was at school, on detention slips, sick notes and stuff.

Leeanne, Jason and I go to the supermarket. We buy twenty B&H and a roll of foil and get fifty pounds cashback. It's safer than going to the bank, where they might examine the signature on the card more carefully. Jason scores for us again. We do the gear in my car, which I park on Mum's drive.

The following day I get another fifty quid. I can't wait for Leeanne and Jason, so I decide to score off Mick on my own.

His girlfriend opens the door when I arrive to collect the gear. She doesn't look much older than me and has a pretty face with a sprinkle of freckles across her nose. They have three children aged between four and eight. The kids are all like him, tall and dark.

Inside, the house is like a dirty squat. There's nothing in it. It looks as if it was once nice – patterned wallpaper on the walls with a matching border – but there's no TV or comfort. Smoke stains on the walls trace shadows of things that were once there: pictures, the TV. Junkies are like that when their habit gets bad – they sell anything of value.

Mick can't get a vein, not even the big one in his groin, so he smokes a large amount on the foil. It's quite a tricky process, fragile – you could easily heat it too much and lose some of it.

He's having one of these huge boots while I'm there when his eldest daughter runs in from the garden. 'Daddy, Daddy you'll never guess what I've done,' she cries, accidentally sticking her hand in his foil. She has burning hot heroin on two of her fingers, and she starts to scream in pain. Her instinct is to get it off as quickly as possible.

Mick's reaction is instant.

Grabbing her hand by the wrist, he holds her body back by the shoulder. If you get the heroin off while it's hot, it'll shatter into little pieces and you'll lose it, but if you wait till it cools you can peel it off in one piece.

'Daddy! Daddy! It hurts! It's burning!' she screams, tears streaming down her face.

'I know it hurts,' Mick says as if he understands, 'but I've got to pick it off when it's dry.'

Something inside me wants to reach out and do what's right, to get it off her fingers, but I'm not about to piss him off. The moments pass and I stare at the floor. I know my emotions are obvious on my face. Eventually, Mick peels the gear off his daughter's finger and sticks it straight back on the foil. She sinks to the floor, sobbing in pain.

Once he sorts me out the gear I've bought, I leave quickly; I don't want to be near him. I don't look back – it's not my business.

Waiting in my car for Leeanne to finish work, I gaze at the rush-hour traffic going past. I feel removed, somehow, from everyday life. She's got an office job at a place called Landscape Contracts. They run a maintenance contract for the local council, cutting the grass on school playing fields and communal grounds. She wanders across the road and gets in the front. No-one's in at her house so we go back there for a boot. I throw my bag on her bed and sit down.

'Why didn't you come round after the raid?' Leeanne asks me.

'Guess I didn't know how to just show up on your doorstep, and you never called me.'

'If I said anything about you, you know I didn't mean it.'

'I know, let's forget it. Anyway, I've got my mum on my case big time. Can't shit or sneeze without her knowing. I'll have to cluck again when she gets back.'

'You'll need to be clean when you go back to court.'

'I know I've gotta do it. I'm dreading having to face her. I'll have to get a job or something to pacify her.'

'Well, you do gardening. Come and see me at work – they're always looking for people. I'll help you do a CV and we'll blag it a bit, tell them I know you.'

'Yeah, I could do that.'

I smoke a line, draw in the heavy, brown, viscous smoke; it's thick like Marmite or gravy. I lie back. A good feeling sweeps over me, as if the sun is shining on my skin. I think of Dave, cold and alone in his cell, and wonder when he last had a hit.

'I feel sorry for Dave, being inside.'

'Why would you feel sorry for him, Amber? After what he did to me?'

'What?' I sit up. 'What did he do to you?'

'He spread it around his dealers not to serve me.'

I'm stunned. I want to say it isn't true, that Dave wouldn't do that to her, but then I remember something. I'd come downstairs late one night when we were living at the house. Dave often sat up half the night playing computer games and talking to people on his mobile. I heard him say to someone 'Yeah, spread it around anyone who works for me, if they serve her up, I'm cutting them off.'

At the time there were loads of people who pissed him off. He could have been talking about anyone. I never knew the details of his business. I'd gone back to bed thinking a dealer had been ticked and not paid. I never questioned Dave – I was so dependent on him, I never would, not about anything. I had to be on his side, always – that's the way he liked things.

It's the cruellest thing you can do to an addict, make it difficult to score. They have to give their money to another addict, get them to score, and then they have to share it. Dave knew that. He knew Leeanne was already vulnerable, struggling to afford her habit. 'Oh Leeanne, I didn't know.'

'At first no-one would tell me. When I called they just said there's none about or it's dry. After a while I thought – hang on, there's more to it than that. If one dealer had a problem I could have understood, but not all Dave's dealers. Then I got Mick to tell me the truth. He said it was Dave's instructions. I thought you were in on it, that's why I never called you.'

Fourteen

Christine

'Amber! Amber!' Lauren and Sam run down the hallway as soon as we open the door.

'Hiya, did you guys have a good time?' she says.

'Yes, but we missed you,' Sam says as he grabs her waist and hugs her. 'We got you a present. Mummy, where's Amber's present?'

'It's on top of the suitcase. You can get it.'

Sam finds the decorated paper bag and hands it to her. 'We chose it ourselves. Do you like it?' Lauren says.

Taking out a delicate bracelet made of shells, Amber studies it carefully before saying 'I love it.' She fiddles with the clasp and then shakes her wrist to show them. 'Can I talk to you, Mum?' She glances sideways at the kids. 'On your own.'

Now that I am home and everything is okay, I am not so worried. Whatever she has to tell me, I'll cope with. 'Let's go up to your room.'

Amber sits down on her bed and rests her hands on her knees, lets out a long breath. 'I've been doing gear while you've been away, Mum. I'm sorry.'

I sink down to sit beside her. In my heart I had already

accepted that she would; I would have been naive to think she wouldn't. 'At least you told me right away. Now I want you straight back on the blocker. You must stay in until you're ready to take it. Give me your car keys and your mobile.'

'There's something else. You're gonna hate me when I tell you.'

I had expected the relapse. What else could she have done?

'Just tell me.'

'Promise you won't hate me?'

I sigh. 'Tell me.'

'I took your cash card; don't know how many times I've used it.'

I jerk back. 'What? You took it? Just like that? Where did you find it?' I stand up, put some distance between us and lean against the windowsill.

'It wasn't difficult, Mum. You left it in the study.'

'What about my signature? Did you forge it?'

'Well, yeah.'

'Where is it? I want it back.'

Amber takes the card out of her pocket and passes it to me. 'Did you do this on your own or did someone suggest it to you? Have you been hanging around with addicts?'

'It was my idea, Mum, it was all my idea. But I've got a job,' her face brightens up. 'Start a week Monday.'

'How did you get that?'

'Leeanne works there – it's a gardening job. It'll be good for me to get up every morning. I think that's been my problem.'

'I need to check how much money is missing from my account before we can talk about this. You'd better be here when I get back.'

'Just popping up the shop,' I call out to Tony as I shut the front door behind me. There is a cashpoint at the top of the road outside Onestop. I'll walk.

The sun is shining and the heat prickles my skin despite being tanned from Portugal. Marching up the road, I am hot before I have got very far and my face feels red. I can't believe it. I take her in, pay for everything and put my marriage and two young children on the line to get her off drugs, then I go away for one week, ask her to do one bloody thing and she can't do that! And to top it off she steals my card and forges my signature. How insulting. So, how much has she cleared me out? A thousand pounds is accessible from that account with my overdraft facility before the bank would even start to ask questions.

I could give DS Thompson a call. She's on bail, she would go to prison, she can't take heroin in prison. Is that the right way to handle things after I promised to help her? She's frightened enough with the court case looming.

I put my card in the machine and the white printout appears. I count up the minuses I know are not mine – over two hundred pounds in total.

I have to believe we can still make progress.

Anyway, how bad is it really? This isn't the worst thing that could be happening to me. Something much more frightening is constantly at the back of my mind; I could be dying of cancer. Cancer is a silent disease. In the beginning it has no pain – it could be growing inside me now. If I became ill again, if it were untreatable, how could I face it unless I knew I had done everything I could to help my daughter? Maybe my forgiveness will show her I will never give up on her, that she will have to come to terms with the fact that she *is* going to stop using heroin.

Walking home, a friend drives past and slows up. She winds down the window as I reach her. 'Did you enjoy your holiday?' she asks.

'Yeah, it was great. Let's catch up next week?' I smile as if I'm living a normal life. But I am holding all the grief and worry inside, and my pride makes it impossible for me to share it.

Upstairs, Amber is in the middle of her double bed, Lauren on one side of her and Sam the other. They are telling her about the holiday. 'Outside, you two, it's a lovely sunny day.'

They jump up and go.

I am wheezy and over-emotional as I say 'I've looked at my account and you've taken over two hundred pounds. But I'm going to forgive you.'

She sits up, wraps her slender arms around her knees. 'Don't make me feel any worse. How can you just forgive me?'

'I love you, remember.'

'I'll pay you back, I promise.'

'We'll start again.'

'Yeah, I'm so relieved. I wanted to tell you but I didn't want to ruin things between us. I'll stay home and cluck again; I've only been doing it for a few days, it's hardly a habit.' She squeezes my hand. 'Thanks, Mum. Now you're back I feel stronger.'

I wait until the kids are in bed before telling Tony.

'Well, no surprise there; Amber's back on heroin,' he says.

'I'm home now and supervising her more closely. You can't do something as hard as quitting a drug habit and think it'll be easy.'

'By expecting her to relapse, you make it okay for her to do it.'

'There's no point in arguing about it or getting upset, Tone, anyway she's got a job. When she has to get up for work each morning she'll have less time to think about it.'

'How did she get a job?'

'Leeanne helped her, she works there.'

'Leeanne? Is that who she's been doing it with? Are you sure that's a good idea, them working together?'

I know he's right, but there's a closeness between them that I can't break. The first time I met Leeanne she was thirteen, but even then she didn't seem young – there was nothing fluffy or giggly about her. Leeanne would never chat to me or try to make me like her. The two of them would simply disappear upstairs to Amber's room. Sometimes Amber came down to make tea and toast, but other than that I never saw them. I don't want to make her stop seeing her friend and somehow I can't see the bad in it.

'No, it'll be okay, she's promised me she'll take the blocker and it's a job. She needs to be working.'

'If you think so. What surprises me is where she gets the money for drugs.'

I shrug my shoulders.

The sound of cartoons on the TV drifts into the kitchen while I make breakfast. Amber is lying on the sofa. Her face is pasty white.

'What's wrong with Amber, Mummy? Is she ill?' Lauren says.

'It's her own fault, Lauren. It's self-inflicted,' Tony says as he opens the patio doors and goes out into the garden.

'Are you not well?' Lauren kneels down beside the sofa and stares right into Amber's face. 'Do you want a drink?'

'You could go and get my duvet,' Amber says.

Lauren rushes off upstairs. I hear a whoosh and a thud as

she chucks the duvet over the banister to land in the hallway. 'And my pillow!' Amber shouts.

I pick up the duvet and bring it the sofa. 'How you doing?'

'It's alright, Mum, I'm not too bad.'

Amber has one day of feeling ill and not eating; on the second day she picks at her food and by the third day she is starving hungry again. I know she is back to normal when she says 'Mum, can you lend me some money?'

'What do you need money for?'

'I've got no fags or petrol; I'm running on vapour.'

'I've bought you ten – they're in my bag.'

'Petrol?'

'We'll go up the garage together. I'll put a fiver in for you.'

'I'm gonna take the blocker soon. Wouldn't it be easier to give me the money?'

Amber stands up tall on her feet and stares me straight in the eye, a technique she perfected in childhood to make me believe her when she was lying. Her eyes glaze over and the expression doesn't change.

'Don't be so suspicious, Mum. What do you think I'm going to do?' she says.

'If I make my life easy now, I'm only saving the difficult bit for later.'

She chews her bottom lip.

'Once you start work you won't have time to laze about all day and think about drugs. Things will soon get better.'

Fifteen

Amber

The wonderful smell of cut grass fills the air. Tiny pieces fly up in front of me as I push the heavy, old mower along the edges of the field, where the grass is long and thick, deep green. My stomach rumbles. I may as well head back to the yard, see what Leeanne's doing and spend my lunch hour there.

Pulling up in the van, I see the door to her office is open. I bound over and poke my head through; where she works is just a whitewashed room with a plastic table and a computer. 'What you up to? I've got an hour to kill,' I say.

Leeanne's sitting with her back to me and doesn't turn around. She runs a comb through her hair, making the static electricity blow it out to the side. 'Wanna smoke some gear, then?' she says and puts the comb back in her bag.

My head jumps back. 'Where? My car's blocked in, and there's a camera in the yard.'

'I've got the perfect place,' she says nonchalantly and stands up from her desk.

I follow her to the men's locker room.

'What! Hang on.' I hold back and look around as she boldly goes inside.

'I do it in here all the time. They're not coming back.'

Inside it's dirty and reeks of stale piss and ammonia, as if old men have been pissing on the floor for centuries. It's a vast space with a rickety wooden bench running down the centre. The bench doesn't look like it could hold the weight of one man, let alone the whole gang who work here. There are three showers with no doors on them, and something green is growing up the inside of the one on the end. I'm on edge – keep thinking I can hear someone walk across the yard.

Leeanne sits down and takes out a packet of fags. Inside is her gear, the foil carefully folded and ready to go. We share a smoke. Even though I can't feel anything because I've taken the blocker, I still have the want for it. It's a tease, it makes me more determined to have it. We're only in there ten minutes.

'They'll never smell it in here,' Leeanne giggles as we leave.

I can't find the strength to keep fighting; taking drugs feels natural, normal. Mum thinks the blocker is more likely to dissolve in my stomach if I eat after I've taken it, but that just gives me something to puke up.

Turning the corner at the end of the football field, I line up the blades of the mower to make sure I get a nice straight line. I love cutting grass; it's methodical, up and down while my mind wanders. I've got that afternoon feeling.

Suddenly there's a hell of a noise. My hands jerk with a hard vibration and the punch of contact. A cog or gear must have come loose. Out of the corner of my eye I see something shiny whack against the fence and drop into the grass.

I take the mower to Ian, the mechanic, to fix it for me. He's short, about five feet four, and lean, but he's all muscle. His face is rugged, with deep lines and wrinkles making him appear older than he really is. Ian works in the garage, where there are no windows, just the artificial brightness from a single strip light suspended from the ceiling.

Ian emerges from the shadows in one of the pits. His face is covered in grease, making the whites of his eyes seem brighter – he looks like an animal approaching from a cage.

'Something's wrong with my mower. It's not working properly,' I tell him.

Ian wipes his hands on his arse. I don't believe his green overalls ever get to go home and be washed. He turns the mower over to have a look; the blades are bent. 'How'd you do that?'

I show him the heavy silver bracelet I found on the grass. 'That's worth something, that is,' Ian says.

'Do you know where I can sell it?'

'Yeah, I do know somewhere. I'll take you after work if you like.'

The inside of Ian's car is covered in newspapers, screws and metal shavings. The seats are ripped and stained with oil. I try to brush off the worst of the mess before I get in.

He takes me to a pawnshop in Aldershot. The shop front has a huge glass window with a big orange sign saying 'Cash for Gold'. The bell rings as we open the door. There's a prominent camera and a sign on the counter that says 'We Cash Cheques'. A guy appears from the back; he's big and hairy.

'What you want?' he grunts. He smells of stale sweat.

I let Ian do the talking. He gets me fifteen quid for the bracelet.

'What do you need money for?' Ian asks when we step outside.

'Drugs.'

'Oh,' he says, and shrugs his shoulders, 'okay'.

I save the cash for a few days until I've puked up the blocker.

Then I give it to Leeanne to score for us.

The outside door to the men's locker room has a dent in the bottom where someone's kicked it. The paint is white, flaking and dull. I push it open.

'Still feels weird being in the men's, but after a while you don't notice the smell of piss,' I say to Leeanne.

She sits down on the wooden bench, takes out her gear and smokes a boot. 'I want it! I want it!' are the only thoughts in my head.

The handle of the door clicks as it opens. My eyes widen. 'Shit!'

We both jump when Ian walks in.

'What you two doing in the men's changing room?' he asks.

'Seriously Ian,' I say, laying my hand on my chest, 'I've just shit my pants.'

'What you doing?' he asks again, looking down and tapping the leg of the bench with his foot.

'Smoking drugs, now fuck off,' Leeanne says.

He raises his eyes to her face. 'What drugs?'

'Just drugs.'

'So, what if I go tell the big man you're up to something in here?'

Leeanne and I stare at each other and then look back at him.

'It's gear, why? Do you want some?' I say.

'Don't know, might do,' Ian says.

'Yeah, you're not hard enough for this,' Leeanne says.

'I am,' he says.

'Here you are, then'. She passes him the foil. 'Try not to spend the afternoon puking.'

He doesn't smoke it properly, but his face turns all serene; he likes it.

At the end of the day, Ian bounds across the yard and grabs my arm. 'Can you get me any more of that stuff? Teach me how to run it on the foil?'

I suck my teeth. 'Not sure I can, Ian.'

As if he understands, he says, 'I've got money for it.' That changes things.

'Well… give us twenty quid, I'll see what I can do, call you in a bit.' Ian gives me the note and then drives away.

I perch on the bonnet of my car while I wait for Leeanne.

'I've solved all our problems,' I say when she walks towards me; I can tell she's a bit down. 'Ian wants me to score for him.'

'Why the fuck would we score for him? Why do you even talk to him, Amber?'

'No, you see,' I slide down from the bonnet, open my hands and smile my big Muppet impression, 'we can just give him half of what we get, so we score for free. Ta-dah!'

Leeanne's face changes and she laughs.

We score for Ian on a regular basis. Sometimes Mum forgets about the blocker altogether and if she doesn't I simply make myself sick.

One Friday afternoon I'm hanging around in the workshop, just floating, trying not to touch anything because everywhere is covered in grease. 'Alright?' I say to Ian.

'Yeah, not too bad,' he says, rubbing his hands together, 'especially as we've just been paid.'

'I've set up the score.'

'Why don't I go with you so they know me, then I can get it myself sometimes. We could get a bit of white tonight as well.'

'Okay,' I say, 'but it's not great doing white in the car.'

'Why don't you come back to mine?'

There's one tight space in the car park at Ian's flat; doesn't seem like much of a spot, but he squeezes his car in. The building reminds me of an old estate farmhouse, as if it was here first and the town grew up around it. There's a staircase all the way up the outside of the building, so you don't need to go in through the front; it must have been the servants' quarters years ago.

Inside, the flat smells of that musty man smell. I gaze out of the windows onto the town below. I feel like a princess in a castle tower. The flat is snug and warm with tiny rooms and low ceilings. I don't think anyone's cracked a window open in a month, but once we've sat in his bedroom and smoked some gear, I don't care.

To me, Ian is vulnerable. Other people see the evil intent in him, the anger issues, the violence. I once heard him drop a tool in his workshop and he went off on one like a Tasmanian devil. His hands are always covered in cuts and grazes where he's punched things. But Ian's face is etched in pain – I can see the agony where that anger comes from.

'Shit!' I say when we've done the lot, 'I'm too stoned to go home.'

'You could always stay here.'

I can hardly keep my eyes open; I'm so wrecked, I'm drifting. I bury my head in Ian's neck – I like the close human contact. He tickles my back, soothing me to sleep.

Spending time at Ian's flat means I'm not at home to take the blocker, and I don't need to puke it up or lie to Mum. She makes a fuss, but I just don't go home.

The guy in charge of green-keeping is called Alan. He's wide and stocky, like a gnome, but stern. Alan is easily old enough to be my father.

I've been working at Landscape Contracts for two months

when, arriving at work one morning in Ian's car, I notice Alan's eyes watching us. I feel guilty like I've done something wrong. I glance at the clock on the dashboard; I'm late. Jumping out, I slam the door and hurry across the yard, try to get into work with my head down.

Alan catches up with me, grabs the back of my arm as if I'm a child.

'What the fuck are you doing with that piece of shit!' he shouts in my face.

'He lives near me, just gave me a lift.'

Alan gives me a look of disgust. 'Bullshit!' He must know I live in the village and Ian lives in the other direction. He lets go of me. 'If you come in late one more time, young lady, you're out.'

'Yeah, yeah, whatever.' I walk away.

The next day I'm late again, but only by a couple of minutes.

'You're sacked. Get your stuff and leave now,' Alan spits at me.

I'm resigned to it; there's nothing I can do to save my job. And at least it was quick, like ripping off a plaster. My first thought is – wicked, I don't have to work today. Later I realise I'll have no money, nothing to do all day, and I'll have to tell Mum.

Christine

On the way back from school it starts to spit with rain. I think about Amber. The old behaviour is returning. I know I've got to face it. My pace slows. I am tired already and my chest is tight. I think she's using again. I don't want to believe it. I question her but she's always so reassuring; maybe I'm going slightly mad. I feel beaten. I want to take the easy route. Wouldn't it be easier to just walk away and let her get on with it?

The children's toys are scattered around the sitting room. Methodically, I go from room to room tidying the house, keeping everything in manageable boxes I can cope with, shutting the door behind me when each room is done. Until I can't distract myself any longer and the only room left in the house is Amber's.

I stand in front of her door. I can't shuffle off my responsibilities because things are tough. Inside, the curtains are shut but it is light enough to see. 'You awake?'

'Am now,' she turns over and groans. 'What's the time?'

'Nearly eleven. I've brought you a cup of tea.'

'Thanks, Mum.' I pass her the cup and she shuffles up the bed. 'You didn't need to do that.'

Even though Amber's awake, she still looks like she's asleep. I know she struggles to sleep when she's clean. I pull back the curtains. She winces and shuts her eyes when the brightness hits her face. When she opens them again they appear alien. My suspicions are confirmed; she's been doing heroin. It's as if she's deliberately trying to destroy herself.

'You're using again, aren't you? Little something to get over being sacked, was it?'

'Don't be silly, Mum, I'm not.'

I am fed up with all the lying. 'It's always a mistake to think I'm stupid. Do you remember all those nasty side effects you get if you take naltrexone with heroin in your system? Well, I'm going to grind it down to a powder, mix it with a drink and give it to you.'

She chokes on her tea, spitting the mouthful back into the

mug. Brown spots splash back and settle on her cheeks. 'Would you really do that?'

'Well, if you tell me you're clean, why wouldn't I? Don't worry, it's not in *that* tea.'

'Okay, okay, you're right. I've been using.'

'You've got to go to court in a few weeks; we need to prove you're clean. Graham's due to come any day for one of his random tests. You have to keep yourself out of jail; I can't do everything.'

Holding the mug with both hands, she looks down as if she's ashamed. 'I know, I'm sorry.'

Is drug addiction genetic? My genes. My fault. Or is it a disease? If it is, she has infected herself. But I know that if it's not treated she will get worse and die young. There is something pathetic about her that makes me believe she is sorry – I don't know why.

'This is a setback, Amber, but we must keep moving forward – decide what we can do now to get you clean, and what else we can do to help you stay clean.'

'Why are you so good to me? I don't deserve it.' She places the mug on her bedside table then cuddles into her pillow.

'I guess I feel responsible for the way things turned out. I can't walk away from that. I know I left you a lot when you were small, but we needed the money. I couldn't stay home all day and manage on benefits. I couldn't live like that.'

'I do understand a bit more now I'm older.'

'I was so busy worrying about money and what we had, I should have thought about you, what you needed emotionally. I should have been there for you more.' The mistakes of her childhood were my mistakes. The loneliness she felt was down to my choices.

'It's my own fault I started to do gear. No-one made me. I've messed up my own life. I never thought you knew how unhappy I was.'

She's right – I didn't see it back then. I never considered that she might have been unhappy. I always thought about how naughty and difficult Amber was as a child. 'I guess I didn't really, until now.'

'When we've talked about it before, you've always defended your actions and I defended mine. Now we're both speaking the same language. Knowing you understand changes everything.' A few large tears well up in her eyes and spill onto her face. 'If the emptiness from my childhood can start to disappear, maybe the bad feelings from being an addict will start to disappear too.'

'It'll take time, but those feelings will go. You can heal yourself.'

'I'll make you a promise; I'll try my hardest to get clean. You make me feel there is a way back for me.'

'One day you'll find the strength. You fall down, you get back up and start again. I'll never give up on you, never let you go.'

I see her as others never did, as the child she was once, trying to do the right thing but never quite being able to, and I want to be sure she doesn't drift away, as if I'm a large ship in deep water and Amber is a tiny boat tied up alongside. All the time I have hold of her, she can't sink, can't go under.

'Listen Mum, it'll be fine, I've learnt my lesson. Once I'm back on the blocker this time, I'll never take heroin again, promise.'

'But how? How can you when you hang around with other drug users? Something's got to change, you have to stay away from Leeanne.'

'I don't have anyone else.'

'She'll always be your friend, Amber, but you can't see her until you're both clean, and you must finish with Ian. I know you two are taking drugs together. I can't believe you're going to quit when you continue to go out with him. I don't want you staying at his place any more.'

'It's not that easy, I owe him money.'

'Well it's his own fault. He shouldn't have been stupid enough to lend it to you.'

'He can't afford it. He's living on the edge as it is. If he hasn't got enough to pay his rent, he'll get kicked out.'

'How much do you owe him?'

She avoids my gaze and picks at the edge of her blanket. 'Fifty.'

'Okay, I'll give you fifty quid. You finish with him and no more going back. I mean it.'

'Yeah, I'll give him the money and finish it.' She lifts her security blanket to her face and then tucks it under her pillow.

I have to accept the relapse and move forward again. There is no quick fix to what she has done. Maybe the mistakes are part of her recovery?

Amber walks with me to school to collect Sam and Lauren. They shout her name and run towards us when they see her waiting in the playground with me. They are still so pleased to have their big sister back in her old room; they think she's great.

'Mummy, can we get a DVD from the library?' Lauren says.

The three of them choose a film and cuddle up together on the sofa to watch it. From the kitchen I can hear them chatter. 'Who do you want to be Amber? I'm Ariel,' Lauren says.

'I'm Sebastian,' Sam says.

'Don't want to be anyone, now, there's no-one good left,' Amber says.

I feel protective of Amber, finding security in a childish situation. This is where she belongs; at home, surrounded by her family.

The garage door creaks as it lifts, and I hear Tony rev the engine of his car and drive it into the garage. He walks through to the kitchen, places his hand on my shoulder and kisses my cheek.

'Been busy today, love. Phones haven't stopped ringing and I've got three quotes to get out tomorrow.'

Amber shuffles in and stands in the doorway. She is pale and already has her pyjamas on. 'I'm not feeling too good, Mum, gonna take some Night Nurse and go up to bed.' She disappears upstairs to her room.

Tony's eyes widen. 'Is she clucking again?' He turns to me. 'All she does is sneak off and do drugs or lay about ill. Hope you've had it out with her.'

'We've talked it through properly. It's going to be okay this time.'

'You've said that before, but it just doesn't work. She's using you. She knows you're too soft. I bet you're giving her money again.'

'No... well only what she owes Ian.'

'You gave her money to "pay back" that little shit?'

'He needs it for his rent.'

He leans forward. 'And you believed that?'

'She's not going to see him or Leeanne any more. She'll concentrate on being clean.'

'She won't. She cares more about her druggie friends than she does about you.'

'Things are different now.'

'Amber's weak, she's always been weak. She has to take things that little bit further than anyone else. She's done it to herself. She took everything she could until she hit the big one. You have to start being realistic.'

'What do you mean?'

'We both know she'll never do it.'

'She will!'

'She won't, and the sooner you accept it the better. She's your daughter, you deal with it. I'm going down the gym.'

He takes his bag from the under-stairs cupboard and walks out the front door. I sit at the kitchen table and listen to his car drive away.

This isn't what I want. This is not how I want things to be between us. I know I must find the time to concentrate on my marriage. I can't remember when Tony and I last spent any quality time together without the Amber issue coming between us. Is he right? Do I give her too much trust when she can't trust herself? Perhaps no-one can stop the path she's on.

While the kids are playing quietly upstairs I call my mum; I need someone to talk to. The stress is pumping inside my head like a child repeatedly throwing a tennis ball against a wall.

'How are things with Amber? Is she working yet?' she asks me.

'No, not since she got sacked.'

'Why does she take drugs? Why can't she just stop? She's a naughty girl. What does Tony say? I bet he's cross.'

'Yeah he is, but I wish he could be there for me to lean on. I'm not asking him to fix it or help me, just to not make it any worse than it already is. I feel I have to pretend I'm coping, handling it all effortlessly, otherwise I'd have to admit he's right about Amber and give up on her. What can I do, Mum? I can't abandon her.'

'You've got to think about your own health, and you've got Lauren and Sam to care for.'

'I can't turn her out, she's trying to get clean. I know I make mistakes but I want to believe her when she tells me everything will be alright, that she'll stop. I guess Tone isn't quite so taken in. Maybe he's the voice of reason, protecting me from myself.'

'It's not all down to you. I wish that bloody Dave would get out of prison; then he could take care of her.'

'Oh Mum, don't make me cry. Do you think I'll let him destroy her again? He can't even face up to what he's done, admit his guilt and protect her from prison. Still she can't see it. Maybe when we actually get to court he'll do the decent thing. Be the hero at the last moment.'

'Let's hope so, Chrissie, let's just hope so.'

Amber

'Katie's at the door for you,' Mum says with a smile.

'Popped round to make sure you're alright before court next week, Amber,' she says.

Katie's plain but pretty, kind, not nasty in any way. She's wearing a long skirt and boring shoes. She has huge boobs but hides them under a large, loose-fitting jumper. She hands me a present.

'What's that for?' I ask her.

'Your salvation.'

I unwrap it to find a Bible. The cover is navy-blue leather

and it's trimmed in silver. I don't remember telling her, but those are my favourite colours.

Dave and his family have been going to church in Guildford since he was small. The congregation is a tight-knit community – Dave's family are always doing something involving the church.

The first time he took me there I felt awkward when people jumped up and shouted 'I can feel Jesus!' Some of them chanted 'Heal me! Heal me!' and swayed and swooned in their seats. My eyes widened in disbelief and I remember looking around for some way to escape. I thought they were all nutty, but there was a sort of energy inside the church, a bubbling of people talking and singing.

Katie is the pastor's daughter. Dave and Katie went to school together; they were childhood sweethearts before he started doing drugs.

'Shall we go for a drink? We can take my car if you like,' Katie says.

She has a long, white estate car. Sitting forward in her seat, she peers over the steering wheel and drives really slowly. She's not confident on the road and it makes me nervous. When we get to the pub, she doesn't try and park but abandons the car on a verge.

Inside I go straight to the bar, try to catch the barman's attention. 'What would you like, Katie?'

'Thank you, Amber. I'll have lemonade.'

'Oh, go on, try a Fosters-top or shandy, live dangerously,' I nudge her with my elbow.

'No, no, I'll have lemonade,' she insists. I never know why people bother with the pub if all they drink is lemonade. You can sit at home with lemonade – it's half the price and just as exciting. I order a beer.

'Have you heard from Dave lately?' she asks me.

'Had a letter last week.'

'I'd like to see him, but he never sends me a visiting order. I write to him though. And I'm going to be in court.'

'That's nice,' I smile at her. I fiddle with my nails. Thinking about Dave, there's an emptiness in my stomach. 'It's hard without him.'

'You must talk to Jesus, ask him to help you.'

'Yeah, I will.'

'No, Amber, you don't understand. If you ask Jesus he really will help you.'

Katie chatters on about Jesus, making me uncomfortable. *Okay, you loony* I feel like saying. I do believe in God, but I think you have to help yourself – he's not going to do it for you. I'm not listening and after I while I make excuses to go home. Katie's such a good person, she'd never do anything to hurt someone. But I can't spend my time with her if she's going to lecture me about God.

Sixteen

Amber

The sound of cars at the end of the road has increased from one every few minutes to a constant drone; it must be nearly morning. I pick up my mobile from beside the bed and check the time. A gentle breeze comes in through the top window, drawing the shadow of the curtains back and forth, like the ebb and flow of the tide. I slept in this room when I was a child; compared to this my life was simple then.

I take out the letter I received from Dave addressed to 'my princess'. He tells me *life isn't the same without you by my side. I cannot wait to hold you. I'm only alive when you're in my arms.* He says nothing about the court case, but he's probably not allowed to. He knows how worried I am.

Turning over in bed, I stare at the wall. I've been thinking about court, worrying about it, but now the day has arrived I'm more petrified than I could have imagined.

I'm shaking as I struggle to do up the buttons on my fresh, white blouse. The zip of my trousers pinches my finger and won't move. I pause, blow my hair away from my face and try again.

'Amber. Are you ready?' Mum calls up the stairs. My hands

are sweating and my stomach is churning like a washing machine.

Mum reverses her car round to the front of the house and leans across to pull the door catch for me. We don't talk. We've said everything there is to say, gone over every eventuality.

Mum puts a CD in the player and I stare out the window, watch the trees and houses drift past. After the raid, when I was in the cell, I had to stay in the same clothes for three days. If I get a jail sentence they'll take me there straight from court. I'll be stuck in these clothes for a week. I'll only have the knickers I'm wearing.

The trial is being held at Winchester Crown Court. The outside walls are built of large, pale grey stone. The building looks like its stood for a hundred years. Mum and I are stopped by security and searched before going into the foyer. Inside there is a whirr and drone of people talking, barristers in wigs and black gowns, solicitors carrying files and heavy briefcases. The sound of all these people chatting and moving around melds into one and makes me anxious.

April and my defence counsel, Richard Morley, are waiting for us. He's tall and lanky, with dark hair and a pleasant, open face that smiles easily. He's very professional; doesn't discuss anything unless it's relevant to the case, not even the weather.

'We're going to be delayed. We're about to be offered a change of plea,' April says, then looks at her watch.

My heart starts to beat really fast. I take a couple of rasping breaths.

'A change of plea? What does that mean?' Mum asks.

'The police prosecution, David's defence and Amber's defence are going before the judge now,' April explains. 'There's been a mix-up with the police paperwork. David's been convicted twice before for drug dealing but their computer shows it as once. The police have agreed to accept it as once if he pleads guilty. This is important: drug dealing is three strikes and you're out; if David's convicted a third time, he'll get life. But David's defence team can't accept it unless we agree, so I've asked for some of the charges against Amber to be dropped if she pleads guilty to a lesser offence. Kelly will come and find you when we know what's happening. Go get a coffee.'

April and Richard dash down the hallway; his black gown billows out at the sides like a wizard's robe.

'What do you think, Mum? Pleading guilty to anything doesn't sound like a good idea to me.'

Mum places her hand on my arm. 'I trust April; she'll only do what's right for you.'

The cafeteria is like a school canteen – cheap tables and chairs in a large, open room. Mum orders a coffee and I try to find a cold bottle of water from the back of the fridge. I've no strength in my grip to crack the seal and I struggle to open it. When I try to pull back one of the chairs to sit down it doesn't move. I realise all the furniture is screwed to the floor.

Mum reaches for my hand across the table. 'I know you're nervous, Amber, but there's nothing more we can do now but wait.'

A bit later, Kelly appears in the entrance and looks around. Spotting us, she strides over in a short skirt and heels. Three or four blokes turn to check out her arse.

'April's outside court number two. Are you ready? We're in next,' she says.

Am I ready? Is she joking? Mum pushes her coffee cup into the middle of the table and stands up.

Outside the courtroom, DS Thompson and another officer are waiting. Their faces are impassive, emotionless, standing there in their over-pressed, shiny grey suits. Linda and Dave's step-dad wait further down the corridor.

April leans towards Mum and me. 'The judge has approved the proposal,' she says. 'The charges against Amber of intent to supply and handling stolen goods have been dropped. I've agreed she'll plead guilty to one matter: possession of diamorphine. David will plead guilty to the original charges in return for this being treated as his second offence.'

Mum nods her head and looks at me. 'Okay.'

DS Thompson pushes the heavy wooden door to the court and everyone files in behind him. A security guard is waiting by the entrance to escort me to a box at the front of the court. It's like a display case: panels of shatterproof glass framed in wood. There are marks on the front at the height of my forehead, as if when someone's been sentenced they've gone a bit skittie and smacked their head against the glass.

Locked in this box, I know I'll have to look the judge in the eye and say the word 'guilty'. Nothing is certain. I feel like I'm wearing a mask that shows the face of a criminal drug dealer, but that's not who I am. I'm a human being, a child who made a mistake.

The guard opens another door and brings Dave up to stand beside me. Dave is fatter than I've ever seen him, and smart in a dark suit and tie.

Dave and I stare into each other's eyes before facing straight ahead. I can feel the judge watching me so I don't speak. Behind my back I move my hand out towards his. I hold on tight, feeling the soft warmth of his skin. To be with him again is a relief. I'm not in this mess on my own any more. Make it right, Dave, make it right; plead guilty.

The judge is wearing a chalk-white wig and has a fat,

bulbous nose, but his face is kind. The clerk of the court reads out the charges against Dave. 'How do you plead?' she asks him.

The lights inside the courtroom get brighter. Everything is in slow motion, like I'm going to faint. I don't care if I faint; it would be an escape. The fear is all consuming.

'Guilty,' he says.

The clerk turns to me and reads out the charge of possession of diamorphine. 'How do you plead?'

'Guilty,' I say.

The proceedings begin. There are things going on that aren't registering with me. It's like getting beaten up: you cover your head for protection – you don't watch the punches coming.

DS Thompson is called to summarise the details of the case. He steps into the witness box. The clerk hands him the Bible and says 'Repeat after me – I promise to tell the truth the whole truth and nothing but the truth, so help me God.'

DS Thompson presents the police evidence regarding the extent to which Dave's been dealing. Hearing it all read out makes me feel ill. The proof of all Dave's illegal activities is overwhelming. The judge seems to listen meticulously to all the information. Because we're both pleading guilty, there's no jury, only the question of what sentence the judge decides on.

Dave's barrister asks for leniency. He talks about Dave's addiction and his previous attempts at rehab. My ears are buzzing and I'm not certain what's going to happen.

Richard Morley makes a statement about my pre-sentence report; how it wasn't thought that I would benefit from a custodial sentence.

'Before I sum up,' the judge folds his arms on the edge of his bench and studies Dave, 'have you anything else to say in your defence?'

Dave's step-father stands up. 'May I say a few words, your honour?'

The judge nods his permission.

Dave's step-father makes his way into the witness box. He has unruly hair and under his suit he's wearing a yellow tank-top. There's nothing rushed about his manner. He carefully lays out his notes and pauses before he starts, as if he's in church and about to read a sermon. He starts by telling the Bible story of the prodigal son.

'David is our prodigal son.' He pushes his glasses back up his nose with his forefinger before looking around the court. 'But we want him home.'

He explains how Dave's drug-taking has affected the family. 'He will return to us. His faith will cure him of his afflictions,' he says.

It's a fair old speech and people start to turn to each other and whisper. I bet they're thinking 'Shut up, mate'. It's all very godly.

I'm glad the judge didn't ask me to say something in my defence. Anyway, I'm small fry here. I guess he asked Dave because if you're gonna put someone away you have to give them a chance to speak first.

When Dave's step-father returns to his seat, the judge looks directly at me.

'Amber, I am sentencing you to a conditional discharge to run for a period of two years. So long as you remain out of trouble for that period, this will be the end of the matter. Should you, however, re-offend during the next two years and are brought back to court and plead guilty or are found guilty, then the magistrate or the Crown Court dealing with the new matter can also re-sentence you for this offence. I order you to pay two hundred pounds in costs.'

The judge turns to Dave. 'David Jenkins, I sentence you to four years, of which you will serve a minimum of two. Time spent on remand will count towards this. The court will decide at a later date what assets belonging to you are to be seized by the Crown. You will now be taken back into custody.'

I think the judge can see Dave dealt to fund his own habit and I got caught up in it with him. In the scheme of things we're not as bad as some of the criminals who come before his court.

The judge bangs a wooden gavel on the bench. 'Court dismissed.'

Immediately there's a prison guard behind us grabbing Dave's arm. I try to say everything with my eyes; the urge to lean forward and kiss him is immense, tears trickle down my cheeks. Now I'm back to being completely alone.

Christine

Picking up my bag, I shuffle along the bench towards the aisle, waiting for others to join the queue to leave. In the corridor I see April and Richard. 'Thank you for everything,' I say.

I smile and we shake hands.

Turning around to wait for Amber, I notice DS Thompson in the crowd. He looks past me, distracted. Perhaps he didn't see me. I want to thank him too; if he hadn't raided Amber's house, she would still be using heroin. I hope this court case has taught her that you can't break the law and get away with it.

Walking out of the court, I take Amber's hand. I can't stop grinning. After what Dave's done he got off lightly, but it's a good result for Amber.

Driving back, I feel the relief sweep over me. Amber's not

going to jail. As if she feels it too, she turns to me and says 'I'm going to start looking forward now.'

'You're right, we can think about your future. This is a major step in your recovery. You don't need to worry about it any more. I promised you a holiday. Why don't we go away somewhere warm and sunny? Just the two of us.'

She thinks for a few seconds. 'I've always wanted to go to Kefalonia; it's one of the Greek Islands.'

'I'll talk to Tony when we get home, try and book something straight away.'

The smell of garlic greets us when we walk through the door. Tony is home from work early and making pasta with the kids. Standing on a chair stirring mince and onions, Lauren says 'I'm making tea tonight.'

'How did it go, then?' Tony asks.

I recount the details of what happened in court and ask him about looking after Lauren and Sam while we go on holiday.

'I'm glad it went well for you today.' He adjusts the gas and turns to give Amber a hug. 'You have a nice holiday with your mum. I'll take care of the monsters.'

'Thanks, Tone,' she says, closing her eyes and putting her arms around his waist. 'I've never had her all to myself for a week before.'

Seventeen

Christine

Stepping off the plane, the heat hits me like someone opened an oven door and I almost melt. The air smells of aircraft fuel and roasting tarmac. We follow the line of people into the terminal and collect our cases.

Our hotel is set back from the beach, on the side of a steep hill. The pool has a wide view out to a piercing blue sea, and the grass and shrubs nearby are full of the sound of crickets. I turn the wooden, slatted sunbed around to face the sun, adjust the back to the right height, and lay out a nice fat beach towel. Closing my eyes, I inhale the feel and smell of our holiday. I am not thinking about drugs or worrying about her addiction; I am free of it.

I start to watch the other holidaymakers, wondering if their lives are as simple as they appear or whether like us they hide a dark secret. I take my book and some magazines out of my bag, read for a bit, then get bored. 'See that woman over there in the pink bikini? Have you seen the bloke she's with?' I say to Amber.

'I know, I saw her earlier at the bar. She looks like a Barbie doll, but he's no Ken.'

We giggle. 'Didn't know you were like me, a people watcher.'

'We're bound to have things in common, Mum; I am your daughter.'

I notice the sun has highlighted her hair and her shoulders are pink. She has a brightness about her as if she's more alive. 'You look well, Amber – better than I've seen you for ages.'

'Yeah, the sun does feel amazing. I'm gonna eat fresh fruit and salads this week. There's no need for me to take the blocker, and my body is starting to recover. I'm healing.'

'I want to concentrate on getting you back to normal. The walk up and down that hill each day will get you fit.'

Amber picks up my book and studies the cover. It must have sparked her interest. *Descent into Death* by Howard Storm. What's that about?'

'It's a true story about an American guy who almost died and had an out-of-body experience, then changed the focus of his life to serving God.'

She lifts up her sunglasses. 'Can I read it when you're finished?'

'You can have it now.' I want her to read it. She might find some comfort in the deeper meaning of the story.

'Do you believe in God, Mum?'

'Yes I do. I believe we're all a part of God. The addict on the street is still a part of God.'

I shuffle up the sunbed and look at the afternoon sun sparkling on the ocean. The water is a vibrant blue and in the distance I can see the outline of two silver ships.

'We don't live this precious life without a purpose and the only purpose that makes sense to me is a testing of the soul. We don't always welcome tough times, but God only gives us what we can cope with. I've learnt to accept that. The situations we find ourselves in are like exams, and we have to pass them before we can move on.'

'Do you think drug addiction is a test? For me? For us?'

'It's your test, Amber, not mine. I can't do it for you.'

'What's your test, then?'

'For me, it's to know I've no regrets about what I've done and how I've behaved. In the end that's all we do have; our principles, what we stand by – that's what makes us who we are.'

She's silent for a moment. 'I'm beginning to believe in myself. I feel so much better not taking that awful blocker.'

'You can't take it forever; one day you'll have to rely on your own willpower. Try and find the strength within yourself,' I say.

'Yeah, I think I'm past all that.'

Now the court case is over and she's stopped seeing Leeanne and Ian, everything is going back to normal. I hope she'll finish with Dave soon. I know if I bring it up, try and make her, she'd say 'yes' just to please me. I want her to *want* to do it.

I have my daughter back and our relationship is better than it ever was before. She's starting to open up to me. In the end, it wasn't that bad.

I am missing the little ones, Lauren and Sam. When I get home perhaps I'll be able to go back to my normal worries – has Lauren got her PE kit and lunch money – rather than worrying about whether Amber's using heroin today.

I watch her turn the pages of the book. 'Maybe you'll be able to stabilise yourself now. Perhaps you don't need the blocker any more.'

Amber

I wake with a start. For a moment I struggle to pull my mind back from my nightmare and concentrate to remember where I am. My bed is soggy and my body is hot. The duvet is tangled around my legs. I wipe my forehead with the edge of the pillowcase. There is a faint glow radiating from the edges of the curtains; I'm safe at home.

I've dreamt I'm smoking heroin with Leeanne. I can smell it and feel the effect. I'm relieved in some way, like I've had a respite.

In my dreams an imaginary world springs up around me and dark shadows and voices draw me into a dream-world of possession. It plays games with my mind. Part of me is convinced I'm going to die and the only thing that will make me live is gear.

I must try to believe I can feel normal again without heroin. It's a daily fight not to take hard drugs.

My phone rings with a number I don't recognise. I answer it anyway; it's Leeanne. 'I've moved in with Matt. Come and see me.'

I'm not sure what to say. There's a silence on the line. 'I just want to see you,' she says.

I'm not about to say no; she's my best friend and I love her.

I know Matt – Leeanne went out with him when we were teenagers. He has a podgy belly with man boobs; he's intelligent, but he's not my kind of person.

When I call round, he answers the door. 'Leeanne, its Amber!' he shouts, then strolls away, leaving me standing there.

The hall carpet has a dirty trail where everyone's walked, yet around the edges it's still a pretty pink. By the TV there are tall piles of DVDs leaning haphazardly and there's a stack of books by the sofa with a mug on top. The sitting-room curtains are thin and pale; they don't meet in the middle and wouldn't keep the light out if they did. At one end of the room there's a table where Leeanne's eating her dinner.

I wait on the sofa for a few minutes, then I feel uncomfortable. I lean forward and sit on my hands. 'Do you want to come out for a bit when you've finished that?' I ask her.

Matt butts in. 'She's not going anywhere.'

Leeanne huffs and pushes her plate into the middle of the table; her food is only half eaten.

'I make the food then you go out? No way,' he spits.

I know Matt's trying to take care of her, control her addiction, but he always was obsessive; he has to be with her the whole time. Maybe Matt and I are jealous of each other.

'I'll go then, catch up with you later.'

The little envelope appears on my phone the next day; it's a text from Leeanne. I pick her up while Matt's at work.

'What was that all about last night? He's a moody git,' I say as she gets in the car.

'He won't even let me go out. He knows I'm a smack head and he uses it against me.'

'I don't know why you're with him. He can't even tolerate your friends.'

'It's cheaper to live with him. Things are tight now I'm not working.'

'When did that happen?'

'Had to leave before I was sacked.'

I glare at her. 'Why?'

'Couldn't get up in the mornings. I'll find another job. I have to. I've extended my loan again, spent it already.'

Leeanne used to be strong, emotionally and physically, but

that's all gone. Her face has changed – she's not as stunning as she used to be.

'You're gonna get off the gear one day, we both are.'

'Am I? I'm scared, Amber. Look what I've done.'

She holds out her forearm to reveal a purple puncture mark and a brown patch. 'I fuckin' missed, wasted all my gear. Do you think I should go to hospital?' She touches the puncture and flinches. 'It hurts.'

'You can go to hospital and they'll syringe it off, but they'll ask questions. I've seen it on Dave before – it'll go down. Why are you banging up, anyway?'

'Matt gives me a tenner to score, then waits outside for me. If I smoke it it's not enough, so Mick's started to give me a hit while I'm there.'

'Leeanne! That's so dangerous! Why would you let that dirty bastard bang you up? If he does it for you he could kill you – he won't know when to stop, when you've had too much. Loads of times I found Dave passed out with a needle stuck in his arm with a small amount of gear still in it.'

I want to take care of her but I know I can't. It's hard enough trying to take care of myself. I drop her back at Matt's flat.

Pulling up at the traffic lights, I realise I'm nearly home yet can't remember driving the last two miles. I can't bear the thought of Leeanne being banged up by that wanker. It's quite an intimate thing – it gives someone a lot of power over you. For me it would be a step too far.

I'm going to get some dope. I know I'm replacing one drug with another, but maybe it'll take me back down that hill. Stave off the weakness I felt when I was with Leeanne again.

I ring a bloke I've got weed from before. 'You alright, mate? It's Amber, got any green?'

'Err, no, but I've got a bit of solid.'

'That'll do. How long?'

'Pick it up in twenty.'

I smoke it in my car. It's really good, wet and squidgy. When I burn it with a lighter it goes fluffy. I pull off the fluffed up bit, gently roll it between my thumb and forefinger and sprinkle it nicely into the joint. It gets stuck in the lines of my fingers and I rub it off on my jeans.

'Post for you, Amber,' Mum says and chucks an envelope at me when I walk in. 'From Her Majesty's Prison Service.' Her face is hard and her voice is cold.

Inside there's a letter from Dave telling me he's been transferred to Winchester, and a visiting order for this Sunday. Now the court case is over I'm not on bail any more and there's nothing to stop me seeing him.

'I'm not budging from what I said; when Dave gets out, it's me or him,' Mum says.

I know I'd choose my family over him. What I have at home is real, right, and what I had with Dave was drug-fuelled and hollow – only good on the surface. But somehow I'm obsessed, as if he's a pop star.

I'm up early on Sunday but not early enough to pick out a new outfit. I throw on the same clothes. Winchester Prison is quite high security. I have to take my passport for ID and I've been told to arrive at least half an hour before the visit so they can process me. The building is like a fortress – high exterior walls with CCTV and barbed wire. Huge spotlights are placed every few feet along the perimeter; I bet they could light up the place like a Christmas tree if someone tried to escape at night.

I follow the signs to a communal room for visitors. It's a

makeshift metal shack – no privacy, no door, no nothing. No money has been wasted building this. Inside it's cold, only a few lockers and a bench. The other women are chatting to each other, relaxed. They stop when I enter while they turn to watch me, then go back to their conversation.

'Leave all your possessions in a locker,' the warden tells me. 'Handbag, keys, everything, then go through the metal detector.' She points to an archway.

A female prison officer is waiting on the other side; she pats me down all over. She's not afraid to feel around my crotch and the wire in my bra.

'Right. Outside you'll see a processing queue, up the steps.' She points vaguely into the distance. 'Have your ID ready.'

The stone steps are worn down in the centre where so many people have trodden on them. The guard studies my passport photo carefully and checks my name against the visiting order. Another prison officer goes to get Dave from his cell and escort him to the visiting room.

'Through the metal gates into the courtyard,' the guard says. 'There's three white circles painted on the concrete. Stand in one and wait until you're told to move on.'

I walk through with two other people. They seem to know what they're doing and go directly to the first two circles. I stand in the remaining one at the back. Two dog handlers approach from a side door attached to the building, each with a dog on a tight leash. The handlers walk the dogs past quite fast, one on each side. I guess there are two dogs so you can't pass something from one hand to another to hide it.

Not much longer and I'll see Dave.

One of the dogs stops near me, pulls on its leash and then sits on my foot.

The prison officer huffs impatiently and gives me a hard stare. 'Do you have anything on you?'

'No,' I reply, which is the truth.

He waves the other two people through and moves me forward to the first circle. I think he's trying to ensure the dog has smelt something on me rather than where I was standing. He brings out a different dog from the one that sat on my foot. I hope it'll be okay this time.

The next two visitors come in from the security queue. The dogs walk up and down the three people again. The new dog walks past and immediately sits on my foot, then wags its tail as its handler pulls it away by the collar.

'You know you're not going to get in there without a cavity search,' the prison officer says.

Why did I wear these bloody jeans? They must have the smell of dope ground into them.

I think about Dave. I want to see him and he'll already be waiting for me. I've come all this way and I'm nearly there. It might be a long time before I can see him again. I love him.

But it's not happening.

There is no way I'm being bent over a metal table, naked, while a prison officer with plastic gloves on sticks her fingers up my arse.

Then I remember my secret joy at home: the rest of the solid. Dope helps me to control my emotions, blocks out everything when I feel too much. I can go home and get stoned – easy option. 'No. You're alright. I'll just go.'

After all those gates and procedures I've gone through to get there – the place is a maze – all he has to do is open a quick-release door by the fence. He pushes me out.

'Off you go, fuck off,' he seems to say.

Suddenly I'm back in the outside world. I have to walk for ages back to the car park.

What will I say to Dave? He was looking forward to my visit and I've wasted a visiting order. He'll be cross.

'What happened on Sunday, princess?' he asks when he rings me a few days later. 'You must have been there 'cause they got me out of the cell and everything. I was waiting for you.'

In my head I've been through all the excuses I can think of, but none of them seem believable. I tell him the truth.

I take a deep breath. 'Well, Dave, the dog sat on my foot...'

He interrupts me. 'Oh, babe, did you try and bring me something in?'

I catch on in a second. 'I tried, Dave, I tried.'

Yeah, believe that one if you want to.

Eighteen

Amber

It's raining hard. I can hear intermittent volleys of hailstones hitting the front door. I pick at a thread in my jumper while I sit on the stairs and wait for Mum's car to pull up.

I have a neediness for her, for her love and attention. I follow her around the house most days. Mum's brought me up to believe that if I was trying, she would help me. But today is hard. I haven't walked away from trying – I've been fighting it the whole time and I'm still fighting. Fighting the 'fuck it I'm going to do gear forever' attitude. But every now and then I have moments of utter weakness and I feel like breaking down.

Through the glass I see a bright orange Sainsbury's carrier bag appear, quickly followed by a couple more. I open the door to see her journeying back and forth from the boot of the car.

'Mum, can you lend me some money?' The hood of her jacket is pulled over her head and she rolls her eyes at me.

Standing in the hallway I stare at the rain splashing on the carrier bags. I take a couple into the kitchen and start to take out the shopping and place it on the worktop, not sure where it all goes.

Mum hurries in, shaking the rain off her jacket. 'What do

you need money for? What have you done about finding a job?'

'I am trying. It's hard, that's all.'

'You've got to stop moping around. I've bought a local newspaper; it came out today. Have a look and see if there're any jobs you can do, even if it's only part time, then I'll help you do a CV on the computer.'

I take the newspaper into the sitting room and open it out on the carpet. Fetching a cushion from the sofa, I lie on the floor, turning the large pages until I find the situations vacant. Some of the adverts are difficult to understand: 'the candidate requires excellent customer service skills' – I know what the individual words mean, but what do they want? Then I spot an advertisement for an assistant manager at The Body Shop in Camberley.

'What do you think, Mum?' I show her the advert.

'You could do the job easily.'

I ring the number and speak to the manager. She asks me a few questions then invites me to come in for an interview a few days later.

Inside The Body Shop it's like a multi-flavoured sweet shop. Areas of the shop smell different, lavender over here, then coconut and white musk as I walk through to the back.

The manager has fragile blonde hair and a round face, and she's wearing round glasses. She's a nice person but not very sure of herself, easily manipulated. I put on a sweet, posh voice while she interviews me, using demure body language and sitting with my back straight, hands together on my knees. I make my behaviour childlike so she doesn't feel threatened or dominated. I do a lot of the talking. I tell her all about my retail experience and how much I believe in the natural products and ethics of The Body Shop.

A few days later she rings me and offers me the job.

'Can you start straight away, Amber? We're short-staffed,' she says.

She doesn't mention a reference, which is lucky because there's no way I can get one.

It's a small shop in a large shopping centre. Only a few people work there: the manager, one full-time member of staff, a couple of part-timers and me. The full-time person is called James. He's gay and a bit of a Goth – black fingernails and eyeliner, and dyed black hair.

It's warm inside. The customers are friendly and I chat a lot. If I get tired I can sit down – it's easier than working outside. Some days I think about gear all the time, and some days I just feel it, the need for it, with my body rather than thinking about it in my mind. It's always there. But each day I try to be normal, manage to keep up the pretence.

Part of my job as assistant manager is to cash up at the end of the day. The office is a long, thin room, just a cheap, chipboard desk and a big, chunky safe in the corner pushed against the wall. I clear away some of the papers to make a space. I scoop up the change from the till with a tiny shovel and throw it on the scale. It smells coppery, like blood. The notes are old and dog-eared and they're never the right way round. I turn them so that all the queen's heads are facing the same way. I want to go home and my feet are throbbing.

My pocket vibrates with a text message. It's from Leeanne. *I need help to score.*

No, I shouldn't.

I slow up, count the notes again.

Now she's asked me, I know I'm going to. It's too tempting, too sweet. I'm rotten and worthless so what difference will it make? I won't always do gear, it's just today.

My demons are quietly smug – even before I've replied to Leeanne, found the cash or rung the dealer, they know they've won tonight.

I pick Leeanne up. She pulls the seat belt across and slides it into the catch. I glance across at her, notice how small and frail she's become. She seems so weak and defenceless and I want to stop the sick emptiness in my stomach. 'What do you need?' I ask her.

'Haven't got anything.'

I reach down for my purse. I've got a fiver and some pound coins. 'Phone?' I pass it to her.

'Give us one of your fags,' Leeanne says as we drive to meet the dealer.

I feel for the packet in the door pocket and chuck it on her lap. I notice the wide expanse of her hands, remember how she always protected me from bullies at school. Leeanne takes a long draw on her cigarette and blows the smoke out of the inch that's open at the top of the window.

'You know what matters most to me? Don't you, Amber?'

'Yeah,' I laugh, 'gear'.

Leeanne turns her head. She's silent for a moment before replying. 'No… if I wasn't here…'

I repeat the words back to her slowly. 'If… I… wasn't… here?'

'You know, what's important?'

I remember when she'd said this to me once before. When she had a great job, earning good money, she'd applied for a pension policy. Filling in the application form in her car, she'd got to the part that said 'Who to pay out to in case of death'. She'd turned to me, tucked a loose piece of hair behind her ear, and smiled. 'Well, you know who that is, don't you?'

'Aww, sweetheart, I love you too. Might have to knock you off now. How much do I get, then?'

She had laughed. 'Not you, you dickhead, Claire!'

I'd realised she'd meant her younger sister. 'Yeah, of course.' It'd struck me as one of my more stupid moments, so I know now who she means. 'Well, Claire.'

'Thank you, yes.'

I'm silent. The realisation that she might take her own life is too terrible to admit. 'Don't do anything stupid will you? I can't cope with all this shit without you.'

'Fuck off, Amber.' She winds the window down further and throws the butt out. 'I'll do as I like.'

I see the dealer waiting on the corner and put it out of my mind. She's being emotional and silly. She's just playing up.

We smoke the gear in my car.

Later, when I'm sober, I know that even though I've come so far this one slip has taken me right back there, like trying to get out of a deep ditch. I've spent hours climbing up the side and it takes two seconds for me to slide back into the mud. I think I'm strong enough to do it once and stop, but I'm not.

Why am I so stupid? Even a dog is smarter than that – call it once and kick it in the head, it won't come next time you call.

My connection to Dave is starting to fragment. Writing to him and visiting him are falling further down my priority list. If I'm clucking I don't write, and if I'm high I don't write and can't visit as I need all my money to score.

I start hanging around with Ian again.

The office at The Body Shop has a heavy metal door that automatically locks from the inside. I smoke gear in there, after work if I'm locking up, and when the manager's not in. I push my hands against the cool, silver metal and walk out onto the shop floor. Nicely stoned, I catch a glimpse of myself in the mirror and step back. The trousers of my suit hang low on my hips – I'm constantly yanking them up. Pushing my long hair away from my face, I lean in for a closer look. Yeah, my pupils are pin-pricks – good job no-one else knows why.

'Would you like me to do your make-up?' James offers when the shop is quiet.

I shut my eyes and relax back in the chair. 'Where did you learn to do this?' I ask him.

'I think I've always been interested in make-up. I've been wearing it since I was twelve, much to the disgust of my parents.'

'Don't they like it?'

'They're religious – they think being gay is a sin against God. According to them it says so in the Bible. They won't allow me in the house now, so I rent a bedsit with my boyfriend. My mum said I'd burn in hell.'

James smiles and turns the chair around to face the large mirror.

'You're done. What do you think?' he asks.

I sit up and view my reflection. I seem different, more like the person I used to be before heroin.

The manager smiles at me. 'You look pretty with a bit more make-up on, Amber. There's a lot in the stockroom that's gone out of date that you can take if you like – perhaps some of your friends would like it.'

I take the lot.

In the evening Leeanne and I go to the pub. Women will give you a couple of quid for a mascara or a foundation; we soon walk out with a tenner.

Next time we've no cash to score, Leeanne says, 'Can you

get any more of that make-up? It was a good earner.'

'I'll have to take it off the shelves, and I can't be the one to walk out with it in my bag.'

'I'll come in and get it.'

'Yeah, when no-one else is there.'

I take loads.

Leeanne and I sell the make-up on, a few quid here and there, but it adds up.

Thursday evening, strolling in for my late shift, I find the manager waiting for me. 'Amber, can you come through to the back?' She doesn't seem angry but upset.

All last night's cashing up is laid out on her desk in the office. Maybe I made a mistake and the till was wrong? Maybe she's noticed the missing make-up? She hands me a letter. I open it and find that she has invited me to attend a tribunal. My hands are shaking. I read more: *an incident has been reported to me about you using illegal substances at work while closing up last night.*

I look up at her and raise my hand. 'Two minutes,' I say as if I'd just remembered I hadn't locked my car and would be straight back. I walk out.

James' black hair bobs down behind the till. He pokes his head up again as I leave and I glare at him. What would I say to a tribunal? No, it's better to jump before you're pushed.

Heroin narrows everything down; it's the only thing I really care about. It makes me calm as if it's all disconnected, someone else's pain. I'll leave for work at the normal time each morning and stay out all day.

I ring Ian. 'Alright? What you doing tomorrow?'

'Going to work.'

'Really? Do you have to? There's that flu going around,

everyone's had it. It's just I haven't got anything to do tomorrow; I'm free all day.'

'Well… I've had a bit of a cough.'

'See, you're coming down with it. Best ring work now, tell them you're ill. You need to rest before it gets any worse. We can score tomorrow, spend the whole day tucked up in bed.'

Christine

'The Body Shop phoned for you this morning.'

I scan Amber's face. Her eyes are sunken, blank. Over the past few weeks she's lost weight again – her arms are skin and bone. I don't think she's going to work. I can't prove anything: she always has the right answers and so much more energy to defend herself and deny it all than I have to prove it.

Amber looks at me tentatively. 'What did they say?'

'Have you got something to tell me?'

'What do you mean?'

'You know what I mean. It's the same as when you were a child. Tell me the truth and I'll help you; lie and you're in more trouble.'

She tells me all of it: smoking gear in the office, getting the sack, how she's been spending the days with Ian. My chest tightens; the stress and anger make my head buzz.

Nothing I do makes Amber take drugs and nothing I do can make her stop. Am I making it worse? Enabling her to use by giving her a roof over her head, food on the table, and hiding it from Tony? Am I making it too easy for her?

'So what did they say when they phoned?' she asks.

'They didn't phone, Amber.'

'I want to tell you, I always do; it's just I can't believe you'll help me again, that you can forgive me again,' she brushes the hair from her face. 'That you'll still love me.'

Each time she lets me down it's hard, so hard. But when I see the state she's in I can see the self-harm. Her eyes are empty and watchful, as if expecting the rejection.

Then I see something in her, some glimmer of innocence or goodness, and I know I have to go on. Instead of making her hate herself for what she's done, I must try and understand, to forgive her. It has to be me, her mother – no-one else can play my part. Something inside me believes she's getting stronger.

'I did a lot of stupid things when I was young,' I say. 'Not on purpose, I just didn't know any better. I believe it's the same for you. You didn't get yourself into this mess on purpose, you got mixed up and lost. Now you can't find your way back.'

'You don't blame me?'

'What good is blame? You're my daughter, I still love you the same, I just hate the things heroin makes you do.' I reach out for her thin little hand. Her nails are ragged and dirty and there's a large orange stain on the inside of her forefinger.

'I've done some pretty shitty things since I've been on the gear, Mum. It has a way of turning people nasty.'

'Let's start again from today, slate clean, you and me. I forgive you for every time you've lied to me, for all the times you've let me down.'

'I'll stay home for a few days, till I take the blocker, I promise…'

'No! Don't promise me anything, promise yourself. It's your life you're wasting.' I shake my head, let her hand fall. 'Don't say you can do it if you can't.'

'I can. I will. It's been hard coming to terms with things but that's over now.'

I want to believe her. I am gullible. I've been gullible before, but she doesn't have to lie. I've told her I know it's hard, that I'll help her anyway.

I must bring some balance back into my life. I can't watch her all the time, and I've got to stop obsessing about it. I need to spend more time with Lauren and Sam; although they can sense the atmosphere at home, they're too young to know what's been going on.

The winter evenings are coming in fast. I draw all the curtains to keep in the warmth and turn the heating up. I want us to be a normal family. 'Shall we go out on Saturday? Make an early start on the Christmas shopping?' I ask Tony.

Sitting beside him in the car, I watch his face as he concentrates on the traffic and my love for him wells up inside me, a solid physical thing that can't be broken. He has done nothing wrong and yet the issue of my support for Amber sits between us, sits inside our marriage.

There was a time when we could almost read each other's thoughts, but now I conceal my mind from him, afraid he'll see the thoughts I'm thinking. There is a fear starting to come over me, a fear of being trapped between what seems hopeless and what seems right.

If Amber can't break free of heroin, I have to know it isn't because she never had a chance to change but because for whatever reason she just can't do it, that her little body can't take the strain of withdrawal and she truly wants me to let her go.

Monday morning I wake to a pounding head. I can't go to work today. Everything's been building up. I want to rest and take some time for myself.

I ring Jane. 'I'm not coming in, I've got a migraine.'

Tony is concerned. 'I'll take the kids to school, you go back to bed.'

'Bye Mummy. See you, don't wanna be you!' Lauren runs in and kisses me before running out again.

Stretching across both sides of the bed, I drift into a shallow sleep.

When I wake, the headache has lifted. Gazing out of my bedroom window, I see the November frost still on the grass and the rooftops, yet the sun is shining. I make a cup of tea, put on my coat and sit on the wooden bench at the front of the house. The air outside is fresh and invigorating. Cybil, my cat, comes out and nuzzles my leg. She sits there for a few minutes while I tickle her ear and then chases after a bird.

A car pulls up the drive. My eyes squint half shut and I place my hand on my forehead to shade the late morning sun. It's Amber. My temper stirs – what's she doing?

Amber, Leeanne and Ian get out of the car. They don't notice me until they stroll up the path. When she's closer I look into her eyes; the eyes always give it away, pinpricks. The black dots bore into my soul. The three of them are stoned.

Anger starts to rise in my chest. I am angry for being manipulated, angry for being too soft, angry at myself for not telling Tony.

I jump up. 'What's the matter with you!' I scream.

They jerk back in surprise. My voice sounds strange in my ears, high and squeaking. 'Can't stop for five bloody minutes can you? You're off your face again! And what about him!'

My hand springs up to point at Ian. 'I told you to get rid of him!'

Ian moves his mouth to say something. His eyes meet mine

for a moment, then he looks away. Amber steps in front of him. 'Don't shout and upset yourself, Mum.'

'Fuck off all of you! Just fuck off!'

I am on the verge of losing control. I want to lunge at her and grab her by the throat. How can she do this to me again? I hate her.

They walk away.

'I was going to quit tomorrow!' Amber shouts over her shoulder.

I suppose that's a valid answer if you're a drug addict.

She shouts something else but it's lost in the wind. It doesn't matter; there is nothing she can say now.

Her dark green Fiesta reverses back fast, the engine moaning at the strain, then disappears down the road.

Breathing hard, I stand on the path for a moment.

Amber can't live in this house and use heroin; I must stand by that. How long will it be before she's stealing from us? Putting the kids' safety at risk? Is it time to come to terms with the fact that she cannot, or will not, ever stop using heroin? I'm living two lives. One is safe and simple; I have a husband who loves me and two children who need me. The other life involves just me and a daughter who lies, steals and takes hard drugs. I could just choose the easy one, say goodbye to her.

Inside I am starting to break. Like trying to push an elephant up a hill single-handed, the strain is immense. I need to take my mind away from all this, to make my life about me again. I can't be drained any more; I don't have anything else to give.

Am I just prolonging the inevitable? There comes a time when being stubborn becomes being stupid. Maybe Tony's been right all along and I'm the fool.

I drive miles to a shopping centre no-one from work would ever go to.

I walk around, distracted by the bright lights and shiny floors. A beautifully groomed sales assistant argues the benefits of a top-of-the-range face cream; whilst I talk to her I am just another customer, ordinary, normal. I buy a very expensive handbag that takes me quite a while to choose, and a suit for work that's like every other suit in my wardrobe.

Why does Amber do it? Is her self-worth so fragile? Is her need to get high so strong she can't see the truth – that it's killing her? Will I finally have to find the strength to throw her out?

Of the choices I can make now, which one is still going to feel right in twenty years time? Which choice will leave me with my integrity and which choice will rob me of my self-esteem?

Can I make one final push to support her? This is all I have left.

By the time I get home I am calmer.

Sitting on the sofa, the long shadow from the hallway divides the room. Tony comes home. I make as if to pour him a glass of wine but only a dribble comes out; I must have drunk the bottle. Tony notices and looks at me. 'What's the matter?'

'Amber's on heroin again.' I place the bottle on the table, wait for his response.

His face sets into a rigid stare. 'Why would a person who's supposed to love their mother do that to themselves?' he says. 'If you drove yourself into a brick wall and survived, why would you do it again? I'd feel lucky I was still alive, not see if could kill myself a second time.'

'She's not trying to kill herself. She doesn't want to do it. She's addicted.'

'You can't cure someone who doesn't want to be cured. Give it up.'

'I can't.'

'Do you think she cares about you? Because she fucking doesn't! Stress is the worst thing for you – it could bring back your cancer. What are you going to do then?'

'If I lose her I'll be destroyed. I won't be the person I am now. I won't be able to forgive myself.'

'You can't go on like this forever. What if she's still doing it this time next year and the year after? What then? And what's going to happen when Dave gets out? If you think you can stop them being together you can't.'

I take a deep breath. 'There will come a time when I can...' I start.

But not yet. The maternal side of me won't let go. I made a commitment when I became a mother and the consequences of that choice are mine. The things I believe in can't be cast aside. It's probably some of that strength that made Tony fall in love with me in the beginning – what impressed him when we first met.

Tony's face softens. He sinks down beside me on the sofa, lets out a long, lingering breath. Taking a stray piece of hair from my shoulder, he twists it around his finger before letting it fall.

I turn my face towards him.

His eyebrows draw together, his face is questioning, as if to find the answer, the right words to say to make it all go away.

'What about us? What about our children?' he says.

A tear wells up and spills out of my eye. I shake my head. 'I can't give up yet.'

He sighs, and I watch him walk out.

I open another bottle of wine. The alcohol has no effect. I sit up alone waiting for Amber. It's late and the house is silent when she comes in.

'This time, Amber, I think you'd better go away,' I say. 'I need a break.'

'What do you mean go away? Where will I go?'

'You'll have to go abroad somewhere, away from all your junkie friends. You're old enough to go on your own. It'll do you good, give you a chance to think things through in peace.'

'Cluck on my own abroad?' She seems to panic.

'Don't bother to make a fuss because I don't care.'

Her handbag falls to the floor. 'Where you gonna send me?'

'Somewhere cheap. The Canary Islands, it's got to be quick, I can't put up with you being at home. You'll have to take the blocker at the airport before you can come home. Get used to it, you're going.'

'I want to stay clean but I feel so lost without heroin. I don't know if I can live without it. I hate the cluck, it fuckin' hurts!'

I am cold and emotionless.

'Put up with it Amber or die. If you want to die, ask me and I'll smother you with a pillow while you sleep. Either way, you're not going to die from heroin. I bloody well won't let you. Have you got that?'

Nineteen

Amber

I switch off the light and slide my back down the wall. I sit on my bedroom floor in the darkness and listen to the fight going on downstairs. Pulling my knees up to my chin, I hug my legs. Mum is crying.

'She lets you down again and you send her on holiday, great!' Tony shouts at her.

It must have woken Lauren. I hear her little feet on the stairs.

'Daddy, Daddy, you've made Mummy cry.'

'Go back to bed, Lauren, you're too young to understand,' he tells her.

The effect my addiction is having on Mum, on her marriage and my brother and sister – she's risking everything to help me. If this is how it's going to be at home, I'd rather go – but I know if I carry on taking drugs, I'll have to go.

Mum manages to book the trip for two days later. My flight is at six a.m. I'm nervous, tetchy, and I'm sweating and starting to cluck.

The short-stay car park is cold and dark and it smells of kerosene. Wrapping my coat up around my ears, I follow Mum into the airport. She helps me find the check-in desk for my flight. My suitcase disappears down the luggage chute and I lean against the counter while I answer the security questions, then clutch my boarding pass and passport.

'Let's get a hot drink,' Mum says. We find the only café that's open. The tables are all empty. Someone is sweeping aimlessly down the large expanse of concourse.

'Sorry I can't stay,' Mum takes a sip of her coffee. 'Your flight will be boarding in a few hours.' She looks at her watch. 'If I go now, it'll only be an hour on the car park.'

Half her coffee is left on the table. I sense she wants to get away. 'Bye then,' Mum says, and hugs me. Her soft hair brushes my face and she smells safe. 'Just smoke fags, eat McDonald's and get on the plane.'

I want to do the right thing, so she'll want me back when this is over.

Slinging her bag over her shoulder, she walks away.

The airport is almost empty. Staff sit behind their desks staring blankly out into the night. There's nothing much going on. A few people lie along the seats trying to sleep, positioning their coats or bags as pillows.

I feel the itch for heroin.

If I don't want to, I don't have to go all the way to the Canaries. I could get my suitcase back and hide at a friend's house for the week. I bet there's a train station here. I glance around and see the yellow sign for railway information. I'll have to stay out of Mum's way, couldn't afford to let her catch me in Aldershot. I could even get a couple of sun-bed treatments, to make my skin look tanned.

I put my hand on the seat to push myself up, but feel so dizzy it scares me. I have a pain in my chest, as if someone's stabbing me. I slump back.

If I sit here and rest, I'll be okay in a minute.

I try to stand again, but the pain comes back even worse. I can't get up, let alone walk. It's like I have a hook in my chest and it's pulling me down.

I feel sick and it's hard to get enough air. My eyes start to water. People are looking at me; I may be having a panic attack. I try to stay calm minute by minute and inhale deeply. A lonely traveller is watching me; he seems concerned. I hope he doesn't come over.

On the other side of the hall I spot a sign for a chapel. It's bound to be empty and I can be alone in there. It's not like a normal church, just another room in the airport. There are five or six rows of individual chairs and at the front is a table covered in a white cloth.

Now I'm alone I can be myself, and I have a little cry. Why am I still taking drugs? What am I getting out of it? What will I have if I lose my family? I'll be a homeless drug addict. But will I ever feel right again without heroin?

There's a selection of leaflets at the back of the chapel. I shuffle through them and take one titled 'I Am with You Fellowship'. I'm so alone it seems to speak to me. I ask God to help me find a way to stay clean, to help Mum, to give her the strength not to give up on me. It'll be hard for her to forgive me if I don't get on the plane. When this is over I want to come home, want her to want me again. Somehow, please, please, get me on the plane.

I take everything out of my hand luggage, sort through my money and ticket, then pack it all again. I pick up my bag and walk out of the chapel. I try not to think about anything or turn around, just go straight through passport control. I'm committed now.

The departure lounge is calm and noiseless. I don't sleep but wander around looking in shop windows, their metal grates pulled down shut. I spend a lot of time in the smoking area.

People suddenly materialise from nowhere. There's a smell of breakfast. Everywhere is busy; the airport has woken up. My flight is called.

On the aircraft I think 'sod it, I need alcohol'. The wine relaxes me.

The guy sitting next to me says 'Bit early for a drink.'

'I don't normally; I'm extra-nervous travelling alone.'

He starts to chat, just small talk. He's also alone. He's quite handsome and a lot older than me. He looks tanned already and his face is weathered.

When we land at Gran Canaria, he gets on the same coach as me and we get off at the same resort. There's a pool and a bar on the ground floor and a lot of steps up to the apartments. He can see I'm weak.

'Here,' he grabs my suitcase. 'Let me take that for you.'

His room is opposite mine. He knocks for me in the evening and we have dinner together. It's good to have another person to talk to.

'Why are you so thin, Amber, yet you're so unfit?' he asks. 'You struggled to walk up the hill yet you're only in your twenties.' He seems like he's into fitness and obviously takes care of his body.

'I've been really ill, that's why I've come away. I'm still recovering.' I imply it's serious, that way he won't ask questions.

'Of course, I have a daughter your age. Anything I can do?'

I shake my head and look away.

Pulling back the heavy-lined curtains in my apartment, I see the morning sun. I step out onto the balcony, let it shine on my skin. I pack my sun cream and a towel and walk down to a beach I can see nearby. In the afternoon the clouds build up and I'm cold, so I walk back to my apartment and lie on the couch watching films.

But when the daylight fades I feel the loneliness; it comes on with the darkness.

I send a text message to Mum, wait for a reply that doesn't come.

I make a mess and leave all the jobs, the tidying and washing up, so I'll have something to do tomorrow. I run a deep, hot bath, hoping it'll warm me right through. The cluck is making me wet from sweating – at least in a bath I'm meant to be wet. I lay there so long the water begins to cool, so I pull out the plug until it's half empty and then refill it with the hot.

The duty-free shop in the town has Mum's brand of perfume. I spray it on my sleeve, then lift it to my face all day to remind me of her. Even though I've got two more days before I come home, I pack my case. Then I get everything out again and repack it.

Mum's waiting for me at Gatwick airport. I feel a great sense of achievement, as if I've got something out of the way. She has the naltrexone tablet with her.

'We're not leaving until you take it. I've brought you a drink to wash it down,' she says.

I'd forgotten this part. I take the pill into my mouth, push it to the back of my throat and swallow it.

I hate the blocker. Each time I take it is as horrific as the last, like swallowing pure poison. It has a foul taste, as if it's something unnatural, a cold stone that I can feel dissolving in my gut and spreading around my body like a virus.

I read all the verses in the leaflet I took from the chapel.

They're from a book called *I Am with You – Divine Help for Today's Needs* written by Father John Woolley. I write to Father John telling him how much he has helped me. He sends me the book free of charge and writes me a personal note. Reading the book every day makes me feel someone is working with me. It opens the door to a range of thoughts and feelings I've suppressed, things I haven't allowed myself to consider before. Maybe I'm not worthless. Maybe God does love me in spite of everything.

The weather has turned cold and icy in the short time I've been away. I'm still very delicate and I can't seem to get warm. Immediately, Mum's on my case about getting a job. Apparently there are lots of temporary positions in the shops for the weeks running up to Christmas. I end up landing a job working for Tie Rack in Guildford.

I huddle behind the till. Where I have to work is just a kiosk in the shopping centre, open plan with a display of ties and scarves. I'm next to the automatic doors. Each time people walk in and out, a blast of cold air rushes up the walkway. It contains tiny fragments of ice that bite into me. I can't wear my coat while I'm working, so I have no protection from it. I rub my hands together. My nose is constantly running and is red on the end.

A man with pure white hair and a camel overcoat picks up a scarf and unfolds it. He puts it down before moving away. The shopping centre is busy, people hurry past, but no-one buys anything from me and the time passes slowly.

The desire to take heroin is still there. It's massive, like trying to hold my breath. The urge to breathe out is immense.

I'm not going have a boot, but knowing I haven't swallowed the blocker gives me some relief, stops me thinking about it so much. There's this gap at the back of my mouth, where I've had my wisdom teeth removed. The tablet fits neatly into it. I can position it easily with my tongue. I start hiding it there when Mum gives it to me, then spitting it out.

Driving down the hill into Guildford on my way to work, the traffic is already backing up from the roundabout; Christmas shoppers are out early this morning. I slide the car into neutral and squeeze the brake to control my speed in the queue of cars.

My stomach turns over as if I've just dropped three floors in a lift.

Why do I feel anxious? I check the clock on the dashboard; I'm not even late. My hands are sweating. What's the matter with me?

The pressure inside my head builds, like a volcano about to erupt. Something's happening to me that I can't identify. Then the heavy, red molten lava comes pouring out, smothering my willpower – the fear that heroin will kill me, the fact that I don't want to hurt Mum. It's laughing as it engulfs me.

I have no control.

I can't go on like this. I don't have the strength to go into work, face people and be normal. Fuck it! I can't do it! Now the thought of drugs is in my head, I can't stop it.

And there's the panic.

I have to mentally go with the thought of drugs. If I struggle to resist the urge, the panic gets worse.

I turn the car around.

I drive to a dealer. I know he'll be there. I know it like I know it's cold outside. I buy heroin, all the money I have on me, and he ticks me some.

Once I've got it there are no thoughts. Just do it! Do it!

It's frightening to have no self-control. I've lost my mind

and I don't know if I'll get it back. I know I'm in trouble and I'm ashamed of my behaviour, but knowing my mother's going to kill me hasn't stopped me.

Back home, the front door slams behind me, the keys are still in my hand. I'm feeling high. Mum's right in my face. I'm instantly sobered by her stern expression. What I've done comes rushing back to me.

'Why are you back early?' she demands.

Shit, am I early? I'm stoned so I think everything will be okay. 'Oh, we were quiet today so they let me go.'

'Don't think you're fooling me, Amber!' she shouts. 'You're using again! How can you do this to me after everything I've done for you? Everything I'm still doing!'

I leave. I know I'll make it ten times worse if I say anything. She's a woman on the edge, having a go at me but holding a lot back. I can see it in her eyes.

I'll go and stay with Ian for a few days, let things cool down.

Christine

Through the open window I feel a breeze of cold night air on my face. I'm wide awake in bed, hoping Amber will come home. I'm always waiting for her. It's taken a long time for me to be prepared to let go of the veil of hope I surrounded myself in. In my heart I know I lost her a long time ago. I've been lying to myself, hiding it from myself for too long.

She's off on a binge somewhere. Her habit will escalate again after everything I have tried to reduce it. I must have done it all wrong. Handled her addiction wrong, brought her up wrong – wrong to lose touch with her father.

Tomorrow is Christmas Eve. I have no idea where she is. Her phone is switched off. Each hour I don't hear from her is a quiet torture. I want a life for Amber, a husband and a baby one day. I refuse to believe she will always be a drug addict.

A car pulls up. My heart starts to pound as I listen for her key in the door, but the sound of my neighbour's voice takes away my hope. I stare into the dark. The worry is beginning to consume me.

I hate my inability to cope. Why aren't I strong enough? I need to think of a way to punish myself for being such a bad mother, bad wife, bad person. I want to take a knife, something sharp, and cut myself. It would distract my brain from the emotional pain to the physical pain. I can cope with the physical pain. But the scar would label me for the weak person I am.

My ears are wet. The tears have spilled silently out of my eyes and filled them. My pillow is soggy from the overflow.

In my life I have spent a lot of nights crying and many times I've thought about dying. If it were possible to die of a broken heart, I would die here, in my bed, tonight.

But it's not and I don't.

Part Four

Redemption

Twenty

Christine

The newly lit open fire crackles and spits, giving off a dull heat. The sharp smell of burning coal catches the back of my throat. The lights on the Christmas tree change colour in a never-ending reel, blue then red, then yellow, then green.

'Is this big one for me?' Sam asks, sliding a large present out from under the tree. He pushes it into the middle of the room and rips off the red shiny bow. Sitting back on his heels, he stares at it for moment.

'Open it, then,' Tony smiles.

Sam tears back the wrapping paper to revel a remote-control racing car. 'Wow!'

I glance down the hallway. Amber is moving shakily towards me, steadying herself with one hand against the wall. Her face is a violet-grey.

'Any there for me, Sam?' she asks, lowering herself onto the sofa.

After opening a few presents, Amber discards the contents, only seeming interested in the envelopes with money in. She's empty yet suffocating, like a child dying of boredom.

I swing back the fridge door and pour myself a glass of

champagne. I know it's early but I need it. I am not about to make a scene in front of the family on Christmas Day. When lunch is ready we settle into the dining room. The table is decorated with crackers and Christmas napkins; festive songs play softly in the background.

Amber picks at her food and pushes it around the plate.

'Aren't you at least going to eat that?' Tony asks, staring across at her, waiting for a reply.

She gets up from the table. 'Just popping out for a bit, Mum, won't be long.'

While everyone relaxes on the sofa to watch TV, I clear away the plates and glasses. Waiting by the window as Amber goes out to her car, I watch her make a call on her mobile before driving away.

I close my eyes, trying to keep the thoughts in my head under control, to take all my feelings of resentment and disappointment and frustration and control them, to slow them down, to stop them. I want to sleep for a very long time and, when I wake again, for all this to be over. I am powerless, as if I'm trying to halt the force of a ten-ton truck hurtling down an icy slope.

Yet, as I feel the fear, I remember: I believe in God. My life is guided by a divine force. I wouldn't have been given these challenging circumstances if I weren't capable of dealing with them. So help me, God, to rescue her if I can and to let go if I have to. The thought of this makes me feel stronger, gives me comfort. I'm not alone.

I place the tablet in the dishwasher and shut the door, listen to the sound of water rushing in as the cycle starts. Washing up the pan from the oven, I think about it, the fact that I'll surrender to God. Everything seems alright; a mellow state of calm wraps itself around me.

Amber

Orange, sodium streetlights shine a warm glow on the road, but inside my car Leeanne and I are cold. We're parked a short distance from the flat she shares with Matt. Slouched down in our seats, Leeanne has her feet on the dashboard and my knee is resting on the steering wheel. The radio is on low, playing the top hundred songs of 2002.

'Is he gone?' I ask, biting down the last of my nails.

'No, he'll be a bit longer yet.'

'So what are we going to do tonight? It *is* New Year's Eve.'

'Well, I'm not going to that stupid party with Matt and his friends,' Leeanne says.

'Fuck it, we'll just stay in, then.'

'Don't be like that, we'll find something. Ring Jason.'

I take out my mobile and select his name; he answers straight away.

'What's he's doing?' she asks. 'Tell him we'll pick him up. Duck down – Matt's leaving now.'

Peering over the dashboard, I see Matt get into a car with two blokes and they drive away.

We pick up Jason. He jumps in the back, claps his hands loudly and rubs them together. 'Right, what we doing then?' he says.

'Bloody hell, give us a chance,' I say.

'How much money you girls got?' He turns his head slightly to one side and flashes me a cheeky smile. 'I've got seventy.'

'We've got sixty together,' Leeanne says.

'Okay, we could go to the pub,' Jason says.

'Yeah, it can cost you a tenner each to get in and then they put the price of the drinks up – it's ridiculous. Three skinny smack heads – who's going to talk to us?' I say.

Leeanne looks down at her lap. 'It's not the brightest idea,' she says.

'We could get some Es and drive to London, see if we can find a street party,' Jason says, leaning forward between the seats. 'All we'll need is petrol, fags and some water.'

'Let's do that,' I say.

'If we're gonna get some pills and get high, we're gonna need some gear for the comedown,' Leeanne says.

When we get to the dealer, Leeanne and Jason get two bags of gear each and I get one. 'Do you know where we can get any Es?' Jason asks him.

'No, but I've got some white,' the dealer says.

I look across at Leeanne.

She shrugs her shoulders. 'Yeah.'

We spend the rest of the money on white.

Back in the car I realise I haven't got enough petrol to get to London.

'Well, Matt won't be back till late,' Leeanne says.

No-one speaks while we drive to her flat. I feel a yearning for those times Leeanne and I went to London to a club for New Year's. We used to spend the day talking about it, planning what to wear, taking ages to get ready. I wonder if she feels it too.

In the sparse back bedroom we sit on the floor in a circle. Leeanne switches on a small lamp and tilts it away, casting a dim glow. She finds an old CD case and places it in the centre. Jason gets out the crack and empties it onto the flat surface. We've more white than dark, a big lump of crack, so we put loads on each time.

When the white's gone we do the gear.

240

Now we're twitching and pranged, but there's not enough gear to bring us back down. All the drugs we bought are finished way before it's even midnight. What idiots we've been – spent all that money and hardly got high. There's not that satisfying feeling of being wrecked. We can't take it back, can't change what we've done. We listen to the fireworks and celebrations going on outside, people in the street laughing and singing. This is shit: no music, no fags, not even a can of beer between us.

Jason sits back against the wall, places his hands on his knees. 'Whose fuckin' idea was that, then?'

'It was as much your idea as it was mine,' I reply.

'No, come on, we all agreed,' Leeanne says.

'I didn't want the white, I only wanted the dark. It was you girls that wasted all the money.'

'Yeah, well you can smoke it quick enough, Jason,' I say.

For the first time, I can see that when the three of us are together we become something else. A moment ago we were going to the pub. But no, we had to waste all our money on drugs. This is as high as it's gonna get. I feel an overwhelming urge to shove them away, to stand up and walk out. We're influencing each other. We don't mean to, but it's the way we are. If I have any hope, I have to get away from them – not in a hateful way, but together we're all sinking faster.

I look at what's happening around me and know I have to make things change; the life I'm living is not who I truly am. I feel a strange epiphany as if I'm looking at my situation objectively, not from Amber's point of view but as if I'm having an out-of-body experience; I'm watching the events from outside myself.

At midnight I send Mum a text wishing her a happy New

Year. Then I send another saying *I've been bad tonight but this year I'll be different. Don't give up on me yet.*

Waking up on New Year's Day, I feel rough as hell. Closing my eyes, I wretch, puking up some bile into the toilet. My throat burns and the smell of sick surrounds me. There's something weird floating in the water like a piece of skin – the lining of my stomach?

I study my face in the bathroom mirror and promise myself I'm not doing this again. I don't have to live like this.

I have no concept of who I am any more – not a drug dealer's girlfriend but not quite part of my middle-class family. Like this I still hate myself. No-one else can make me okay, no-one can help me until I help myself.

I close the lid of the toilet seat and sit there with my head in my hands, staring at the large, natural stone tiles on the floor. The idea that I can do heroin here and there, that I can dabble, isn't working. Last year I had a glimpse of real life before diving back into the drug world. Each time I cluck it takes something out of me; it's as if I've been chasing the gear for a hundred years and it's taken its toll on me – the want for it is starting to collapse. I can't be fucked with all this any more. Using heroin is hard work and being clean is becoming easier.

Mum believes I'll have the strength to stay clean one day. While I have her support I have a chance, but I can sense she won't go on forever. Taking the blocker works. It gives me a taste of freedom, not having to fight the urge for it, but it's the idyllic calm, the eye of the storm, before I go back to sabotaging it myself.

I know you can get a blocker that lasts six months, a large dose placed inside you by a doctor. That's what I need. This last step would take away my free will. Is it my free will? Or is it heroin making me believe I want to be an addict?

Mick's girlfriend answers the door when I knock.

'He's not here, but he'll only be a minute if you wanna wait.' She looks at her feet and leaves the door open for me. I glance into the kitchen as I go past. She's standing at the window blowing her cigarette smoke out through the crack.

I step over a German Shepherd dog and sit on the dirty old sofa in their lounge. There's dog hair everywhere and it smells of wet dog. There's a guy there called Kevin. He's before me in the queue. Kevin's older than me; he's in his thirties but he looks sixty.

'I've been doing this for fifteen fuckin' years,' Kevin says as his eyebrows meet in an expression of desperation. 'It ain't easy, mate,' he shakes his head. He speaks in a slow drawl, as if his brain works a beat slower than everyone else's.

I cross my legs. 'I'm not doing it much longer. I'm going to get clean; my mum's going to help me.'

He's surprised. 'Do something now, it ain't gonna get any better. If you're offered help, take it.'

'Yeah.' I look at him. His fingers are swollen and his whole body is shaking. I don't want to end up like him.

'Feel pretty bad today. My ankles hurt, knees hurt… so tired.' He leans forward to rest his forearms on his legs. 'Why the fuck do I do this? My body's packed up and I still fuckin' do this.'

The front door opens and Mick strolls in. Pushing his greasy hair back with slender fingers, he sits down between us and drags the coffee table towards him. Moving aside the crap – spoons, foil and ashtrays – he lays out the gear in the space he's made.

Instantly, Kevin is cooking up his hit. 'Here mate, Amber says she's getting clean, her mum's gonna help her,' he laughs.

'I'm gonna get a six-month implant of naltrexone,' I say.

'Fancy them inventing something like that.' Mick widens his eyes and looks at me, his fag butt resting precariously on his bottom lip. 'It's torture, forcing us to have that done. Imagine it, no matter how much smack you do, you can't get high for six months. How do people think up such a torturous device?'

Kevin pulls down the front of his trousers and injects into his groin. He chucks the needle down, his eyes glaze over and he slumps back. I lay out my gear on the foil, do a couple of lines, then wrap up the rest, folding it neatly in half and then in half again. I tuck it in my fag packet and leave.

I haven't seen Leeanne and Jason since New Year's Eve; I usually do my gear with them. I call Jason. 'What you doing, mate?'

'Not much. You?'

'Having a boot in the car. You seen Leeanne?'

'Jay reckons she's trying to bang up, making a right mess of her arms. He told me I should give her a few tips on how to do it properly.'

'Do you think she's alright?'

'If you can't bang up then you shouldn't *be* banging up. I'm not going to teach someone how to make their habit worse.'

'She's not getting people to do it for her, is she?'

'You know what she's like.'

'Will you come with me? Help me find her?'

I pick Jason up and we start at her flat. The light is on and Matt's silhouette walks past the curtain. 'At least he's home,' Jason says.

I knock on the door and a few moments pass before we hear footsteps and a lock being pulled back. Matt opens the door an inch. He's wearing an old tee shirt and trackies; his long hair hangs like curtains around his face. In the background I can hear the sound of the TV.

'She's not here,' he says.

A kitten is curling around his ankles.

'Where is she? I need to talk to her,' I say.

'Out, don't know where.'

'Well, can I talk to you then?'

Jason tugs at my sleeve, gives me a frozen smile. His eyes are wide, glaring. 'Amber!' His head jerks towards the car.

I'm not just going to leave. I can help Leeanne. Matt nods his head inwards, opens the door a fraction further. I step into the hallway. 'Any idea where she might be?' I ask.

Matt lets out a long sigh. 'Look, Amber, there's nothing you can do.' He reaches down and picks up the kitten.

'Did you drop her off somewhere?'

Jason's fidgeting behind me. He shifts his weight, pushes his hands into the pockets of his jeans.

'Amber, let's go, we can find her ourselves,' he says. His elbows push outwards and he jerks his head again. I understand the importance of the gesture. He means: fucking move.

'Stop interfering,' Matt says. 'I'm taking care of her, not you. You always have to get involved, don't you? I'm giving her a tenner a day and that's all she's doing. It's not that bad, alright.'

Matt doesn't know her like I do. He'll never be as close to her as I am. What makes him think he can help her and I can't?

'Well actually, for your information, it is that bad,' I say. Jason grabs my arm, tries to pull me away. 'She's banging up, asking dealers to do it for her. I need to find her, help her. Tell me where she is.'

Matt's face changes. 'Get out!' He pushes the door against me, trying to close it.

I stumble back. 'Tell me, Matt, I need to know.'

'Let's get out of here,' Jason says. We walk back down the concrete stairwell. It smells cold, like shaved metal. 'What the fuck did you do that for?' he says.

'I'm helping her.'

He shakes his head and looks at the ground. 'Don't ever try to help me.'

I get in the car and slam the door, turn my head to reverse down the road.

'Where do you think she might be?'

We drive around the neighbourhood, searching lonely car parks we've done gear in before, ringing people we know, but she's nowhere. I think she goes to deeper, darker places that neither Jason nor I have any knowledge of. After a couple of hours, Jason says 'We're never gonna find her. Take me home.'

Back in my room I switch on the TV and kick off my shoes. Arranging my hair away from my neck, I lean back on the pillows. I watch the dwindling daylight through the open curtains.

My mobile rings. It's Leeanne – she's come back to me for help; I knew I was doing the right thing. 'Hiya, you alright?' I say.

She's shouting, hysterical. 'Fuck you! Fuck you! Do you know what you've done? I've got nowhere to live now! Fuck you!'

'Oh, Leeanne…'

She bursts in, 'Do you know what it's like for me? Do you? Do you? Nah, you haven't got a fuckin' clue have you?' The phone clicks. She's hung up.

The sky starts to darken. I press the off button on the remote, stand to draw the curtains and sit back down on my bed.

I don't understand. She's being melodramatic – I only want to help her. It was difficult for me when everyone found out about the heroin but in the end it turned out alright. I'll leave her for a bit, focus on getting clean for the six-month blocker.

In a way it'll be easier now. I won't need to explain why I can't see her. Maybe when I've helped myself I can help her.

I'll go back to work tomorrow. It's better to be out all day. I've signed on with an agency. It's casual work in a factory, so I only get paid when I turn up and they don't seem to mind if I'm off a bit.

I come home to find Mum in the kitchen cutting up vegetables for dinner. She reaches for a carrot; her knife is loud and hard as she slices it in half on the board. I pull back a chair and sit down, clasping my hands together on the kitchen table. I say 'I want to talk to you about something.' My voice is clear and calm.

'Go on,' she says and stops chopping. Turning to face me, she widens her eyes. 'Got something to tell me?'

'You know I have trouble taking the blocker every day? Well, they do one that lasts six months. I know a bloke who's had it done. He's been clean for a year, put on weight, got a job and everything. That's what I want, a six-month implant.'

'So where can you get that done?'

'There's a place in London called the Stapleford Clinic. I thought we could ring them.'

'You mean *I* could ring them.'

'Well, yeah.'

'And you think this will work, do you? What if I pay for it and then you change your mind and take it out?'

'No, you can't take it out. It's put deep under the skin of

your stomach. Once it's in, the clinic won't take it out again, no matter what you say.'

It's like it's not me saying it. I can't stop – the words just come out of my mouth. A voice shouts in my ear: *why can't you keep your big mouth shut?*

'So…' Mum points the vegetable knife in my direction. 'It's a guaranteed six months clean? Why didn't you tell me about this before, Amber? It's a great idea. How much do you think it'll cost? You know what, I don't care: it'll be worth every penny.'

She's so totally up for it, I almost wish I hadn't told her straight away. I thought we might discuss it over a longer period, so I could think about it a bit more.

'But you're not clean now, are you? You can't get it done while you're using.'

'No, but I will be. I can get clean, I just can't *stay* clean.'

Mum tilts her head to one side and her mouth shows the beginning of a smile. 'Give me the number and I'll call them, but if you let me down that's it.'

'Thanks, Mum.' I push back the chair and stand up to hold her. I'm taller than her but she's always my mum. I feel safe in her arms. 'I won't let you down.'

Christine

We peer over the edge of the tank at the large koi carp, their orange and white bodies writhing together in the shallow water. My mother stands behind Lauren and Sam. 'I thought you'd finished with Amber after that last time,' she says.

'I guess when it comes down to it I don't know how to let

her go. I just don't know how to do it. People say "you have to want to stop" – well, she does, and I have to find a way to help her.'

The kids walk on further, but it's cold so we go inside to find the guinea pigs.

'I can't stand there and watch my daughter slowly kill herself. I can't. What if she turns to prostitution to feed her habit? And when she's lost all her looks and her teeth have fallen out I'll have to lie to Lauren and Sam about where she is and what she's become. What then? At least I can tell myself I tried.'

'But can you afford it, Christine? I know you earn good money but it's a lot to pay out for. What does Tony say? Does he know how much you're spending?'

'I'm lucky I can afford it, Mum. The amount her addiction's cost me is immense. I haven't told Tone what I've spent. He knows, we just don't discuss it.'

'Amber wants it done? She told you so? What if you're wasting your money?'

'There's something different about it now. I can't explain it but this time it's *her* driving things forward. Maybe she knows I can't go on much longer. If she has it done she'll be clean for six months. If she stays away from other addicts she could get well.'

Until I discussed it with someone else I hadn't seen how it could go wrong, but there are no guarantees. I can't control Amber's behaviour; I never could.

'Mummy, can we go and look at the fish again?' Lauren asks.

We stroll around the aquarium and then wander inside to choose a house plant for the living room. 'Why does someone from a loving home start taking drugs in the first place?' my mum says. 'I know she was a bit wild but I never thought she'd get addicted to something like heroin.'

'Amber has a self-destruct button. Ever since she was a child she's had to take things that little bit further than everyone else. I don't know why.'

'Still is a child if you ask me,' my mum grumbles.

'If Amber kicked heroin for good, I would be so proud. I know it's not what most parents hope for, but it'd be enough for me.'

The application form from the Stapleford Clinic arrives in the post. It's addressed to Amber, but I open it.

'I think we'd better fill it in together. They want a lot of information, and an initial payment of a thousand pounds,' I tell her. I spread the pages on the dining-room table. 'I'll get a pencil, in case you make a mistake.'

Amber reads through the form, then groans and leans back in her chair. 'They want to know my drug history – every drug I've ever taken and what I'm taking now.'

'Is that hard?'

'For some reason, yes it is. I don't want to admit to it by actually writing it down.'

'It has to be filled in tonight so I can post it back tomorrow.'

Amber looks down at the pencil in her hand, passing it between her fingers like a miniature twirling baton. Staring up at me, her eyes are more grey than blue, large and soulful.

'Come on, let's start at the beginning.' I take the pencil and read out the first question. 'What was the first drug you ever took and how old were you?'

She screws up her face until her nose wrinkles down the middle. 'Well… dope.'

'How old?'

'How old was I when I got expelled from boarding school?'

'Thirteen.'

'So, thirteen.'

'Really? When did you sneak off and do that?'

She shrugs her shoulders.

'No wonder it's messed with your mind if you were smoking it at that age. That's where you started to go down the wrong path.'

What was in her world back then? What idea did I hold of Amber at thirteen? Did I even know what she was like? Her presence had been there at home, but she'd seemed to have a dull disinterest. I had been too wrapped up with my own life to sense the jeopardy that surrounded her, that in some way her childish vulnerability made her susceptible to the quick fix offered by drugs, that something about her made her that way. Only now can I see it.

My eyes stay on her face, waiting for a moment of recognition, maybe forgiveness, but it doesn't come. I take her hand and draw it protectively towards me. I sense we're standing at a crossroads together and I know she's free to choose which path she'll take.

Amber

Fragments of sunlight shine through the glass in the front door and make a pattern on the wall. The wind blows the tree outside and the fragments of light move. Cybil jumps up as if to pounce and claw one of them – stupid cat.

A white envelope emerges through the letterbox and gently lands on the mat. I reach down to see it's addressed to me. It's from the Stapleford Clinic, giving me an appointment for the beginning of March. They say that after a short interview, if I'm suitable, they'll put the implant in on that day. I take it out to my car and read it again.

Although I'm afraid, I know I can live off Mum's strength, not my own.

I remember years ago when Jason and I were in a pub in Farnham, a guy we knew from school was standing at the bar. He'd always been a bit of a boffin – really intelligent. As Jason and I waited to get another round in, we chatted to him. We were both pretty wasted. 'I always knew you two would go off the rails,' the guy had said.

'Well, my parents can't control me,' I'd said, boasting. 'No-one can.'

The guy had laughed and shook his head. 'It's not about being controlled, Amber. No-one can control another person. You can only *allow* someone to control you. You give that control to someone who loves you, someone who knows what's best for you. It's a relationship, not a battle of wills.'

By giving Mum control now I can rely on her determination. I have faith in her and can trust and surrender to her, rather than use all my strength to wriggle out of what she wants me to do. I'll work with her to achieve our common goal.

Clucking is a process. I know I can do it, and the measure of how painful the cluck will be is how long I've been doing heroin again. It's the same as when you drink too much – the next day you have a hangover. But, if you drank continually for a week, when you finally stopped your hangover would be much worse.

But it's never as bad as the first time. I'm not afraid of it any more. It doesn't control me. You can make a long, difficult journey if you know the way.

I start to get back on track.

I finish with Ian. 'It's over and I'm not coming back, you'll have to accept it. We never were a couple,' I tell him.

'We were a couple! We were! I love you.'

'It doesn't matter now. Things have changed.'

I walk away. When I look back he's standing on the path; then I watch him turn and fade into the darkness.

Ian has a habit now. He didn't understand in the beginning. People warn you you'll get addicted. 'Yeah, yeah,' you say while you kid yourself you're in control. You don't realise till it happens. Then you're fucked and on the street.

The date of my appointment at the Stapleford Clinic draws closer. I'm into the last seventy-two hours – if I smoke a boot now I won't be able to have the implant. My only option for the future would be to pimp myself on the street. There are no more naïve blokes to get cash from, no more stealing from Mum or blagging off relatives – everyone knows what I am. I've had tick off every dealer I know and not paid them, even taken from kids with a lot less than me. 'Yeah mate, give us a bit of yours today and I'll sort you out tomorrow,' I'd promise them, but never did. Now all my resources are gone.

There are cracks in my defences; the walls are breaking down.

I remember a passage I read about why God made man; I find it again in a book of quotes Mum bought me.

> *God created the angels, with their natural propensity to good. Later, he made beasts with their animal desires. But God was pleased with neither. So he fashioned man, a combination of angel and beast, free to follow good or evil.*

Without both aspects of myself – angel and beast – I would not be who I am. Angel is my good side. She wants to quit, do what Mummy says. But she's weak, she can't do it alone. It was that strong, rebellious energy that got me into drugs and it's that animalistic strength I need to tap into now, to focus and control that brutal frame of mind – use its power to change.

Fuck it if I'm in pain. Fuck it if I can't cope. Fuck it if I can't do gear for six months. How hard am I?

I'm hanging on tight; it's a white-knuckle ride.

Twenty-One

Christine

'This is it,' Amber says. The silver plaque on the wall reads 'The Stapleford Clinic'.

It is a tall, narrow building down a smart residential street. Do the people who live in these houses know they've got junkies on their doorstep? We climb a tight staircase into a stuffy waiting room. Pictures of poppies are hung on the walls and spider plants in terracotta pots line the windowsill; their long tendrils drop down with mini versions of themselves.

Amber slides back the glass hatch and gives her name to the receptionist, a no-nonsense type with straight blonde hair and thin lips.

We choose a couple of empty seats and wait.

The atmosphere is soaked in anxiety and fear. A woman in her forties is staring at us; at first I think she's talking to me and then I realise she's talking to herself. There's a smell of unwashed hair around her. The man in the corner is clicking his teeth, twitching and grinning as he does it. He starts to pat his thigh, creating a complicated rhythm. The woman constantly gets up and down to ask the receptionist a petty question, as if her attention span doesn't allow her to sit still, seeming unaware that she asked the same question two minutes ago.

Through the open window I can hear the sound of the busy London traffic; its reassuring drone breaks the silent awkwardness inside the room.

I notice a flash of petrol-blue material appear at the top of the stairs. It covers a slim woman from head to toe. A silver thread runs through the sari and sparkles as she moves. There's a man with her but he can't make it up the steps, just collapses on the floor.

'Please, look at him, please take it out,' the woman says to the receptionist.

She turns back and gestures towards the man. 'Help him! Help him!' she pleads, holding the edge of her sari to her chin. She can't be more than twenty.

The receptionist stands up and peers through the hatch. She tightens her lips. 'It's not the implant making him ill; it's the heroin in his system. He told us he was clean.'

'But I am clean, I am,' the man moans.

'If you hadn't lied to us this wouldn't have happened. I'll ask the doctor to see you, but he won't take it out, not under any circumstances.'

Amber nudges me. 'I'm going outside for a smoke.'

'Don't be long, we might be next.'

Has she used heroin in the last few days? Is she worried about side effects. Perhaps she might leg it?

I wait, edgy about whether to go outside and find her, but then a faint waft of cigarettes drifts my way as she drops her handbag on the floor and sits back in the empty seat beside me. She's not wearing any make-up and her face is fresh. 'Are you afraid?' I ask her.

Straightening her back, she turns to me with a slight smile.

'What, of the implant? Nah. Took a naltrexone tablet yesterday, found it in the bottom of my bag.'

The door of an adjoining office opens. 'Amber Cameron?' a young man asks expectantly. He's attractive in an intellectual kind of way, slim with pale brown hair, not cut in any style, just left as it grows.

We stand up to go in.

'No,' he says directly to me. 'Amber needs to do this on her own.'

Thank you, God; at last someone other than me is going to help her. I sit back in my seat, pick up a magazine and flick the pages to pass the time. I have to take my mind away from the urge to watch the other addicts in the waiting room; as if on cue they turn and stare at me.

Fifteen minutes later Amber emerges, smiling.

'How did it go?' I ask her.

'Yeah, good. Told him my life story in a few sentences and he says I'm okay to have it done.' Her head nods towards the door. 'We need to go over the road to their surgical unit.'

I observe the rather controlled act she's assuming and wonder what's going on inside her head. Was this her way of coping? When it actually comes down to it, will she go through with it?

Amber lights a fag as soon as we step outside, and although she hasn't smoked it all by the time we've crossed the road she throws the butt on the pavement and squashes it with her foot. 'I think it's down here.'

We descend a cramped staircase to a basement. It's like a horror movie; there are no windows and a strange man in a white coat is waiting in the corridor. He has a skinny frame but his head and feet are big. There's not much colour in his face and his head is completely bald.

'Please come in, you're next,' he says.

He gestures to the room behind him. Inside there is a harsh strip light that buzzes slightly and blinks. The walls are plain and it smells sterile, clinical.

'Lie down on the bed,' he says and moves across to where a stainless steel tray is laid out with a selection of instruments. Preparing a large needle with what appears to be milk, he injects it into the soft flesh of Amber's stomach, beneath her belly button. She gasps and her face contorts.

'You can sit outside for five minutes while the anaesthetic takes effect,' the skinny doctor says.

I sit down on one of the three white plastic chairs lined up against the wall. Amber gently lowers herself beside me, one hand on the back of the chair and the other on the site of the injection.

'So tell me what the psychiatrist said, then,' I say.

'Well, his name's Anthony,' she says as a sparkle flashes in her eyes. 'First, he asked me what I thought was my best feature.'

'Oh, I'm fascinated, what did you say?'

'I said my eyes, my heart and my soul. Then he asked me what I didn't like about myself and I said my destructive nature and that I can't rely on myself.'

'What do you mean?'

'Well, I want to stop using gear, Mum, but I can't.'

'What else did he say?'

'He asked me if I'd ever been sexually abused or beaten up, and what sort of relationship I have with my parents.'

'Did you tell him you never see your dad?'

'I told him I've never seen my parents in the same room together, which he thought was odd. But when I told him that you and I are close and that you're here with me and paying for everything, he said he thought I had the right support to come out of the addiction swiftly.'

A big smile beams across my face. 'Swiftly, I like that, that's good news, sweetie. Did he say you'd get any side effects?'

'No, he said the human body has an amazing ability to heal itself and it was significant that I could still hold down food and water while I'm withdrawing. He thought my addiction hadn't started because of any psychological damage but because I'm a bit of a rebel. I didn't need any further counselling. He said if I have my family around me that's the best way to recover.'

Why didn't I do this sooner? Why did I accept it so easily when she said she didn't want rehab? Because I didn't want to spend the money? But it still cost me so much. Why did I waste all that time and energy trying to control her uncontrollable behaviour?

The door opens and the skinny doctor reappears. 'You can come back in now; I think it'll be ready.'

Amber hoists herself up on the table, then lies down and shuts her eyes. The doctor selects a scalpel and then cuts a slice into her flesh. I turn away for a moment. Although he appears quite old, he's an expert, as if in the past he's performed complicated surgery. I turn him back to see him place a long capsule inside the cut, manipulating it into the soft tissue. Satisfied, he stitches it up.

'Can I have a bath with the stitches in?' Amber asks him.

'Oh yes, you can have a bath.' He closes his eyes, nods slowly. 'I think everyone should have a bath every morning.'

The guy's definitely a weirdo.

We climb the stairwell out of the dingy darkness and step back onto the pavement, blinking in the sunlight.

'How do you feel?' I ask.

She peers down her jeans. 'The injection was the most painful.'

The scar on her stomach is pretty savage; the skin is raised where the implant stands up proud, like a large caterpillar placed under her flesh. I can see ridges in it.

She runs her fingers over it.

'Over the next six months, as it slowly releases the naltrexone, that should get smaller,' I say.

'Actually, I feel okay,' she says.

'Wait till the anaesthetic wears off.'

'Hadn't thought of that.'

At home I give her some painkillers and try to play nurse for a while, fussing over her. 'Why don't you go to bed and I'll bring you up some supper on a tray?'

But Amber is like a wild animal released from a trap; she goes straight out. I let her go.

Amber

Placing my hand on the roof of my car, I try to stand up straight but it hurts. I have to bend over as if my shoulder has been stitched to my knee. A smoke of heroin would make all this pain disappear.

The implant is like icicles in my veins. I can trace the changing chemistry inside my body. When I smoke the heroin that's doing me so much harm it always feels so good, warm and soothing, yet the medicine to make me better feels cold, dirty and impure.

I have to try and score. I'm possessed. During the last vital days leading up to my appointment, the gear has been trying to get inside my mind; it hasn't stopped, not even to sleep. Now it's over, my willpower is zero; I give in, let it in and let it take me. Maybe the implant will take a while to kick in and I can have one last hit?

I phone Mick. 'Come over,' he says.

I show him where I've had the implant. The lump is big and tender now, like a tumour; the stitches are fresh and raw.

Mick's black eyes flash. 'You can cut that out. If it's just gone in it'll come out easy with a knife.' he looks around the kitchen as if to find something suitable to do the job.

I buy a bag of gear from him. Can't wait, can't contain myself, I do it there and then. Can I feel it? Can I? I wait for it to build up gently. Was that a tingle I felt? Maybe? Was it? A tweak from the pain of the stitches tells me no; it's my imagination.

I'm aware something has taken my free will. I'm a prisoner in my own body unable to have the thing I love the most.

I start to cane it, smoking loads; the tears are running down my face, I can't hold them back. I screw up the foil and throw it at the wall.

Mick looks confused, squeezing another puff from his fag.

'It's not fuckin' working!' I shout.

'I don't mean to be funny, right,' he points the butt at me. 'Just cut it out.'

'Yeah right!' I leave.

How will I recover from the panic and the insomnia and the resulting exhaustion? I've been clean for weeks before and the symptoms didn't get any better. Will I ever feel normal again? What have I done to myself?

Twenty-Two

Amber

'I've got the job, Mum!' I shout down the phone.

'What? They offered it to you already?'

'Yep, he asked me some questions about plant names and their care – I stuttered a bit, but I must have done enough to convince him I know about horticulture. He wants me to start Monday.'

First day at work. God, I'm nervous. My hands are sweating and my brain feels like it's been frazzled; I can't think straight.

Opening the doors to the polytunnel, the smell of freesias and stocks fills the air. I breathe in to savour the fragrance. Inside it's damp as if there's been a gentle rain; a unique microenvironment. Rows and rows of seedlings are lined up together with not a brown leaf in sight. They hum with new life, a mass of living energy. Bees and 'looking flies' are everywhere, I call them looking flies because all they do is look really close and then buzz off – they never seem to settle on a flower.

Standing in the sunlight planting seedlings, I stop what I'm doing and look around me. I smell the wet earth, study the delicate petals on the flowers, the leaves of the plants. Through my sweatshirt I feel the heat of the sun on my back, and I can't remember the last time I was so happy, happy without drugs.

'Amber, can you give us a hand loading this lot?' someone shouts.

Stacking polystyrene trays into a van, I'm sweating for all the right reasons, not because I'm clucking but through physical exertion. I don't feel like a freak. I feel alive.

'Want it loaded today, Amber? Keep up!' The lads think they're funny but they're only one tray ahead of me.

Obtaining heroin and using heroin are moving further down my thought processes. I've stopped sulking. I know there's no point trying to score, so I don't think about it. I'm liberated.

I've lived my life on a tightrope, a thin wire I've had to balance on each day. Sooner or later gravity kept getting the better of me and I'd fall. Now if I fall I land in the lovely safe netting under the wire and can't hurt myself. I embrace it.

But I have moments when it's hard to keep it up. I feel awkward and different. I realise how empty I am; I've nothing normal to talk about. And I'm still me, still the new girl trying too hard to make friends and fit in. Yet without Leeanne I'm still the one on the edge, most days eating my lunch alone. I want to make friends, but I can't tell them what is the biggest part of my life. It creates a barrier to me getting close to someone. I'm nervous as to what I might say in case I let it slip, so I stay on the outskirts so they don't realise.

I don't quite forget the gear; that last little thought is still in my head.

My phone vibrates with a text. It's from Mick: *It's snowing at my house.*

He's got crack, lots of it.

Crack is not like heroin; heroin takes all the pain away. But crack does change the way you feel – it's an escape to the drugged up, fuzzy world that's not real.

It's an opportunity, overwhelming, yet simple. Fuck it; I can still have a pipe.

I ring him. 'Alright mate, it's Amber.'

'Fuckin' hell, hello.'

'You at home?'

'Yeah, yeah, pop round.'

On the way to Mick's my palms are sweating. My stomach has shrunk to the size of a peanut and my bowels feel like I'm about to get a squat of diarrhoea. The need to get in there and get it is intense, mesmerising, messy.

'Ain't seen you for a while; who's got better gear than me, then?'

'Not here about the gear, Mick, you said you'd got white.'

'Yeah, have I ever. Wanna pipe?'

He pulls a tray out from underneath a nearby table. On it is a pipe and a couple of rocks. He hooks me in good with a generous one.

The first pipe is always the best. I light it, take a lengthy breath and get the first kind of rush. I hold it for as long as I can and then let it out bit by bit, really slow, getting the really nice rush. It's taken seconds. Now I want it again, only worse this time. I don't get paid for another week and I owe Mum most of it.

'Can I buy one and tick one?'

'Well... I could tick you another one,' he shrugs his shoulders. 'I'd have to add it to what you already owe me.'

I know something's coming, but my want for the crack is so great I think I'll do anything.

'Oh... yeah, about that.'

He raises his hand to stop me. 'That doesn't matter now. I'm sure we can come to some sort of arrangement,' he says it as if he were a loving, caring father.

'Like what?'

'I know you're keen to get off. We'll talk about it later.'

He hands me two rocks.

Result. I'm out of there and I'm never going back. I feel smug and giggle as I drive away. I park in one of my safe places, do the rocks in my car with a makeshift pipe.

Back home in bed I'm pranged. Everything I was escaping from is marching back at full speed. I'm so over-alert it's scary. I'm paranoid, getting up to peep out from behind the curtain, thinking someone's outside. I'm on the brink of insanity. The walls are closing in.

Next day I want more white. The need overwhelms the fear.

I ring Mick again. 'Hello mate, has the weather changed at your place yet?'

'Nah, we're still in the Arctic.'

'You at home?'

'Nah, nah, I'm out and about. Where do you usually smoke?'

'Little Sands car park at the bottom of the hill.'

'I'll see you there in ten.'

I'm gonna get some white, I'm gonna get some white, I chant in time with the music on my radio.

I pull into the car park. A few minutes later, a large maroon car pulls in beside me. The paintwork is dull, and peeling where it's rusty around the wheel arches. Mick leans forward to look at me, pushes back his greasy hair.

I jump out of my car and slide into the front seat beside him.

He passes me a pipe. In a few seconds the rush is gone.

'By the way, I need to tick again, but you know I'm good for it.'

His arm snakes across behind my head and he grips the back of my neck in a weird kind of way. It feels creepy and inside I start to freak out.

Mick leans back in his seat and unbuttons his fly with one hand. 'I know you're good for something,' he says, then he nudges himself down and lifts up his hips. His eyes are black, emotionless, like the eyes of a shark. He turns to me with a smarmy smile and raises his eyebrows in anticipation of me catching on to what he wants me to do.

Maybe the water's darker and deeper than I thought. Maybe I can't swim out of this one. I panic. 'I don't think so.'

'Don't care what you think, you owe me.'

His grip tightens. His long fingers are like steel as he pushes my head forward.

I brace my feet flat on the floor, one hand on the dashboard and one on my seat, in a desperate attempt to stop my head going down, like a cat when you're trying to get it in the cat box to take it to the vet's and its gone rigid, grabbing the sides with its claws.

I can't see over the dashboard. I need another form of action. Mick's too strong. I bang my fist straight on the horn and hold it there as hard as I can.

My eyes are tight shut and tears are running down my face. This is my last cry for help.

'What's going on in there?' a man shouts and bangs on the back window.

Mick releases his grip and my head flings back. My hand finds the door handle and I fall out of the car into a deep, dry puddle. A large Alsatian dog sniffs in my direction and pulls on its choke chain.

'You alright?' the man asks, helping me up.

The long, maroon car spins out of the car park, kicking up dust and screeching out onto the main road.

'Yes, thank you.' I brush the tiny stones from my jeans.

I must get away quick in case Mick comes back.

Parking on the driveway at home, I rest my head on the steering wheel and sob. How did I get myself in this mess? I delete Mick's number, and any other dealers, from my phone. Best to do it now while I have the strength.

I feel dirty, ugly and soiled. No way I'm telling Mum what just happened. I pull the memory from my mind, place it in a heavy, secure box, and bury it somewhere deep and safe, where I'll never, ever find it again.

Christine

Lowering my weight onto the pristine cream cushion, the garden swing seat immediately sways into motion. Balancing a large glass of wine in one hand, I lift my feet until the movement subsides.

It's a beautiful evening, warm through and through. Even the breeze is warm.

Tony opens up the French doors and walks straight across the grass in his shoes. He smiles at me. He looks good in his work suit, tall and distinguished; I still fancy him after all these years. 'On the wine already?' he laughs.

'Yours is in the fridge.'

He turns back to the house. 'Bring the bottle!' I shout.

A moment later he's back, wine bottle and glass in hand.

'Is that Amber's mess in the kitchen? Looks like she's used every saucepan in the house to cook something.'

'I'll clean it up; just got in from work.'

'You shouldn't have to. It's time she was more independent – you've done enough. We both have. She doesn't have to continue to live here.'

'I can't allow her to rent a cheap room somewhere; those places are always full of addicts.'

'If I find one more fag butt shoved in my plant pots I'm going to kill her. It would be good for us if she moved out, good for our marriage.'

Until Amber stopped using heroin I didn't want her to leave home. Even now I want her to live close by, so I can keep an eye on her. I see it as the next stage in her recovery, like Care in the Community. I want things to get back to normal, no more tension between Tony and me; he wouldn't attack her and I wouldn't need to defend her.

'I could use some of my savings as a deposit and buy her a flat.'

'What, and get a mortgage?'

'I've got enough, so it should be okay.'

'Do it. I'll give you half if you like.'

I turn to face him. 'What, half of the deposit?'

'Yeah, and half of all the fees, you know, the solicitor's fee and the property survey. You deal with it – add it all up and then tell me what I owe you.'

'That would make it a lot easier.'

'Can she afford to pay you some rent?'

'If I look for a two-bedroom place, I could get a lodger in the other room.'

He leans across and places his hand over mine. 'Sure you won't worry?'

'I'll have a key, pop in sometimes. I could let go a bit.'

'And if she wants Leeanne to move in?'

'Well, no.'

'What about when Dave gets out of prison?'

'If she goes back to Dave she'll have to move out. We could always rent it.'

I search the internet for flats for sale. I find something good just around the corner.

The estate agent is waiting in his car when I arrive to view it.

Inside it smells of fresh paint. It has a finely grained wood floor in a lovely shade of beech; I wouldn't even have to buy carpet. The kitchen is new, just needs a fridge and a washing machine. Although it's only got one bedroom, it's perfect. 'Had a lot of interest?' I ask him.

'It's only just come on the market.'

I make an offer, and after a bit of wrangling they accept.

I ring Amber on her mobile. 'I've just bought you a flat!'

'You what?' she shouts. I can hear talking and loud music in the background; she must be in the pub.

'I just bought you a flat!'

'A flat? For me? Oh my God! I can't believe it!'

Within a month we set a completion date. I take a few days off work and help her move in. We buy some inexpensive but stylish furniture and some of the girls at work donate plates and cutlery. Soon Amber has everything she needs to live independently.

It is a risk. I am placing a large amount of trust in her. But I need to let go; I can't watch her forever. Tony is right when he says I have done enough.

Amber

'Coming to the pub?' Peter asks me; he's been staring at me all week.

Peter works on the nursery. He's only eighteen and has a plump face and the kindest smile. He's tall with a round belly; there's nothing skinny about him. But he's cute.

Fridays at work we finish at four, so everyone goes to the pub opposite. After a few weeks I start to tag along. They make really good baguettes with bacon, cheese and brown sauce.

Peter comes to the bar and tries to involve himself in my conversation. I know he fancies me and I like the attention, but I brush him off, turn my back to exclude him. He sits back down and folds his arms across his chest, sulking.

The weekend is looming, and I've nothing to do but sit in the flat on my own. I've no real friends and the reality of weeks without heroin has started to sink in. I need something else to help me face things. I've always found it hard to contain my emotions: most girls go to the loo and cry, I go to the loo and get stoned.

'Anyone get any green?' I ask one of the lads in the pub.

Peter butts in. 'I can get you some dope, Amber.'

'No you can't, Peter,' I dismiss him.

'I can. What do you want? An eighth? I'll get it now.'

I look at him and laugh. 'Alright then, Peter, go and get me an eighth, but I won't pay you until you bring it back.' He puts his pint down and is off on a mission. I turn around. 'He won't be back.'

In less than ten minutes, Peter's back with an eighth solid. He won't let me give him the money for it, so I buy a round with the tenner instead. I give Peter my number. He's more interesting now.

There's a party atmosphere in the bar. We're drinking pints and shots and before long we're all hammered. Normal closing time comes so we have a lock in. It's three in the morning when

I notice someone passed out on a wooden bench, as if they'd slid down sideways and stayed there, mouth open and one arm dangling over the edge.

I don't remember leaving the pub, but now I'm swinging all over the road with Peter coaxing me along. 'You can stay at mine,' he says.

Peter props me against the wall and then fiddles in his pocket for his key. He stops and, taking my wrists, one in each of his hands, slowly brings them together over my head. He kisses me tenderly and gently pushes me back, holding me firmly, not taking advantage, passionate.

For someone to want me so much is such a turn on. He's so warm and loving and yet so intense and lustful. I need to be desired like this, taken.

In the morning the light hurts my eyes so I shut them again. I realise I'm in a strange house. Peter is sleeping beside me with that same smile on his face. I've got such a hangover I have to leave.

When I get back to my car someone has written 'dirty stop out' on the dusty back window.

I go back to Mum's for some breakfast. The sun is shining and it's such a beautiful day that although I need to go to bed I want to stay outside. I lie down on the swinging seat in the back garden. Watching the dappled sunlight through the willow tree, the gentle motion rocks me back and forth until I fall asleep.

'Amber,' Mum shakes me hard.

The day is fading and it's starting to get dark. 'Amber, it's time to go home and get to bed, and your bloody phone's been ringing all day, someone called Peter.'

Christine

My eyes automatically glance to the left as I drive past Amber's flat. Slowing down, I see her car is parked there; why isn't she working? Maybe I'll pop in unannounced, see what she's up to. I concentrate on the road ahead. I might take the kids swimming after school. I don't have to worry about Amber all the time. I don't. She's probably just off sick with a cold.

I drive around the roundabout and go back, park on the road outside. Taking out my house keys, I shuffle through them, check I have Amber's front door key with me.

Weeds have grown up along the outside wall. There's a big fat one splitting through the tarmac. Doesn't she do anything? I thought she worked in horticulture?

Placing my key in the lock, I steel myself; whatever it is I'll deal with it.

Amber is stretched out on the sofa, legs spread wide. She's wearing old tracksuit bottoms and a half-smart top that's inside out. She doesn't even flinch. There's a slight smell of bonfire, tangy, pungent. The sound of cartoons is on in the background. The ashtray is brimming with fag ends.

'Day off today, is it?'

'Yeah… not feeling very well.'

'Dope the cure, is it?'

Amber shuffles up. 'Might be.'

I look around again and fold my arms. 'There's nothing wrong with you, you're just lazy. How're you going to manage if you don't go to work? You just do what you like and expect me to pay for it again! Don't you think it's time you grew up?' I glance at the TV screen. 'Bit old for cartoons, aren't you?'

A pile of plates is stacked up next to the sofa; empty packets of crisps and biscuits are jammed in between. 'Look at all this crap you've been eating.' I pick up the box from a cheesecake. 'Have you eaten the whole thing? You can't live on sugar.'

'I'm always hungry. Whatever I eat it's never enough.'

'Oh get over yourself, Amber, you're not a child.'

Her eyes are glazed and distant. 'Here she goes,' she says under her breath.

'What did you say?' I bark.

'Nothing... look, I don't think you understand, Mum. Reality has been harder to face than I thought. I struggle to cope.' Her lip trembles. 'The nursery let me go. I got a little bit of dope. What's so bad?'

'So I'm paying the bills again, but you've got money for dope? Where did you get it? From a drug dealer?'

'Peter gets it for me. I don't go anywhere near a dealer.'

I notice Peter's grubby shoes on the floor; his clothes are drying on the stand. 'He's eighteen and you're twenty-three. He's too young for you – I don't know why you're with him.'

'I need him around. He helps me do things.'

'Helps you do things? Like what?'

'Go to Tesco.'

'That's not hard, Amber.'

'Well, I'm finding it hard. I have a panic attack if there're too many people in there. They all stare at me.'

'You're being pathetic.'

'No, it's more than that. The walls close in and I'm dizzy. I can't breathe and I choke, then I have to sit down. It's like I can't face reality because I'm not high.'

'You're just replacing one habit with another.'

'Isn't it enough for now that I'm here and not doing gear?'

'Peter shouldn't be staying here every night, he doesn't live here.'

'I need some stability in my life with someone who doesn't use drugs, and Peter gives me that.'

'I don't understand why you can't put it all behind you.'

'Weed helps me cope with things. I've smoked it from such a young age I feel more normal stoned than not. It gives me back the old Amber. I can make decisions and stick to them; it doesn't matter that I've got no friends. It narrows everything down, makes my life simple.'

'But don't you see, Amber? You're living a half-life, accepting less, and all the time you're high you believe it's okay.'

I get back in my car and drive away. I'm tired of it all now. Tired of worrying about her, tired of trying to make her into something else, something she can never really be. I just have to wait and hope that one day it will all be alright. That one day she will grow out of it. Grow up.

I suppose it can't be rushed and I have to be patient. I sense there is a part of her that is still unreachable and essentially alone.

Twenty-Three

Christine

The red light on the answerphone is blinking. The indicator says I have one new message. Opening the tall cupboard in the study, I hang up my coat. The fading sun makes a last effort to shine through the slates in the venetian blind, casting half-shadows on the desk.

I haven't spoken to my mum in ages. I meant to call her yesterday; I expect she rang while I was out.

I press the play button.

Dave's slightly wheezy voice sounds in the room and a frisson of goose bumps cover my skin. I hadn't expected that – thought there would be a bit more time. He's always been there, a dark cloud in the background, waiting. His photo and letters are still under her bed. I delete the message. He'll have to ring back.

Early next morning the phone rings. I answer automatically, without thinking, but still Dave's the last person I expect it to be. 'Is Amber there?' He sounds relaxed, confident, as if he's unashamed of everything he's done.

I think about the humiliation, the social embarrassment and self-doubt he put me through. My body starts to shake. I

275

want to tell him what I think about the drug-taking, the fact that we had to go to court, that I felt like a criminal.

'You can leave a message.' My façade of emotional control is betrayed by a breathless, squeaking voice. He gives me a mobile number and I write it on a piece of paper.

For a moment I allow myself to believe that Amber doesn't want him back. That after all this time she has moved on. Can I trust her not to go back to him? No. Trust her not to lie to me? No. Will she expect me to be there for her when it all goes wrong? Yes.

But I want it out in the open so I can deal with it. I can't change her.

Amber

Inside the pub it stinks of stale cigarettes. The faded Axminster carpet is covered in fag burns and long, red velvet curtains hang at the windows. It's a drinking pub – they don't do food – but there's a pool table.

Peter's working nearby. He comes in straight after work, still in the same clothes, the smell of mud and the open air on them. He sees me come in and goes to the bar to get me half a lager.

My foot taps the leg of the table. Peter has this ability to stare into space with a stupid smile. It always annoys me.

'What are you thinking about, Peter?' I can hear the irritation creep into my voice.

'Nothing,' he says.

'That's impossible. You can't think about nothing.'

I'm always thinking about at least three or four things at a time, but Peter has a talent of just switching off like a computer on standby. I stare at him across the table; I think it makes him uncomfortable.

He sucks in his cheeks and tries to concentrate. 'Just going for a wiz,' he says and stands up.

I pick up a beer mat from the table flick it over in my hand. I lean forward to rest on my elbows. Some guys walk past me. I recognise one of them but can't remember his name. 'Alright Amber, mate. I hear Dave's out.'

What! My world shrinks.

Who else knows me in here? Who else knows Dave and knows I'm sitting in here with another bloke. Oh my God! Peter's gonna get it and that's so unfair!

'We need to go!' I bark when he returns.

He tries to finish his pint. 'What's the rush?'

'We just need to go!'

I'm shocked. Why wasn't I the first person to know Dave was out? I realise our relationship is damaged, yes, but when the judge sentenced him part of me thought I'd never see him on the outside again. I calculate in my head how long it's been; his release has come earlier than expected. Although I haven't sent Dave a letter or spoken to him, or Linda, for months, I still expected him to call me when he got out. Our relationship was shattered the night of the raid and never came to a natural end; prison meant everything was on hold until he came out again.

The last time I saw Dave I'd had the implant two months. He'd just been transferred to a different prison. I had to borrow the petrol money from Mum to visit him; I could tell she didn't want to give it to me, didn't want me to go.

I'd no idea where this prison was. I miscalculated the journey time and got completely lost. By the time I arrived I'd used more than half the petrol and I wasn't sure if I'd make it home.

When I finally found a space to park the car, the fan came on straight away and the engine was ticking.

Because I was so late the prison officers had taken Dave back to his cell. Only when I arrived did they fetch him back to the visiting room. I'd wasted an hour of a two-hour visit.

'You're late, princess,' Dave had said as he pulled back a chair to sit down.

Seeing him had made all my emotions bubble up. 'It's a long way to come on my own. I'd no idea where this place is. I'm not good with directions. I've driven past Stonehenge, was I supposed to?'

'Babe, you look like you're gonna cry, calm down.'

I relaxed back and caught my breath. Dave studied me for a moment. 'You look amazing. You've put on weight and everything, princess.'

Having only a limited time to be with him had made it very intense.

'The implant's working really well for me,' I'd told him.

'Yeah? That's great,' he'd said, holding my hand across the table.

'It might work for you, Dave – just to be sure.'

'Nah, don't need it.'

'You're clean now, but it's hard to stay clean on the outside.'

'Well…' he'd sucked his teeth as if to say *will I be clean?*

Dave had let go of my hand then. He'd leant back in his chair, tilting it on the two back legs. I could see in his eyes that we were not on the same level, not thinking the same thoughts, and a smirk had appeared on his face. 'I can live without the drugs, princess, but not the money.'

I'd known then that he was the same as the day we were raided. Mentally he was still right back there whereas I'd moved on. Without dealing gear he wasn't anybody special, he was just Dave, and maybe that wasn't enough for him.

The hour was up and our visit had ended abruptly.

Walking to my car, I'd stopped and looked back at the prison. It was a grey, square building, alien to the landscape as if it didn't belong, like a carcass in the middle of a field, unmaintained and rotting.

I'd thought about what Dave had said. I'd known then that he'd never stop dealing heroin, and he couldn't sell it without taking it himself. I couldn't live with him, watching him do it, and not do it too. The fear of knowing the police could break down my front door at any time would be immense. Mum's words had come me back to me then; she had known right from the start that he'd never stop. He'd proved her right.

But now Dave's out of prison my feelings for him have erupted. I want to see him, to share the deep love we have for each other. We went to bed one night and when I woke he was ripped away from me, as if he'd gone to war. I've pined for him, idolised him, and I need to see if our relationship is the same when we're sober. I'm desperate to believe Dave and I can still be together, although I'm not sure what the rest of the world will say.

Peter pulls at his grey Beanie hat, adjusting the sides down over his ears before we step out of the pub into the early evening chill and walk to my car.

Dave doesn't have my mobile number, doesn't know I've got the flat; how will he get in touch? I think for a moment; he might have phoned Mum's house.

Back home I evade Peter and ring Mum. 'Dave's out of prison. Has he phoned for me?'

'You didn't tell me he'd been released.'

'Only just found out.'

'He's left a mobile number. You'd better call him, tell him it's over; you're with Peter.'

I write the number down. 'I'm surprised you gave it to me, Mum.'

'I can't stop you seeing Dave by lying to you, hiding it from you. If you want to go back to him, you will. But think about it, Amber, you don't have to settle for Dave, or Peter – you can put the past behind you, find a man you can really love.'

I phone Dave straight away. My heart's racing.

'Alright?' I say excitedly when he answers, 'When did you get out?'

'Can't talk now,' he pauses. 'Let's catch up tomorrow, pick me up.'

Is his voice slightly cool? Did I imagine it? Maybe I should have made more effort to write to him.

When I pull into the parking bay outside his house, I beep the horn and then jump in my seat at the noise. Dave walks down the path with a cowboy swagger; his demeanour is the same, still sure of himself. He's wearing his usual baggy tracksuit bottoms and tee shirt and he's gained a surprising amount of body weight. My tummy flips; he always did have a way that gets to me.

Dave sits in the front and leans towards me. He smells faintly of aftershave. I've waited for him all this time, longed for him, and suddenly he's beside me. He draws me into his arms and we have a cuddle, then he takes my face in his hand, pulls it to him and kisses me hard on the lips.

It's the first time I've felt anything that has started to heal the trauma of the raid. The sun shines in through the windscreen, warm like a shot of morphine, and I'm happy. He's what I've longed for; it's a relief. I want him back.

'Let's go for a beer?' I say.

'Yeah, but out of town.'

I'm all jittery like it's a first date. I check my make-up and suck my stomach in.

The low lighting in the pub is soft and soothing. I find a table with a couple of big worn-out armchairs. Shafts of sunlight shine through the window, making the dust particles glitter in the air. Dave walks back to the table with the drinks; he passes me a glass of wine and as he does our hands touch.

'How long have you been home? How come you're out early?' I pile into him.

'It's all a bit of a shock, really,' he says. 'Got let out early for good behaviour providing I stay at me mum's. Course, gotta be in early, but at least I'm on the outside.'

'Why didn't you call me?'

Dave takes out another fag. He's chain smoking with a kind of desperation, dragging hard on the cigarette so that he smokes each one in three or four draws.

He gazes out through the window into the car park; his face is thoughtful. 'I've spent the last few days getting re-acquainted with my family.'

I want us to be alone, where we can talk more freely and have another cuddle. 'Why don't you come back to my flat? I've got a bit of weed.'

He smiles. 'Haven't had a joint in ages.'

In the flat I fill the kettle and switch it on while he walks in and out of the rooms, looking around and nodding his head. 'Nice place, yeah, shame I can't live in a place like this,' he says.

'Why don't you move in? We're both clean.' I pass him his tea.

'It's a bail condition, babe, gotta live at the family address for two years.'

This doesn't sound like the Dave I knew; he wouldn't have cared about his bail conditions.

I take out my Rizlas and start skinning up. I spark the joint and pass it to him.

'You still make a good joint.' He squeezes it between his fingers and winks at me.

Dave lounges on the sofa, stretching out his legs in front of him. He yawns, rests the joint in the ashtray and reaches across to me and kisses me. My lips linger on his; he still tastes the same, of tea and fags. It's the most natural thing in the world, being in his arms, but because it's been so long since we've been together it's exciting.

It's the first time in our relationship he has a hard on before I've even touched him. I can feel it rubbing against my leg. The thudding of his heart through his tee shirt makes me think of all the times we were too wrecked to make love. I like it now, all this enthusiasm.

We move into my bedroom. Pretty soon we're both naked. 'I'm not on the pill, don't want to be careless and get pregnant,' I say.

'Don't worry, I won't come inside you.'

My body is tingling and I'm starting to perspire when he withdraws. His breathing is heavy and his face has a pained expression. I can tell he hasn't had sex in a long time; he's like a teenage boy, all excited and then it's over. He yelps at the end, as if it hurts, then lets out a long, leisurely sigh.

Sex is not always about sex. This time for me is about wanting to know I'm still special to him and that he finds me attractive. I'm claiming back what's mine.

Now he's come he makes excuses to leave. 'I need to go home,' he says and pulls on his trackies. I sit up against the pillows, draw my knees towards me and hug them, contemplate why he's leaving. It's as if he can't get away fast enough.

Outside his house, Dave gets out of my car and rests his hand on the door frame. He bends in to look at me. 'You can give me back that money, you know, what you took from the house?'

'You're joking? Right? I needed it back then – you know what a state I was in.'

'Yeah, but you can pay me back a bit each week? You're working.'

'I don't have it.' In my head I think *he can't mean it.*

'I'll call you,' he says.

I finish with Peter. 'I love you, Peter, but I'm not *in* love with you.' He doesn't accept it, keeps clinging on.

'How can you say that, Amber?' His lip begins to quiver and I think he's going to stand there and cry. 'I love you.'

I have to be more and more horrible to him, to make him understand. 'Dave's out of prison, and I've slept with him.' I say it so he realises it really is over.

'I'll forgive you, if you say you're sorry.'

I shake my head. I don't want to hurt him, but I want to be with Dave. Peter will meet a sweet girl his own age; he'll be better off without me. We stand there for a moment, holding the silence between us.

'I'm not going to change my mind, Peter.'

He packs his few things into a couple of plastic carrier bags and leaves. He seems like a small boy walking out the door.

Everything is set now for Dave and me to be together.

I reach into my pocket and check my phone in case he's called. Nothing. Every time it rings I expect it to be him. I send him a text message saying I want to speak to him; he doesn't answer.

Sitting on the sofa alone in the flat, I hear the beeping of the pedestrian crossing. I glance out of the window to see a young mum holding the hand of a child as they cross the road. The world is moving on for everyone else and I'm here waiting for Dave. The memory of the smell of his skin, the feel his body on me, it's all fading away. I'm gagging to see him again.

It's been a whole week of waiting.

This isn't good enough for me. Whatever I thought we had together, whatever fantasy is going on in my head, he hasn't contacted me. Clearly I want him more than he wants me. If we're going to be together, it'll happen straight away.

I write him a letter, telling him it's his last chance to be with me. I shove it through his mum's letterbox. He doesn't reply.

After all we've been through, he can't even speak to me. I don't understand.

Maybe it's what I deserve. Why would he bother to contact me? My own father never did.

I start to spend time with Peter again. I don't explain it to him, why I want him back, and he doesn't ask. We settle into our life at the flat.

Aldershot town centre is busy with Saturday-afternoon shoppers. Peter insists on holding my hand. 'Let's get a film from Blockbuster and something special for tea,' he says.

I glance ahead, and in among the crowd of people notice Dave coming towards me. He's holding hands with a girl. Do I know her? Dave looks up and catches me staring at him.

I study the girl again and realise who she is. I'm stunned to see it's Katie, the church girl. She gazes up at Dave, then looks ahead at what he's seen. Her smiling face clouds over and she touches his arm to gain his attention, whispers something in his ear. They start laughing, change direction and head off down a side street. I sense they're laughing at my expense.

They've betrayed me. Katie pretended to be my friend. I want to storm up there and smack that smile right off her face.

What Dave's done isn't dissimilar to what I've done with Ian and Peter. But I didn't love Ian or Peter. Dave must love Katie; why else would he be with her?

It would have been easy for him to write me a letter explaining he didn't feel the same way about me and that he was in love with someone else. It's as if he's done it like this to hurt me the most. I realise what a stupid twat I am. He used me – Katie doesn't believe in sex before marriage.

But I suppose it's easier this way.

Peter pulls at my hand and draws me into Blockbuster. I'm jumpy and agitated, and although I'm glad Peter hasn't noticed it makes me feel even more isolated and alone. I can't tell Mum about this, can't share these feelings with her. I need Leeanne; she'd know the right thing to say to comfort me.

I've always identified myself as Dave's girlfriend. Who am I now? Finally I've woken up from the spell. Now I need to come back to me, to find a different life, something to define *me*. To start with, I need a proper job.

Finding a spot close to the Job Centre, I park the car and scan down the road. I'm never sure who'll be hanging around outside; drug addicts are always out of work.

I step onto the path and lock the car, and notice someone on the pavement with their face tucked under a hoodie. I'm too close to go back now.

Addicts were always so nice and respectful when I was with Dave, wanting to be my best buddy because I was living with a dealer. On my day off from work, Dave would give me cash to go shopping, maybe two hundred pounds, just to blow on clothes.

Walking around Aldershot looking in the shops, I'd often bump into one of Dave's regulars; they could never do enough for me. I'd send them up to McDonald's to get me a Coke. I'd revelled in the attention then, but, since the raid, I know how desperate addicts are. After a while heroin is in your body at a cellular level.

Addicts treat me differently now. They always want something from me – a lift somewhere, a fag, or to borrow my phone. If I give them something, anything, they'll constantly push to see how much more they can get. It's best to let them believe I have exactly what they have: nothing.

The guy on the path is Nick, one of Dave's old dealers. Putting a shaky hand up to his mouth to cover his missing teeth, he shouts 'Oi, Amber! Dave Jenkins' engaged, ain't he?'

'Yeah,' I nod in his direction as if I already know, but I didn't know.

The news that Dave and Katie are getting married hurts me more than seeing them together. How is it so easy for him to find someone else to love? The way he was supposed to love me once. All the things he said to me, they were all lies.

Nick's chin is covered in stubble and he smells of stale alcohol. 'When's the wedding, then?' he asks.

I smile and push open the metal-framed door to the Job Centre.

'How'd he fuckin' get away with it?' Nick shakes his head in disbelief. 'Marrying a church girl?'

The early evening sky is bathed in pink with the promise of a sunny tomorrow. Mum and Tony are in the garden when I pop round. Mum pulls off her gardening gloves and walks along the path to meet me. 'Didn't expect to see you,' she says.

'I'm fed up. I've got nothing in my life, Mum, did nothing at school, got no qualifications.'

'What's brought this on?' she chuckles.

'I need to put some distance between me and the drugs. I want to prove that for once in my life I can do something.'

'Giving up a habit like yours is huge; it certainly counts as something.'

'I want to start again, from the beginning, go back to college and finish the course I started after school. The way I feel about myself has to change.'

'Okay, how would you do that?'

'Study the NVQ in horticulture part-time and work the other days. Will you help me?'

'Course I'll help you, I'm your mother.'

'I'd like another implant, Mum, just to be sure.'

Recently, when I was with Dave, even though we didn't do gear or talk about gear, it was in the room with us.

'That was always the plan, Amber. I'll get the day off work and come with you.'

'No, Peter said he'd take me. We're gonna do some shopping in London.'

Mum studies me thoughtfully. Does she believe I'd lie to her? That I have some clever plan?

Mum does truly love me, she always has; thinking otherwise was just a neurotic fear that I had as a child, my 'nobody loves me and I'm going to sit at the bottom of the garden and eat worms' attitude. I created it myself, blown it all out of proportion.

It's over and I feel a sense of completion, like I'm filling in the last piece of a puzzle, the one that for a long time has been lost. 'Look, Mum, you really don't need to worry,' I laugh.

'What's funny?'

'Hearing myself say it, I know that this time I mean it.'

Spots of rain appear from a colourless sky as Peter and I walk from the tube station to the Stapleford Clinic. The weather's warm and the pavement is crowded with people. I take off my jacket as we stroll along, make Peter carry it.

'You look so well, Amber. You've done great these past months,' Anthony says.

'Yeah,' I relax back in the chair. 'I feel I'm over my addiction. Would you ring my mum, tell her I'm here, don't want her to worry.'

I wait while he dials her work number and asks for her.

'Hi Mrs Lewry, it's Anthony from the Stapleford Clinic. Just wanted to let you know Amber's about to go for her second implant. I think she's made an excellent recovery. You must be very proud.'

Peter's hand feels safe and reassuring as we watch for a break in the traffic and cross the road.

The skinny doctor recognises me. 'Hello again,' he says, closing his eyes and nodding his head. I'm not sure if he has many clients who come back.

I'm shaking but it doesn't hurt as much the second time.

On the way back to the station I notice a large Waterstones bookstore. The shop front is a huge expanse of window with two big double doors. The floor is made of gleaming white tiles. Each wall is lined with cedar wood bookcases, filled top to bottom. My eyes identify each individual book and I'm attracted to all of them. I settle for a book about horticulture.

Sitting on the train I watch the scenery speeding by, notice a cobweb in the top corner of the window, undulating with a gentle breeze I can't feel. I lean back in my seat and take my book out of the carrier bag. Turning it over in my hand, it feels warm. It feels how I want to feel; full of knowledge, full of the future.

The time I've spent staying in bed smoking dope I've been hibernating, recuperating and gaining strength. I'm weak socially, but being away from other drug users has made me resilient. It's allowed my mind and body to heal and mend. As if the winter is over, I've come out stronger now. I'm on my own. I have the choice of what to do with my life.

I'm going to stay clean. I'm going to be the woman I can be.

Part Five

The Price

Twenty-Four

One year later

Amber

My fingers tap the steering wheel until I spot a space in the early morning traffic and join the line of commuting cars. The sun hangs low in the sky; it glints at me and stings the back of my eyes, making me realise I've forgotten my sunglasses.

I glance at my watch. I need to hurry or I'll be late again; I'm supposed to be at work for eight and it's already quarter to. I light a fag, balancing it in the corner of my mouth while winding the window down to let the smoke out. The ash drops, then my phone rings. If I lean over to answer it I might set my hair on fire.

The phone stops ringing and then immediately starts to ring again.

A strange feeling reaches into my gut, a sort of emptiness – thoughts of being late are gone. I flick the fag, half smoked, out of the window and pull over. I drive a little way into a car park and pull the handbrake on. I catch the call on the last ring; the number on the screen is one I don't recognise. 'Hello?' I wait for the person on the line to speak.

'Amber, you've got to come to the hospital.' I know the voice straight away. It's Jo, an old school friend who is a nurse. I trust her completely that this is not a prank.

'Why? What's happened?'

'Stephen Jones was admitted to A&E last night.'

My concern drops away. In the time I've known Stephen he's overdosed at least fifteen times; I guess this was just one more. 'And?'

'Well, Amber, he was stabbed! The doctors here tried to save him, but they've pronounced him dead. Can't talk, I'm working. I think you'd better get here.'

I hear the click of the phone as she hangs up, gaze at the low branches of the tree I've parked under. I don't feel emotional or cry – I find it hard to believe. Is it really Stephen? Or has there been a mistake? Memories of Stephen, Leeanne and me shuffle through my mind, the three of us together in the park, times spent at their house. Leeanne will be devastated by her brother's death. Maybe she's still at the hospital?

The automatic doors of the A&E department open to the sound of squashing rubber. Stepping on the mat, I scan the waiting room for someone I recognise. Jo is hanging around at the reception desk. She greets me with a sad smile and shows me to the relatives' room. 'Is Leeanne here?' I ask.

Jo shuts the door. 'You've missed her, the family have all left. She was here, she's in a bad way.'

I sink into a brightly patterned armchair. The antiseptic smell of the hospital is making it seem real now. I feel dizzy and my hands grip the edges of the seat.

'Why, Jo? Why couldn't they save him?'

'Multiple stab wounds to his chest. He lost so much blood, he was dead really before the ambulance got here.' She sits down beside me and softly rests her hand on my arm. 'He was strong though, always was a fighter.'

I look into her gentle face. 'I always thought he'd die of an overdose. It's so unfair that this should happen now when he's been clean for so long.'

'I'm due a break. Let's go outside for a smoke,' Jo says.

Outside the air is crisp, refreshing, almost sharp; there's a large ashtray attached to the wall and it's overflowing with cigarette ends. Jo is not that childish schoolgirl any more; she's professional in her nurse's uniform, her long hair tied behind her head. After a few minutes she says 'I've got to get back to work.'

My journey home is in slow motion yet takes no time. Although the flat is exactly as I left it, everything has changed. I get stoned on a couple of joints; it helps me to be emotionally detached. I think about phoning my boss to tell him why I'm not at work, but I don't. I feel serene.

Leeanne's house is dark and completely still when I arrive. I walk up the short driveway and knock, standing on her doorstep while the moments tick by, not wanting to leave.

After a while I feel in my pocket for my car keys and go.

I sit in the flat all the next day, listening to the monotonous sound of the TV. The six o'clock news jolts me from a kind of stupor; I have to go back to see Leeanne.

This time there are lots of cars outside: some I recognise as belonging to members of her family and two police cars. Leeanne's aunt opens the door. She stares straight through me for a moment with motionless eyes and then comes to life. 'Oh yeah, it's you, come in then,' she steps back to let me pass. She knows why I'm here.

The family are all leaning against the kitchen worktops. They turn to stare at me.

'Hiya,' I say, 'heard what happened to Stephen. I'm so sorry.' But I can hear how lame it sounds.

I take an empty slot against the wall. They all have fags on the go. The room is filled with blue smoke; it settles in a haze around the light.

Leeanne's not there. I know if she's still upset with me I'll take it with a numbness that tells me I deserve it.

'Cup of tea, Amber?' someone asks as they fill the kettle and plug it in.

'Yeah, thanks.' I place my bag on the kitchen unit. There's a massive amount of sadness in the room. It's thick and heavy as if it has form.

'You look well. Not seen you in a long time. Where've you been?' Leeanne's mum, Rose, asks me. Her eyes are swollen and her face is tight.

'Came round yesterday, Rose. No-one was home.'

'No, at the police station, weren't we?'

'How's Leeanne?'

'Well, she's in a bad way. Whatever made you two start that bloody stuff I'll never know,' Rose shakes her head.

Others in the kitchen nod in agreement and mutter, whispering so I can't hear. I know the family partly blame me for Leeanne's addiction.

'Where is she?' I ask.

'Police are in the other room taking a statement from her. They reckon she knows that junkie who stabbed our Stephen.'

A tense silence settles on us; everyone stares at the floor for a few moments.

'I hear you've given up the gear now, Amber?' Leeanne's aunt asks. 'Is that right?'

'Yeah, I'm clean.' The tension in the room is making me feel sick. I hope one of them doesn't start on me.

A dark blue uniform appears from the sitting room. 'Alright if I get a drink of water?' he asks Rose.

This is my opportunity. I pop my head round the door. My eyes go straight to where I know Leeanne will be sitting. Her bare feet are tucked up beside her on the armchair. She glares at me – an angry look, full of suffering.

'I've gotta go now; do you want me to come back?'

Her face softens. She's almost tearful as she says 'Yeah.'

'I'll wait a couple of hours, let this lot finish.' I check my phone; it's coming up for eight o'clock. 'About ten, then?'

Leeanne raises her chin and tilts her head to one side. She's weak, wide open to the pain she's in. 'On the dot?' she asks hesitantly.

'Yeah, on the dot.' I leave, straight out the door, a collective goodbye to those standing in the kitchen. 'See you later,' and I'm gone.

It's nearly ten when I go back. The police and most of the relatives have gone.

Leeanne opens the door. Her face has more colour now. I sink into the sofa. Rose brings another chair from the kitchen, her fragile frame struggling with the weight. She opens a bottle of wine, pours me a glass and puts the bottle on the floor by her feet. Rose wants to talk about Stephen, to go over the details of his death. She's devastated. Angry.

'What was he doing there?' Rose shakes her head. 'Why would anybody stab our Steve?'

'I hope they catch the bastard that did it,' I say.

'Well, they know who he is, just gotta find him,' Rose replies.

It's getting late now and the exhaustion sweeps over me. 'I'll get off then,' I say, leaning down to pick up my bag.

Leeanne raises herself out of her chair. 'I'll jump in the car,' she says, 'for the ride.' She slips her feet into some shoes and takes a random jacket from a pile jammed onto hooks by the front door.

In the car she leans towards me. 'Got any money? Got a phone?'

'Yeah,' I reach into the door pocket and chuck her my phone.

She calls a dealer; like a takeaway service, you order what you want. The dealer answers but then says nothing. You state who you are and make sure they remember you.

'Alright, mate? It's Leeanne.' She looks across at me and whispers, 'What do we want?' She knows I'm paying.

'What can you get?'

'White and dark.'

'Okay, get a bit of both.'

She shuffles in her seat, sits up taller. 'How much?'

'We'll have two white and four dark.' Ten pounds each: sixty quid.

The dark is for her, the heroin she'll need for tonight and in the morning. Like alcohol, in the evening you can cane the arse out of it, but in the morning you only need a tickle to keep you going.

Leeanne tells me where to meet the dealer. I wait in the car, watching from a dimly lit side street while she stands in the road scanning up and down until a large figure appears from the darkness. She's so defenceless, scoring drugs on a street corner. She pays him the cash and puts a packet in her pocket.

Leeanne knows I'm clean and that I've had the implant; she's heard it from other addicts. Like a community, they talk about each other, who's taking what, whose dealing or clean. We do the crack in the car. I don't really like crack since that time with Mick, but I still have the addict mentality – if she's doing drugs, I'm doing drugs. There's one rock of crack so we share it; hers is bigger than mine, I'm not fussed.

I shiver. Don't want to let go of her. 'Come back to the flat for a bit?' I reach across and place my hand over hers. 'You've never seen my flat.'

Leeanne hesitates. 'Okay, but I'll need to ring Mum, tell her where I am.' She makes the call then passes me back the phone. 'She wants to speak to you.'

'Don't you let her out of your sight, Amber, will you? She's really staying with you? You're not lying for her?' Her voice cracks with emotion.

'She's with me, Rose, and I've bought her some gear. She's staying at mine. You get some rest tonight and we'll see you tomorrow. I'm gonna take care of her.'

The lights are on at the flat when we pull up. It's late but Peter's still waiting up for me. Leeanne wanders around checking out all the rooms; the stainless steel and black kitchen, wood floors and sunken lighting.

She smiles. 'Your mum buy this for you.' It isn't a question, more of a joke, a laugh at me.

'Sorry about your brother,' Peter says. His eyes don't settle on her face but shift around the room. 'I'll make us a cup of tea,' he says and heads for the kitchen.

Leeanne and I sit on the sofa and stare at the TV. We're both pranged after the crack; I need a joint to relax me and bring me back down. I get out the rest of my dope and start skinning up. She needs to do the gear I've bought her, but I don't know where.

It's okay that Peter knows what she's doing, but he's not going to be anywhere near it. If he says 'Let's try it, give us a line,' as much as I protest, I couldn't stop him. It would be so cruel, so wrong. I couldn't live with the guilt. I'm protecting myself. There's no way she's going to smoke it in front of him.

I hand her a roll of foil. 'Use the bathroom. Just need a wee first.'

Walking down the hallway, I go over in my mind all the things of value I have in there. There's not much that's worth anything now, but I don't want to lose what I have. I put my watch, a necklace and some earrings in my pocket, then open a drawer in my bedroom and hide them under some knickers.

Leeanne's in the bathroom an hour or so. She knows I've gone in there first to remove my stuff. She knows because our minds work in the same way; she understands what I'm thinking, as I understand her. To an addict it's common sense: you feel vulnerable, you don't want to think of your friend as a thief, but you really don't want to lose those things.

Peter finds some cushions and a blanket, arranging them on the floor of my small bedroom. He doesn't flap or moan but, like a child, he doesn't want to be left to sleep on the sofa alone; he's a gentleman, a good lad. Leeanne wears her knickers and an old tee shirt of mine and we share the double bed. She draws her knees towards her chin, curls up like a baby in the womb. Her body shudders and she takes a long, slow breath and falls asleep. For the first time since Stephen died I cry a little.

I stay semi-conscious the rest of the night. I listen for every noise, whether it's to hear Leeanne sob or to hear if she's getting up, if she might be stealing from me or phoning some dealer to come and pick her up. Just alert, just slightly watchful, but she doesn't move all night.

I get up when Peter goes to work. Leeanne sleeps in for hours. I hold a silent vigil, checking on her every now and then, watching quietly from the doorway. I make a cup of tea and sit on the sofa; holding the warm mug in my hand, I stare out of the window, try to come to terms with what's happened, the enormity of Stephen's death.

Leeanne and I stay in the flat. She does a little gear and I smoke dope. We don't get washed or dressed but watch TV all day.

I've seen her look bad before, after a binge or if she's had trouble banging up, but not like this. Her skin is grey as if her face is covered in a fine layer of soot. She's so skinny and her luscious B-cups are gone, and her hair is unmanaged and tied back.

'Aren't you meant to be at work?' she asks me.

'Yeah,' I say, 'but so what?'

'Does your mum know?'

'Nope.'

'She's gonna kill you, Amber.'

'Yep.'

Peter comes home with a bottle of Bacardi. We pour ourselves a large tumbler each. 'Coke?' I offer.

'Just a splash,' Leeanne replies.

I lay the table and Peter brings in the meal. Leeanne doesn't touch the food, not one chip. She just drinks large Bacardis with not much Coke in. Her addiction to heroin is so strong the alcohol has no affect.

'I'm tired, Amber, I'm going to bed,' Peter says and pushes back his chair. He collects up his cushions and blanket and disappears into the bedroom.

Now the cushions are gone from one sofa, Leeanne and I

squash up together on the other. 'You know those arguments? The shit that's gone on between us?' I'm always the emotional one who starts these conversations. 'If I did anything to hurt you, you know I didn't mean it, don't you?' I pick up the bottle of Bacardi and pour what's left into her glass.

With everything we're going through it all seems so insignificant. Like brothers and sisters who squabble and fight, when something bad happens, we know we're on the same side.

We're quiet but for the occasional passing car outside the window, the headlights dancing around the room as it disappears up the road.

'I never told you I saw Dave the day he got out of prison,' she says.

'Really?' I choke.

She laughs. 'Yeah, walking up the high street in Aldershot, swinging his little prison bag, big smile on his face. I stopped to chat, made out I was pleased to see him. Told him what you'd been up to while he was inside, all the blokes you'd been out with. Took me so long he bought me a coffee.'

'When were you going to tell me?'

'Well, I'm telling you now. I was never gonna let him have you back.'

In the shadow of Stephen's death it means nothing. Part of me is cross that she did something to control my life. But she didn't do it to spite me; she could see the danger like Mum could, knew how it would turn out if I went back to him. She did it for my own good. It was always *you and me against the world.*

Christine

The knock on the front door startles me. I open it to see Peter standing there. 'Hi Peter, everything alright?' He's never been to the house without Amber before.

'I wanted to tell you.'

'Tell me? Tell me what?'

He peers down the road nervously. 'Do you want to come in?' I open the door wider.

'No, can't stop… I think they're doing drugs together.'

'Who? Amber?'

'Yeah, Amber and Leeanne, I think they're doing it together.'

'Okay, Peter, is she working?'

'She hasn't been for weeks. They're at the flat all day. I've only told you 'cause I love her. You're the only one that can stop it.'

'Thank you Peter,' I say. 'I'll take it from here.'

Twenty-Five

Christine

A yellow leaf is trapped under the windscreen wiper. It flutters for a few moments before a gust of wind takes it high into the air. Although paying attention to the traffic, I'm lulled into a feeling where there's no sense of time, only a journey. Amber sits beside me in the car. Being together reconnects us in a way that's been lost recently; I have hardly seen her.

I'm not sure of her mental state, how well she is coping with Stephen's death. I don't want to come straight out and accuse her of taking drugs, say something hateful I might regret.

Amber spreads her hand across her forehead and rubs her temples.

'You seem tired,' I tell her.

'Yeah, I've had more than a few shitty, restless nights since Stephen died.'

'Any news from the police?'

'Turns out he got into an argument with a junkie and the guy pulled a knife. Stephen didn't stand a chance. They've arrested the bloke, charged him with murder, but it'll be a while before the case goes to court.'

'Was Stephen an addict?'

'He was, but he got himself clean before he died. He'd been well for over a year.'

'How's Leeanne?'

'Pretty bad.'

'You spending much time with her?'

Amber looks across at me and narrows her eyes. She studies my face for clues as to what I'm about to say, as if she's being enticed into a trap she wants to be ready for. 'Yeah, quite a lot.'

'You can't fix her up and make it alright; it's too late for that.'

I think she's about to say something and then she changes her mind, turns again to stare at the cars passing on the inside lane.

Amber rests the side of her face against the windowpane. 'Leeanne rings me all the time, says she needs to be with me. But when I pick her up and we're together she fidgets the whole time and I can't settle her. I love her so much and want to help her, but nothing I do is ever enough. I still get pissed off with her. She constantly wants to talk about Stephen's death and go over the details time and time again. I'm heartbroken he's gone, but it won't bring him back. Sometimes I feel like shouting "Shut the fuck up!" No matter how much I want to, it's hard to solve someone else's problems. After a while my self-preservation kicks in.'

Amber sighs. 'And then there's Peter. He nags me that I'm spending too much time with her. He's driving me mad; he's worried she'll get me back on the gear.'

'Will she?'

Amber's silent for a moment. 'Don't be silly.'

'Peter thinks she will. He's been round to see me. Says you two are doing drugs together.'

'Her brother's just died. I'm not about to turn her away.'

'Don't be naïve. The more time you spend together the more likely you are to start using heroin again.'

'I'm not about to give up what we've done. I'm not that stupid.'

'But you are. You'll trick yourself into believing you can handle it this time, that it'll be different, that it wasn't that bad!'

'I won't.'

'I can't survive it all again. I can't do it.' I promised myself I would stay calm but the thought of it all just makes me so emotional.

'If it wasn't for Leeanne, I wouldn't be clean now.'

'Don't give me that! It was me Amber! Me who saved you! Me who stood by you, paid for you! And it was Leeanne you took drugs with!'

'Yeah, well it was her that broke into our bedsit – that's why the police started watching us and we got raided. Think I'd be clean now if they hadn't? And it was her that saw Dave the day he got out of jail, told him about the other blokes I'd slept with! Ever wonder why I'm not with him? Leeanne loves me and I love her. She'd give up her life for me.'

'You're being dramatic and over-emotional as usual.'

I pull up outside the flat and Amber gets out of the car. She gives me a cold stare and slams the door.

I can't dismiss my worries. I can watch her, try to control her, turn up at the flat unannounced. But I won't be able to stop her.

My sense of apprehension grows. How can I stop the future that I fear from happening? Change the sequence of events that I see unfolding?

Driving home from work, I notice the trees are starting to turn the deep reds and oranges of autumn. The leaves have already settled into drifting piles on the edges of the road. I use the time to think, to try and make sense of what's happening, without crying.

I helped Amber – I could help Leeanne. I know where the family live. I could go to the house, offer to help her get clean, then pay for the naltrexone implant. I go over the plan in my head. Think about what I'll say.

The trees become sparse and shops and houses start to appear. The road opens out. Coming down the hill into the town, I am close to where Leeanne lives. I could pop round. There's no reason why I can't go there now. But the pressure of my foot on the accelerator doesn't change. The speed still reads thirty miles an hour. The moment passes and my intentions are paralysed. I drive on.

It's a shout across a large expanse, a cry in the dark. I want it to be loud but can't manage a whimper. I'm afraid. Afraid that, even if I could save Leeanne this time, together they would eventually be drawn back to heroin.

Maybe Leeanne doesn't want to get clean? I can tell myself that but I won't ever know because I don't give her the opportunity to try. I'm too busy protecting what Amber and I have achieved.

I want to believe it will be okay for Leeanne one day, but I haven't got the courage to reach out my hand and help her. Where's my connection to God now?

I like to think I'm this good person, but really, I'm not.

Later, I think about the future, Amber's future, and I can't see Leeanne there; like the photo in *Back to the Future* where the people fade away.

Amber

Leeanne opens the fridge and takes out a chocolate gateau. It's dry and the topping is cracked like it's been in there for weeks, and it has bits missing as if a mouse has nibbled it. She picks at it around the edges with a fork and then puts it back.

Leeanne rents a room from a guy called Chris. He's an old friend of hers. We're here to get her some clean clothes and spend the evening without Peter.

Sitting cross-legged on her bed, I watch her take out her gear. She's been smoking so much the room stinks of it. Over the last few weeks, I've seen her do it so often I've resisted the urge. It's surreal, like I'm watching me from outside my body. My willpower is fragile at the best of times, but my resolve is always weaker in the evening.

I feel a dread and a revulsion for what I'm about to do, but there's a stronger feeling, an unutterable longing. I crack.

'Give us a line,' I say.

She gives me a funny look. 'You what?'

It's one of the rules of our friendship that we don't control each other, don't judge. Her head is down, concentrating on her boot, and although she doesn't move her eyes stare up at me through mascara-covered lashes. She picks up the foil and the lighter and passes them to me.

The adrenaline rush explodes through me. I start to sweat.

Putting the foil tube to my lips makes me retch. My mind has forgotten how bad this is for me, but my body remembers.

Every single cell is rejecting it, shouting *haven't we just got rid of this poison?* When I was clucking my whole body cried out for heroin; now it's completely the opposite. It's like asking me to eat a spoonful of someone else's sick.

I put my foot down, pull myself together, make myself do it.

I inhale the slightest wisp, a whiff.

The acid sick burns my stomach as it comes up the back of my throat. I drop the gear and the tube and run outside. Instantly, hot bile spurts out of my mouth, stinging my tongue. My eyes are streaming and my nose is running. I need both hands to steady me, pushing against the wall as I jerk in a spasm.

'Silly cow,' Leeanne laughs, 'what's the point in that?'

'Not feeling too good now, gonna get off home,' I tell her.

Like a magnetic pull, I'm being drawn in closer each day. I need to get back to the safety of the flat. Spend more time with Mum. She steadies me, brings me back.

My bedroom is washed in a soft grey glow. Shadows flicker with the changing pictures on the TV screen. Peter's eyes are closed and his breathing is deep and shallow. I take a draw on my joint and blow the smoke in the direction of the open window.

The calm half-silence is interrupted by my mobile ringing. I check the phone on my bedside table. It's Leeanne. I haven't spoken to her for three days.

I think about answering it; I've never in my life not answered her call before.

Peter wakes and, leaning right over me, grabs the phone. When he sees Leeanne's name on the screen he won't give it back.

'No, don't… leave it, she'll be alright tonight,' he says.

Why didn't I answer? I'm stoned, but I let him stop me. I feel empty. I smoke another joint and it takes everything away, any bad emotions, guilt.

Opening my eyes in the morning, I know I'm going to go to

see Leeanne. I'm still concerned after her call. I pull back the curtain, look through the bedroom window to see what the weather's like. It's a sunny day but cold, so I'd better take a jacket.

My phone rings; it's Gav.

Gav is a big, burly bloke but inside he's a sweet boy. He smokes dope sometimes with Leeanne and me. He's always glad of a bit of girly attention and, like a puppy dog, he's eager to please. He lives in the same block of flats as Leeanne and is mates with her landlord, Chris. A few days ago I gave Gav my number, asked him to call me if Leeanne was in any trouble.

'Hi Gav, how's it going?'

'Amber, can you come to the flat?' he sounds calm.

'Yeah, yeah, I'm on my way.'

'What, now? You're on your way now?'

'Yep, leaving now.'

But I don't rush. I put on some make-up. Studying my reflection in the mirror, I wonder why Gav phoned me. Probably because I haven't seen Leeanne recently. Maybe she's in a mess.

I take a slow drive to the flat. Reaching the road where Leeanne lives, I see an ambulance parked up on the kerb. I let out a breath, relax back into my seat. It's okay, can't be that bad, they haven't even left for the hospital yet. There's a police car in the car park.

I pick up my bag and jacket from the seat, stroll along the path to her door. There's a uniformed policeman standing there. Although the door is open he's blocking the entrance. He stops me. 'Sorry love, you're not allowed in, this is a crime scene.'

I walk away – I'm not too bothered. I have a bit of dope on me, don't want to make a fuss. I sit on some steps where I can see the doorway, spark a fag, take a long draw and I wait.

The clouds build up and the sun goes in; the atmosphere feels heavy but it doesn't rain. The concrete step feels cold through my trousers.

Gav and Chris come out of the flat. Their faces appear to be wet and their eyes are red. Have they been crying? Two policemen are with them. They haven't cuffed them and it doesn't look like they're being arrested. Maybe the police have found Leeanne's drugs in the flat.

Reaching out his large hand, Gav tries to touch me. The look on his face is one of pure agony. It's as if he's trying to escape the grip of the police and be with me in his mind. The policeman moves him on; the moment broken, Gav turns away, stunned.

A cold eddy slips through me. What does that look mean? The thought that something terrible has happened pops into my mind. I dismiss it.

Rose arrives with Leeanne's sisters, Claire and Tanya. They don't bother to park, just abandon the car and pile out. Rose walks over to me; her face is white.

'What's going on, then?' she asks.

'Don't know, Rose. They won't let me in.'

Rose stares past me to the doorway; the policeman is still blocking the entrance. Her face pinches slightly and she strides over.

I follow. If she's going in, so am I.

'Out of my way, I need to come in and find out what's happened,' Rose says.

'Sorry madam,' the policeman replies, 'no-one's coming in…'

Rose butts in. 'You don't understand, that's my daughter in there.'

'No,' he puts his hand up to stop her going any further. 'She's gone.'

'What do you mean she's gone? Don't be so stupid. What, has she climbed out the window or something?'

That's perfect. Leeanne has overdosed, the ambulance crew have revived her, fixed her up, and now she can't face us all and she's done a runner out of the window.

'No,' he raises his hand, again stilling her. 'She's dead.'

I reel as if someone's punched me in the face. It's a physical pain that winds me. I can hear a loud buzzing in my head and my vision blurs. Even in that confused split second time stops, and in those first moments I know there will never be another day like this one. I doubt I'm really living and expect to wake at any time.

Rose lets out a long scream, a primal sound that seems to come from deep within her. She's hysterical, crying and shouting 'No! No!' Her body starts to shake and wretch. She drops to the ground on her knees.

I'm cold and shivering. My mind has to let the thought in now, the truth that my Leeanne is dead. In all my nightmares I never let her die. I knew her addiction and depression were spiralling out of control, but among all the ways I thought it might end, I never believed she would die. I wish I'd answered her call. She needed me last night and I should have gone to her.

Slowly, we leave, go back to Rose's house.

I ring Mum. 'You don't need to worry any more; she's dead.'

'Dead! What, Leeanne? How?'

'She died of an overdose last night. I've lost her!' I cry down the phone. Despair and disbelief fill every cell in my body.

I stare into space, draw my knees up to my chin, wrap my arms around my shoulders and rock back and forth.

A doctor comes to the house to sedate Rose.

Leeanne's death happened so fast, as if I was going on a long journey and I lost my concentration for a moment, missed a turning. Now I'm past it and I can't turn back.

All the time her body is at the flat I want to be as close to her as possible. It feels like it isn't true unless I see them bring her body out.

A black van is parked in the car park that has 'Coroner' written down the side. The area in front of Leeanne's door has been cordoned off with bright yellow tape. I sit on the same concrete step where I sat before.

Two police officers wheel out a trolley with an orange bag on it. Why was it orange? Not black? It's stretched where her bottom and her knees are. She must have died curled up in the foetal position, the same way she lay with me the first night after Stephen died. While we were grieving for Steve, the idea that Leeanne might take her own life, that she might die, was so terrible it was too much to be held in one mind. She's a young woman my age; why wouldn't she always be there? I know she's overdosed before but addicts do – it's a hazard they all face.

My earliest memories are of feeling alone, even if I was with other people, of the nothingness that came on before school in the morning and at the end of the day in the shadows and twilight. But when I was with Leeanne somehow I wasn't alone, and the gnawing emptiness didn't come.

A few days later, I receive a message from Dave. *I heard about Leeanne, are you okay?* What, am I more interesting now? Or does he want to be there for me? I'm surprised he still has my number.

Easy for him to send me a text. Later he'll be able to

convince himself he was there for me when she died. My anger is naked and full of venom. I'm furious.

I bombard him with abusive messages, calling him cowardly and gutless. I want to rip into him in any way I can. I know what he did to her. I hate him. I never belonged with him – that was not my destiny.

The days cloud together, lost in tears.

Twenty-Six

Christine

I slump down beside Tony on the sofa and lean back into the plump cushions. He points the remote at the TV and mutes the sound. 'How did the funeral go?'

'Oh, not so good.' Now Leeanne is gone I feel guilty for the things I said, the things I thought.

'Leeanne's mum?'

'Poor love, I feel so bad for her. There's nothing anyone can do to heal the pain of losing her daughter or bring her back.'

'Losing her son, too, how do you cope with that?'

'I don't know,' I shake my head. 'I just don't know.'

'Where's Amber? Did she stay for a bit or go back to the flat?'

'She stayed.'

'Do you think she's faced it? Leeanne's death?'

'She's put it to one side. It's too difficult to deal with. One day, perhaps, but not yet. If you were to ask what the price was that she paid for her addiction, this is it, the thing that can't be replaced: she lost her dearest friend.'

'You were right, you know. I've never actually told you that. You saw the danger from the start. It could have been you now in Rose's place, and Amber dead. I never thought Amber would give up heroin, not permanently. I should have believed in you. I only got angry because I wanted to fix it for you and I couldn't. I thought all the stress would bring back your cancer. I didn't always make it easy for you.'

He pauses and turns his handsome face to look at me. His eyes are tender, caring and deep, as if I can see right inside his soul. 'You know,' he says 'I was always on your side.'

All the time I was worrying about Amber, taking all her crap, Tony was worrying about me – the only person who was. He was my rock, keeping me stable, giving me the strength and courage to be able to help her.

I ring Amber the next day. 'There's always dinner here for you, and a bed for the night, if you don't want to be alone,' I say.

'No, I'm alright at the flat, Mum. It's my home. But I'll come round.'

I try to be there for her; it's difficult to know what to do. Until now she's been busy making the floral arrangements for the funeral – it's given her something to focus on. Now she has to get back to normal life.

A brisk wind blows in as I open the front door. The night air trembles through the beech tree that stands behind the garage, swirling the branches and blowing leaves into the porch. Amber seems to bring the cold inside with her. I feel it on her nose and her cheeks as I lean out to hold her. Her face is stunned as if the intimacy of death has settled on her features. She holds my gaze while tears fill her eyes and tumble down her cheeks, then she shakes her head and wipes them away.

'I need a drink,' she says, stepping inside. 'Something to ease the pain, take my mind off things.'

'There's some wine in the fridge. I'll join you.'

I bring in two glasses. Her hand shakes as she takes one from me. 'How are you? How are you coping?' I ask.

'It's hard, but I'm finally sorting out my life. I've finished with Peter. It's not right to be with him when I don't really love him. He's moved out. I'd rather be on my own.'

'What about Rose? Have you seen her since the funeral?'

'I went this morning. Although she was pleased to see me, she said when I walked through the door she still expected to see Leeanne walk in behind me 'cause we were always together.'

'I still can't believe it. Do you think Leeanne did it because of Stephen's death?'

'His death destroyed her. He was more than a brother to her; he understood what she was going through as an addict, the things she had to do, the lifestyle she led. He was a sign of hope for her that if he could get clean, one day she could too. All that panic and depression I suffered when trying to quit; it's too much when you're dealing with grief at the same time. And since his death her habit kept growing. I think she was desperately trying to shut out the pain. She's free of pain now.'

She stops talking and we sit in silence for a bit before she continues. 'Towards the end Leeanne had such a neediness, she was so agitated and paranoid, and difficult. But I was weak, too weak to help her. Now I'd give anything to take it all back. I'm gonna miss her so very much.' Amber brushes her hair from her face and wipes the back of her hand across her wet cheek.

We finish the first bottle of wine and I open another.

'You know, Mum, Leeanne's death has saved me. There're only two ways out of heroin addiction. I got out one way and she got out the other. I'll never take drugs again.'

The second bottle finished, a third seems like a good idea. I get one from the garage.

She takes a gulp from the refilled glass and says 'For such a long time I thought I was so hard-done-by not having a dad. But having you is so much more wonderful than having a normal family.'

She's slurring her words as she carries on. 'You know, and listen to what I have to say before jumping to conclusions, I have so much to be thankful for, we've done so much since you had cancer, and each day with you is a blessing. I'm not afraid any more. I have a friend in heaven. There was a time when I thought it would be you up there.'

Amber

Claire leans in and takes a brown cardboard box from the back of her wardrobe. She stares at it for a minute and then folds back the flaps.

'I'm not sure I'm ready to do this, Amber, take out her things and look at them. Makes it all true if I do.'

I take Claire's hand. 'We'll do it together.'

I see Leeanne in Claire's features, the way she swings her hair from her face, something about the shape of her hands. It doesn't hurt quite so much if she's with me. I know she feels the pain more than I do. She's lost a brother and a sister.

Claire takes out a few items of make-up and some clothes – not much to show that Leeanne was ever here. I pick up Leeanne's hairbrush and run my fingers over the bristles; it still has her hair in it.

A thought shows on Claire's face. 'Oh…,' she says, and turns to rummage about in a drawer. She finds what she's looking for and takes it out.

'The last time I saw Leeanne, she told me to give you this,' she says. And she chucks something at me. It's a green ball.

I've always liked things that are bright, colourful and sparkly. One bonfire night I bought a ball at a market stall. It was made out of blue gel and when you squeezed it a small box inside lit up and flashed lots of different colours. I loved the feel of the squishy gel and watching the different-coloured lights.

After Stephen died, when Leeanne and I were hanging around the flat all day, she'd taken the ball off my bookcase and played with it. Standing in the kitchen, I'd heard a loud crack and realised she'd squeezed the box too hard and it had broken. 'Oh,' she said and gave it back to me. I made a face.

Leeanne gave me one of her looks. 'Shut up, Amber, it's not important. It's only a bloody toy,' she'd said.

The ball in my hand now is the same as the one Leeanne broke, except this one is green.

Nighttimes are hard; tiredness comes but not the release of sleep. I toss and turn in the darkness, smoke a fag with the bedroom window open, search through the back of the kitchen cupboards for the remains of a bottle of vodka or Bacardi, anything to get me through the night.

All the time I go over in my mind the events leading up to Leeanne's death.

I know that something stopped me from seeing what Leeanne was going to do. The signs were there but although I saw them they didn't made sense, didn't register. I lived those weeks with her believing she wasn't going to die. But her destiny was so powerful nothing could have prevented it.

Alone, under the covers of my bed, I squeeze the box inside my green ball and I think of her. When I'm ready to sleep, I place it carefully beside my bed.

I dream. A dream of Leeanne. In my dream I'm riding a fine white horse. It has a saddle with stirrups but no bridle or girth. I hold on to its mane, which is soft in my hand. A little way behind me there's a young man riding a brown horse. He has the face of an angel.

Everything else is in pale white colours, surrounded by a mist, and I can't see clearly. As we ride along, a garden with formal flowerbeds opens out in front of me.

People are standing beside the horses; their heads come to where my feet are in the stirrups. I look down to see who they are and I see Leeanne smiling up at me. A tremendous joy fills my body. I cannot control my desire to hold her. I lean down to embrace her but lean over too far and feel myself sliding off my horse. She holds out her arms to catch me and we fall into the grass together.

There is no sensation of the fall, nor of hitting the ground, only the weight of her body in my arms. I can smell the fragrance of her hair, and now she's here, so close to me, I see the fine details of her face, the freckles around her lips – familiar, yet forgotten till I look.

In the background voices are saying 'Oh, isn't that wonderful, they've found each other.'

For that first split second, that moment when I wake, I forget she is dead. Then the realisation comes. It's a tidal wave – the pain of losing her hits me and I'm breathless.

The dream evokes a feeling of her and I try to hold on to the emotion; it's all I have, it's the closest I can get to her without dying too.

By the shaft of white shining through the edges of the bedroom curtains I find the ball and squeeze it. I know I'll have to face many moments in the future without her, but tonight, just for thirty seconds while the lights flash, Leeanne's with me and it's not dark.

I'm living for her now as well as for me. I'm going to do all the things we planned to do back on those summer nights when we sat on her windowsill going twos on a fag.

And, when my grief overwhelms me, when I'm afraid of the future, I run back to the most important person in my life, the one who accepts me in spite of everything.

Just to be with her, in the same room, I feel the strength of our love radiating from her. I don't need drugs to change the way I'm feeling, I have my mum.

I need her more than ever now.

Epilogue

Amber

Heroin offered me an immediate escape from everything, from the reality of life and even from myself. The deeper I fell into addiction, the less I cared. The gear became company, a close friend. I didn't need anything or anyone else. I thought heroin could sort out and solve all my problems. But by the end I'd developed such a self-hatred I was trying not just to destroy myself but to utterly obliterate my very existence.

After the police arrested me I plummeted back to earth with an almighty crash. As though I had been asleep and then thrown into cold water; a sudden impact to my body and mind. The mist cleared and when I saw the reality of my situation it was a shock. In those first few days I didn't have any belief that I could change things, make it right and have a normal life. In fact, I had no idea what normal felt like any more.

But that did change.

From deep within me I had to find a strength, and a belief in myself, that I wouldn't have been able to find without the love, support and acceptance of my mum. All parents love their children and want to help them. Rose loved Leeanne very much and desperately wanted to help her; she just didn't know how. I am not going to start preaching about how to sort your life out and get off drugs – it's not that simple, there's no easy answer. It takes courage and determination and it hurts like hell. It's a hard-won gift.

Before I was clean, other addicts told me a lot of scary stories: if you quit you'll never feel warm again… not true; even when you're clean you can start clucking again years later… not true; you'll become an insomniac and struggle to sleep… not true. It does take a long time to fully recover, but it feels so much better to be clean. When I look at my eyes in the mirror I'm amazed that my pupils are visible: I'm not clucking off drugs. I still get a buzz out of it.

It occurs to me that people who know me will see me in a different light after reading this book. I won't be able to do the same job with the same people because something will have changed. I won't be the same Amber any more. Why is that? To some it may explain a lot of my odd behaviour, but once people hear the word heroin they screw up their faces – instantly you are a worthless junkie. Even after being clean for ten years people will see me differently. It's something I'll never escape. I'm different now. But, even though I am not stealing or dealing or taking drugs any more, once I did and that won't ever change.

I think about when Leeanne and I were young, living for the weekend; those are the days I miss the most. I would give anything to recapture them. I also miss the days with her in the future that I'll never have. I remember them only when they arrive and she's not there to share them with me.

Sometimes I'm convinced I could have prevented Leeanne's death; by knowing something was wrong the night she phoned me, by realising how depressed she was after Stephen's death, by never taking drugs with her in the first place. I'm the only person she would have let into her bedroom that night. I'm haunted by that, but I will own it for the rest of my life. I paid for my addiction – I lost my best friend – but Leeanne paid the ultimate price.

I have been lucky, lucky to have my mum stand by me, lucky to have survived heroin.

Amber

Things that helped me quit drugs and may help other addicts

1. Admit to yourself and others that your addiction is out of your control. Find someone who is not using drugs and confide in them. You will be surprised how many people are willing to help. The universe will send you someone. Angels show up ready to help, disguised as ordinary people.

2. Stay away from triggers, anything that carries a memory of drug-taking. These can be people, feelings or situations. Triggers shift the brain automatically into *I need drugs*. Over time, triggers lose their strength.

3. Never give up trying to give up. Eventually you *will* get there! A relapse is just a setback. You may have lost the battle but not the war. A relapse doesn't mean you haven't made progress. You didn't become an addict overnight and you can't always undo it overnight, but you can do it in stages. The only thing that matters is time spent not using drugs.

4. You have to have an anti-drug environment. You may need dramatic intervention. If you're living in a place where drugs are used, move.

5. Deny the mental battle. Let your subconscious mind fight it out. The more you lay in bed moaning about how much it hurts, the more it will hurt. Face it, look at the pain, bring it on, tell yourself 'actually, I can do this'. Go with the flow rather than swimming against the tide.

6. Get a job. Get out of bed in the mornings, draw the curtains and let the light in. Exercise and try to get yourself fit. Go for a walk in the woods; look at the ocean.

7. Try some alternative therapies. Acupuncture can help with the physical symptoms. I found some over-the-counter medications helped. Find a counsellor and go through personal therapy. I put if off for years, but in the end I needed it.

8. You can do anything today so long as it's not drugs. Smoke a hundred fags, eat fifty Mars bars, go to the coast and swim naked in the sea – anything you can think of. Drugs are a mind game; you need a change of focus, a distraction, something that feels good.

9. Think with the end in mind. Visualise it. Believe it. Want it so badly you are willing to release old behaviours. This is your life and your time is now: do not wait.

10. Sometimes you have to go further into the void, into the darkness, to get out the other side. You have to be ready for withdrawal, fed up with how hard it is to score, how difficult life is as an addict.

Christine

Things I learnt helping my daughter quit heroin that may help other parents

1. Deal with it as soon as you can. If you have suspicions about your child's behaviour, you are probably right. Don't ignore your fears – drugs are so dangerous. Do something now and do something big; you can't afford not to. Don't be fobbed off by your child's reassurances that it's okay. Addicts are in denial and parents are often in it with them. Look at the situation without self-deception, and see what you have to do.

2. Make it absolutely clear that doing hard drugs is unacceptable. No compromise. Be strong about this. There is no such thing as casual use or having it under control. This can be hard to understand if you have never taken drugs.

3. Insist on no contact with friends who are using drugs. This will probably mean no friends, as all the friends who are not doing drugs will have got fed up with your child and gone away. In the future, when your child is stronger, new friends will appear.

4. Never give them money for drugs. Giving them money

does not help, nor does paying for things so they have money for drugs. There will always be times when there's some emergency and they are desperate. Say no and, if they seem to genuinely need the money, go with them rather than give them the cash.

5. Get some professional help. Pester everyone you can – your GP, Acorn, private charities, everyone.

6. Ask for help from your God or the universe – whatever you believe that power to be that is greater than yourself. Then appreciate everything you have and say a private thank you each time some help comes your way.

7. You need some barriers to your life. You cannot spend 24/7 worrying about where your child is and what they are doing. You have a life too – maybe a family and a relationship that has a high priority in your life. You will not stay the course if you let yourself get too deeply involved too quickly.

8. Always let them know you love them, you just don't love their behaviour. Caring for an addict is complex. There is no single right answer. They become distant and self-destructive. Believe in them absolutely, otherwise how will they believe in themselves?

9. Each person has free will and you cannot quit for them, you can only support their recovery. They need to be in a place in their life where they are ready to leave the drugs behind. This may involve hitting rock bottom first. You may have to let them go there.

10. Sadly, sometimes the person you love has already gone. What is left is just a shell; they don't live in that body any more and all that remains is a tortured soul. Don't torment yourself. Let them go from your life, knowing

you have no regrets in anything you tried to do. Remember them the way they were. Pray for them and send them love.